THE AUTHOR

JAMES H. MEISEL is Professor of Political Science at The University of Michigan. He is the author of *The Genesis of Georges Sorel, The Myth of the Ruling Class, The Fall of the Republic: Military Revolt in France*, and edited *Makers of Modern Social Science: Pareto and Mosca.*

Counterrevolution

ATHERTON PRESS

New York · 1966

COUNTER-REVOLUTION

How Revolutions Die

JAMES H. MEISEL

THE UNIVERSITY OF MICHIGAN

Preface

"Don't go near the windows, understand?"

"Why?"

"Because they're shooting in the street."

"Who's shooting?"

"Bad people. They stopped Grampa's droshki and made him get out and walk."

"But Grampa's old! How could they do that?"

"Ah! They said, 'This is a revolution, mister! So you foot it now, just like the rest of us!' "

"What is a revolution, Gramma?"

The place: Riga, a city in one of the Baltic provinces of Czarist Russia; the time: 1905. I was then five years old. There was also that bad business of the gun, the black revolver, which my uncle refused to surrender to his parents. Uncle wore a uniform, the black, belted uniform worn by all Russian students. He said he needed the revolver to shoot gardavois, the Czar's policemen.

Like all other students, Uncle was a revolutionary. In the end, he did surrender the revolver, but he was quite angry with his parents. "You're such a liberal," he told his father, "and you hate the Czar. But when they stop your fancy droshki, you complain. Pa, you don't know which side you're on!"

What a way to talk to your own father!

🔲

Twelve years later, then aged seventeen and living with my parents in Berlin, Germany, I heard that there had been a new Russian revolution, and that there was much rejoicing in the streets, because this time the people had won. Whenever strangers met, they would stop and embrace, just as on Easter Sunday they exchanged kisses and the information that Christ had risen.

That was in the spring of 1917, and then for many months the news remained confused, until November, when there was apparently another revolution. Its leader, who took over all of Holy Russia, was a certain Lenin-Trotsky. At least, that was the name by which he remained known for quite a while.

This time, Grandpa did not walk. He ran until he reached the frontier and finally Berlin. Grandfather told us that he had to leave home because of Lenin-Trotsky. It transpired that Lenin-Trotsky was actually two men, and that between them they were turning everything upside down. Their followers had robbed my grandparents of their fur coats and most of their jewels (a few they had overlooked, thank God!)

Following the old people, their children and grandchildren, my cousins, also came to Germany. All except the uncle who had been so troublesome about the gun. He did not think Germany far enough, so he made straight for Belgrade, Serbia. It was a pity, because at the start the revolution had been such a romp, with Lenin and Trotsky making speeches all over town, as was reported by a cousin from St. Petersburg—or rather Petrograd as it was now called.

"Did you see them? Hear them speak?" I asked.

"A dozen times. As soon as we heard that Lenin was going to speak in an hour at such and such a place, we'd jump a streetcar and . . ."

"What's he like?"

"Lenin? A terrible bore. He goes on repeating the same thing

*so long that in the end you think he must be right. And when
you go home, damn it, he just stays with you!"*

"And Trotsky?"

*"Ah, he's different. The greatest orator you ever heard. Danton,
St. Just, they must have been like that. Casting a spell. He's witty
too. You never tire of listening to him."*

"What did he say?"

"Oh, that I don't remember. Does it matter?"

*He had told them that they would be swept into the garbage
pail of history.*

▣

*One year later, again on a November day, a college freshman
now, I cut classes because there had been a rumor that the German navy had raised the red flag in Kiel and that today the
revolution would come to Berlin. So I took a streetcar to where
all the big events took place, Unter den Linden, the broad avenue
between the Kaiser's palace and the Brandenburg gate. In front
of a certain building, many officers were waiting for the loyal
army units to arrive. They never came, and so the officers went
home and changed into civilian dress. Presently the workers arrived, marching from their suburbs, many of them still in uniform, and many of them still mere boys. Some of the boys were
carrying machine guns on their backs. They marched around
in two distinctly separate columns, shouting angry slogans at
each other. Only afterwards I understood that I had seen the
breakup of the Second International; the confrontation between
the two wings of socialism.*

*I also found out later that the revolution had officially begun
ten minutes after I had left the scene to return home for dinner
(my father was a stickler for punctuality). Ten minutes after I
had climbed a streetcar, Philipp Scheidemann, the leader of the
right-wing Social Democrats, from the balcony of the Imperial
palace had solemnly proclaimed the new Republic.*

▣

*Ten years later, a newspaperman now, I finally caught up with
Philipp Scheidemann. The place was a large restaurant fre-
quented by journalists at night. They were chatting. Suddenly
someone lowered his voice and said:*

"Don't look now, but behind us the Man with the Withered Hand is just raising it to drink his beer."

I looked around and recognized the aging socialist, no longer in office.

"I don't see it," I said. "Where's the withered hand?"

"Don't you remember? When they made peace at Versailles back in '19, the man swore, 'My hand shall wither 'ere I sign this document of shame!' "

"Well, did he sign it?"

"No, he didn't. But the name stuck just the same."

Without realizing it, I had received an example of the indestructibility of myth.

Then came the days when brown-shirted men, young and old, went marching through the streets in serried ranks, singing raucously. At night, they filled the beer halls to cheer their leaders. The reporters dutifully covered the major meetings: it was a chore like any other. But to cover a Hitler rally with the Fuehrer himself speaking was a plum for which young journalists would fight; this assignment might make their career.

One of them, who had drawn the lucky lot, returned from a rally one night, pale, palpably shaken by the new experience. "How was it?" asked the editor on duty, with a bored expression.

"Frightening. He kept them waiting, so they marked time with a lot of martial music, and the little Hitlers filled in with speeches nobody listened to. Then suddenly there was a shout, 'The Fuehrer has just left the Adlon!' And five minutes later, 'The Fuehrer has arrived outside!' And then, 'The Fuehrer has entered the building!' Until, finally: 'The Fuehrer!' All hell broke loose. Everybody was on his feet, yelling. I myself. . . . Well, then he started talking, and I had a chance to watch him. What a letdown. He doesn't look like much. And as for what they say about him being such a spellbinder, he was dull as dishwater. His face looked empty and his voice as if his heart weren't in it at all.

"But then, all of a sudden, something happened to him. As if a light cord had been plugged into his system: his whole face lit up, and he began to shout, loud, louder, faster, until he seemed beside himself . . . like one possessed! And always looking straight at you with his odd eyes, and talking to you, you alone. . . ."

"Yes," the night editor said, not unkindly. "And what did he have to say tonight?"

*"Oh, that?" the young man shook his head like one awaking
from a bad dream. "That I don't remember."*

*We smiled indulgently. We were so bored with the whole
business—Hitler, The Republic, our own helplessness. We were
all waiting for the end, not knowing that, in one way or another,
it would also be our own.*

THE RULES OF THE GAME

There is no lack of studies dealing with precipitous and violent
communal change.[1] If only the bewildering variety of revolutionary evidence could simply be explained by scientific laws of
motion and summed up in a coherent system, the result might
even have important practical significance. Like Kremlinology,
the novel science (should one call it revolutionology?) might
furnish an effective recipe, or rather two—one suitable to induce
the bacillus of revolt, if that is the objective; the other to contain, if not prevent, the contagion of rebellion.[2]

The handbook will no doubt some day be written that will
contain a computerized codification of the lessons to be learned
from past upheavals. The difficulty is that violence, both individual and collective, tends to permit only the very vaguest and
most general predictions. And revolutions in particular, in addition to being outbursts of collective violence, are doing violence
precisely to all the existent rules. We are not thinking here of
the immense fluidity of revolutionary situations that permits
the most surprising combination of forces in a civil war and
knows one rule only: that there are no rules.[3] Rather: once
rebellion has become overt, the whole society finds itself in a
moral twilight zone. Treasonable acts against the state now
become commonplace; the line that separates betrayers and betrayed becomes obliterated. This discovery discourages commit-
ment on the part of the defenders of the *status quo*, for in a
situation where all may conceivably commit acts of disobedience,
nobody is a traitor. But this knowledge only helps the mutineers;

1. See the Conclusions and the *Bibliography* to this study.
2. "We shall regard revolutions—wholly, be it understood, for conven-
ience, and with no implications of eternal and absolute validity, and with
no moral overtones—as a kind of fever." Crane Brinton, *The Anatomy of
Revolution* (New York, 1952), p. 17.
3. See chapter 1.

it paralyzes the regime. For the regime knows only how to fight the insurrection by the rules, whereas the revolutionary is forced, by the very superiority of governmental means of repression, to improvise. Not always will he be so lucky as to dispose of the advanced devices in the modern armory. Unless the army is won over to the side of the insurgents, they will have to fight with weapons that are obsolete. For this deficiency, the revolutionary compensates by not playing the war game by its accepted laws. It is David with his sling against the armored colossus, the guerrilla against mechanized units and bombing planes, just as in military history the archers, representing an old-fashioned mode of fighting, bested the French knights at Crécy, the charging masses of the French revolution the professional robots of eighteenth-century warfare. There is a counterrevolutionary element in this reversion to archaic weapons against which advanced technology is helpless.

It is this intractability of revolution, its relative immunity to the countermeasures of a baffled regime that is the secret weapon of the rebels, a fact that has perhaps not received sufficient attention. It is one of the reasons, although not the only one why this study (which stops short of revolutions still in progress) attempts to provide neither manual nor system. But it has a thesis nonetheless, banal as it might seem. Its emphasis, with a few exceptions only, on the *closing* phases of historic revolutions, is not arbitrarily chosen. It would be wrong to say that the last chapters of great social cataclysms remained so neglected by historians because they found them unimportant. A better explanation may be that they find the final stages of most revolutions so embarrassing. To say that most revolutions fall short of their professed objectives is only to proclaim the obvious. The hiatus between human ends and historic outcomes, between aspiration and achievement, may however be a blessing in disguise.[4] Too much success can kill a revolution prematurely. Disappointment is not merely the result of failure; it may equally accompany success.[5] Supplanted by the pragmatists of revolution (who in turn must lean on the professionals of violence, here

---

4. The assumption that the "end of ideology" would spell the end of Western man is central to Fred L. Polak's study of utopias, *The Image of the Future*, 2 vols. (Leyden–New York, 1961).

5. "The truth of all revolutions is not that they turn into counterrevolutions but that they become boring." Kenneth Allsop, "Beaten," *The Spectator* (March, 1959), p. 350.

called praetorians), the utopians of the revolutionary dawn are soon heard to lament, with Trotsky, "The Revolution Betrayed."

But no revolution is in vain. Although we may agree with Robert Michels that "the socialists might conquer, but not socialism, which would perish in the moment of its adherents' triumph," [6] the Revolution Lost is also Something Vital Regained. If some rebellions die of their success, their failure may supply the jolt we needed to become once more aware of our humanity. So if, as Camus stated it, "in order to exist, man must rebel" while at the same time keep in mind that murder would "destroy the reasons for his insurrection," the inverse is also true: the rebel too fastidious to risk dirtying his hands surrenders the initiative to those less scrupulous; too proud to fight, he prompts the very outrage he abhors. "Thus the rebel can never find peace. . . ." [7]

6. *Political Parties* (Glencoe, 1949), p. 391.
7. Albert Camus, *The Rebel* (New York, 1956), p. 285.

▣ Contents

■ Counterrevolution

Prologue: The Revolution of the Intellectuals

The first revolt took place in heaven. Long before the first man discovered the tree of knowledge to be the tree of death, the angel Satan-Lucifer rose up against his Lord to charge Him, in the words of Milton, "Whom reason hath equal'd, force hath made supreme above his equals." This was the first revolt against authority, with Satan the first critic, arguing from reason. Because he belonged to the celestial family, they called him a traitor to his class. It was the first recorded split within a ruling group, the worst threat to political stability, and the arch rebel with his followers was penalized accordingly with expulsion from the party and exile, in a vertical (downward) direction.

The Bible records in Numbers 16 the first conspiracy of mortals: "Now Korah with two hundred fifty princes of the assembly, . . . men of renown . . . gathered themselves together against

This is the revised and enlarged version of a piece first presented at a symposium held at Wayne State University, Detroit, in May, 1960, and published in that institution's *Graduate Comment* (Vol. 4, No. 3, December, 1960), pp. 8-10, and 15 as "The Conspiracy of the Intellectuals." Reprinted by permission.

Moses and against Aaron, and said unto them, . . . 'wherefore then lift ye up yourselves against the congregation of the Lord?' "

The question was satanic, and the backbenchers of the assembly suffered the satanic fate: all two hundred fifty-one of them were swallowed by fire and earthquake. The high authority was clearly siding with the front bench. Korah, like his late descendant, Trotsky, was not rehabilitated by a later generation more inclined toward committee rule. The opposition, literally driven under ground, has remained there, its reputation blackened, ever since.

Halfway between immortal gods and mortal men, we find Prometheus, semi-divine thief of divine fire, chained to his penal rock. He was the first inventor-scientist to set a bad example: unendowed, he had to pay his way to do research. Prometheus started the Greek mythology and martyrology of the inquiring mind, the chronicle of Western intellectual protest, which is also existential protest. For "man is the only creature who refuses to be what he is." [1] The children of Prometheus will continue to reach for the Light that blinds, the light that singed the waxen wings of Icarus and that ultimately blinded Oedipus when he tried to outwit his fate.

The human quest for truth, then, seems to call for both success *and* failure. Success will be crime that asks for punishment. The Mind Triumphant must be crucified, or poisoned, or burned at the stake. Was Nietzsche right in making the arch-intellectual, Socrates, a *criminal?* Perversity! Did we not cheer Archimedes when he exclaimed: "Give me a foothold yon, and I shall move the earth!" We cheered indeed. But whenever we cheered, it was with misgivings: "When Pythagoras discovered his great law, he sacrificed a hundred head of cattle to the gods. Since then, all oxen tremble whenever a new truth is found." [2]

As the carrier of the flame that is life-giving as well as life-destroying, mind itself is neither life nor death. Mind moves in the category of means, not ends. Hume said that reason is, or ought to be, the slave of the passions.

This master-slave relationship the mind wishes to correct. Had not God created man in His image? How could man help but

1. Albert Camus, *The Rebel* (New York, 1956), p. 11.
2. Ludwig Börne, *Gesammelte Schriften*, 2. Aufl., VI, p. 187. Heinrich Heine liked the saying so much that he paraphrased it twice: once in *Reisebilder*, Zweiter Teil, Die Nordsee iii, and again in *Götter in Exil*.

try to form the earth after *his?* He is commanded to transcend himself and simultaneously obstructed in this task. What causes the obstruction? Could it be that it is Mind itself?

The first step in restoring reason to its rightful place must be the abolition of Hume's self-denying ordinance. The last step will be the reversal of the master-slave relationship. But not too fast! The safe way to proceed is to announce that there ought to be neither slave nor master.

The battle was fought between mind and mind; a civil war in which the front lines changed incessantly, and nothing was more common than conspiracy and treason. In this struggle, only *organized* rebellion had a chance to win, the solitary rebel none. To his distress did Plato discover this when he staged his one-man experiment in intellectual persuasion. Dionysius, tired of acting the philosopher, sold the great educator into slavery.

But Plato's brainchild, his Republic of an intellectual aristocracy, survived. In vain was the child exiled to the far shores of Utopia. There it grew until it returned to claim its kingdom. It was ready to pay almost any price to gain control; it was prepared to compromise, even with the devil. Power over matter was worth any intellectual sacrifice.

So Mind began to build, to tame the world—first as the Church, then as Aquinas' latter-day unaided reason. In surveying history, the great Italian thinker, Giambattista Vico, could write in his *Scienza Nuova*, a full hundred years before Karl Marx discovered him, "That which did all this was mind, for man did it with intelligence. . . ." [3] But Vico also knew that it was Divine Providence that steered mankind, against its own perverted will, along the spiral cycles of historic destiny.

If Providence could work by indirection, could not the human mind too achieve ultimate control by working through instead of against human folly? Might the road not lead to Dostoevskii's Grand Inquisitor through the three arches inscribed "Mystery, Miracle, Authority"? Had Plato not already unveiled these same secrets when he argued the use of the Golden Lie? In our terms only *myth* is capable of mobilizing the emotions. Plato's Golden Lie does, after all, express a truth—even if it should

---

3. *The New Science of Giambattista Vico.* Transl. from the 3rd ed. (9, 1744) by Thomas Goddard Bergin and Max Harold Fisch (Ithaca, New York, 1948), p. 382, ¶ 1108. The sentence continues, "it was not fate, for they did it by choice; not chance, for the results . . . are perpetually the same."

mean that there is no truth. The Grand Inquisitor, who works with the First Critic, is prepared for the advent of Luciferic nihilism: "Ages are yet to come of the confusion of free thought, of their science and cannibalism. For having begun to build their tower of Babel, they will end, of course, with cannibalism. But then the beast will crawl back to us and lick our feet. . . ."[4]

The old man, who holds neither with God nor with human reason, foresees intellectual terrorism. As Anatole France would later say of the French Revolution, "If you start with the premise that men are naturally good . . . you invariably end by wanting to kill all those who disagree with you." For Mind, equating ever since Socrates the true and the good, insists on unity, and logic permits no contradiction.

Lately, it has become rather tiresome to be told about man in his pride, about the tyranny of progress, about reason on a rampage, turning back upon itself and finally committing suicide. But in itself this reaction to Jacobin and Stalinist excesses is legitimate, and if the intellectuals, having lost all faith in reason, now proclaim man's finiteness and imperfectibility, we need not be intimidated. Reason remains reason, even if it poses as distrust of reason. It may be poor reasoning, or even plain stupidity disguised as reason. But more often than not the contempt of mind is simply mind at the end of its tether. The Romanticist rebellion, Schopenhauer's will or Freud's subconscious, the Bergsonian leap of intuition—these are also moves toward the understanding of existence and its intellectual mastery. But the so-called irrationalist *sides with* life instead of fighting it. In military terminology, he executes a flanking movement or, if you prefer, a sneak attack. Sometimes it is not easy to tell friend from foe; the Saint-Simonians of the early nineteenth century, for instance, combined technocratic tidiness with neo-Christian sentiment, and Saint-Simon's apostatic disciple, Auguste Comte, invented, as the superstructure of his managerial edifice, a fanciful religion of humanity. The heart has its own reasons—so they thought that reason in turn should acquire a heart. It was the heyday of Icarian flights into New Harmony.

Politically, to be sure, there was, after the revolutionary and Napoleonic wars, a lull in the conspiratory movement of the

---

4. The author of the *Brothers Karamazov* was not the first to have these premonitions of totalitarianism. The prophecies made by Proudhon, Nietzsche, and Burckhardt sound strikingly alike.

idéologues. Freemasons, Rosicrucians and Illuminati, even the Conspiracy of Equals, were a danger of the past—for the time being. Reason had returned. That is, it had been reassigned its well-worn back seat of Grey Eminence. As long as they behaved, the many eminences of grey matter had a great time pointing out —*sotto voce*—that mankind had never so ungladly suffered quite so many ruling fools. But because these critics did not always keep their voices down, the time was also great for exiles. Just as Madame de Staël in her Swiss sanctuary had raised her voice against Napoleon the Great, so too from his Channel island Victor Hugo would insult Napoleon the Little, and Giuseppe Mazzini could plot his United Italy in London. Little did it matter. Voices of frustration echoing through the long patient halls of history.

Nor should we omit another great Italian name: Machiavelli, the intellectual activist *par excellence*, the diplomat, historian, playwright, who had been exiled by, but to make things worse, not too far from, his beloved Florence. There he sat and ate his heart out, waiting for the messenger to call him back to active service. Who would that *Prince* be who would be bold enough to call him? And so he fashioned him, the coldly reasonable lion-fox who, at whatever cost to common decency, would unify and liberate the mother country. Mirror for princes indeed! It was a portrait that made people shudder because it made them feel naked. No wonder the true friend of Roman liberty and virtue, Niccolò, became Old Nick, the modern Prince of Darkness. "Hell hath no fury like a woman scorned," and Machiavelli had to pay the penalty for preferring naked truth to the bitch goddess, Fortuna. All stealthy and murderous tyrants claimed him as their patron saint.

Had Machiavelli died in Dante's time, he would have been a prize exhibit in his fellow countryman's poetic hell. For what was the *Inferno* other than a concentration camp to end all concentration camps, in which the exile, Alighieri, prosecutor and judge in one person, could play intellectual torture master to his enemies? The Dantesque hell was a creation of defeat, the darkest night of alienated mind. It had to be suffered through before there could be the apotheosis of the *Paradiso.*

We can think of many other sinners missing from this giant penitentiary, such as Nietzsche, the madman who cried out loud that God was dead. But Nietzsche was mistaken. Men had merely replaced Providence with "the implacable reign of necessity." This was no longer Hegel's dialectic of the spirit, jumping through its world-historic hoops. Marx held with Goethe's *Faust:* In the beginning was not word, but action. That makes Marxism seem to be anti-mind. But what Marx actually meant was that the word had become flesh. The time was ripe. The dreams of Saint-Simon and Comte were to come true—with a vengeance.

The call for proletarians to unite was first heard by some intellectuals exiled at home and abroad. Those who refused to listen could repeat Tolstoy's great *caveat:* "Once admit that human life can be guided by reason, and all possibility of life is annihilated." [5]

The old view that the end of innocence, of *spontaneity,* means death, was revived by nineteenth-century Romanticism and articulated fully in the early decades of our century. The tragic dualism of consciousness and spontaneity pervades the entire work of Thomas Mann. The intellect is sick—life stupid, healthy, glorious; it is paradise from which the chronicler, the artist, has been driven out. The modern Doctor Faustus carries his own hell around, for self-consciousness has seen through life and thereby killed it. Mind's persistent envy of existence becomes self-hatred and self-contempt, and finally mind turns informer: It denounces itself as the enemy. In literature, that self-accusing note was sounded first, with shocking brutality, in *Notes from the Underground,* which establishes Dostoevskii's new, plebeian intellectual, who then, in *Crime and Punishment,* as Raskolnikov, goes on to dream of himself as Napoleon-superman. In philosophical terms this view was spelled out by the German, Ludwig Klages, in *Mind as the Adversary of the Soul.* Doctor Faustus, in the work of Thomas Mann's old age, is now the Adversary of the ancient book.

But this was not the end of Thomas Mann himself. True, during the first World War, he did see Germany as the defender of the soul against the soulless rationality of the democracies. No wonder his *Reflections of a Non-Political Man* were never rendered into English and soon afterwards disowned by Mann, when in the 1920's he fell out of "sympathy with death" and became more appreciative of rationality and its political *ambiente.* He even made some forceful public speeches against Hitler and con-

5. *War and Peace,* Epilogue, Part I, i (The Modern Library edition), p. 1064.

tinued, while an exile in this country, to act as a spokesman of
the allied cause. Like many other intellectuals, he had become a
partisan in the civil war of minds, and Julien Benda, author of
the celebrated book *The Betrayal of the Intellectuals,* could have
taken issue with the German master.

The Frenchman's critical attack on intellectual *engagement* is
as thought-stirring as it is intemperate. It seems there was a time
when all the clerks, to use the author's ecclesiastic term, were
men devoted to the one and undivided truth. They never stooped
to "politics." They did not peddle "ideologies." If they took part
in public life at all, it was only to hold up the mirror of truth to
its falsifiers. It was Plato's knowledge *versus* the "particularism"
of opinion and expediency which to this day is the academic
code of honor.

Unquestionably the debasement of so many modern intellectuals who would sell their birthright for a mess of patronage is
most deplorable. However, was there ever a time when that deplorable state of affairs did *not* exist? Or did Benda merely use
the past as a stick to beat the present? Be that as it may, today
his proud clerk indeed has turned, regretfully or cynically, into
the Organization Man. In his defense, the modern clerk might
plead that organization too is his own, his Viconian artifact. But
it also has become his prison, Kafka's modern labyrinth that the
modern clerk has entered as a latter-day Theseus, hoping against
hope perhaps, for his Ariadne.

At about the time Benda issued his warning, the "open conspiracy" of which H. G. Wells was forever dreaming got under-
way, and nobody suggested treason. That amazing little band of
British intellectuals, the Fabians, conquered without bloodshed
and prepared the way for socialism and the Tory welfare state
alike. They drew the line at revolutionary violence, perhaps the
most successful representatives of Camus' rebel creed. But their
success well demonstrates the shortcomings of sage self-limitation.
Their soberness, their pragmatism left little scope for the utopian
dream, and when they conquered,[6] England yawned. In asking
only for the possible, they had forgotten that man does not live
by bread alone—an observation no less true for being made so
frequently by people who need no longer worry about bread.

6. Indirectly. Fabian practice was not always as astute as Fabian theory.
The influence of the society on the organizational development of British
labor must not be exaggerated.

While the Fabians plotted the "inevitability of gradualism," two Italians, Gaetano Mosca and Vilfredo Pareto, developed the notion of the political class or elite, already anticipated by Henri de Saint-Simon and Auguste Comte. The concept of a dominant minority that can be found in every society infuriated the Marxists because the theory, if true, made a mockery of their claim that the abolition of class would end all abuse of man by man. Beyond that, the elitist version of society reflected, although inadvertently, the interest and status claims of a new class, or rather of a congeries of intellectual skill groups in the widest sense, that had become not only increasingly important but eventually indispensable to a matured industrial society. Likewise, the fast growth of centralized communication systems, the nerve centers of the nascent bureaucratic order, placed the fashioners and handlers of ideas in a strategically central position. Their commodities were more than marketable—they were at a premium. The chances for philosophers not merely to understand but to change the world had never seemed greater. Add to this the fact that political structure assumed a quasi-autonomous character that set it increasingly farther apart from and above the social forces. A distinguished non-Marxist thinker could flatly assert that "the political order is essentially irreducible to the economic order." [7] This statement, though manifestly anti-Marxist, causes no anguish among the disciples of Karl Marx; he had anticipated situations in which the agent of class rule, the state, would become the master of society and rise above the classes.[8]

But that near-disjunction of the political and socioeconomic realms makes the state structure singularly vulnerable to direct attack, particularly in a country weakened by an economic crisis or by a lost war, such as the Russia of Czar Nicholas II.

If Hobbes' Leviathan was, in his words, "an artificial man," the revolutionary party fashioned by Lenin, the Marxist, was a human machine whose cogs were intellectual bearers of light, bringing the First Rebel's message to the underprivileged. The proletariat was to be the coming master, but for the time being

7. Raymond Aron, *Main Currents in Sociological Thought*, I (New York, 1965), p. 173.

8. See Marx, *The Eighteenth Brumaire of Louis Bonaparte:* "Only under the second Bonaparte does the state seem to have made itself completely independent," that is, in the—abnormal—case that the class struggle has reached the point of total deadlock. (Karl Marx and Frederick Engels, *Selected Works*, Vol. 1 (London, 1950), p. 302, and ff. See also below, chapter 6.

an intelligentsia of the happy few would lead, because they knew the goal. True to his Hegelian heritage,[9] the Russian leader spoke almost contemptuously of "mass spontaneity," which at best would achieve only "trade-union consciousness." Political class consciousness was the monopoly of Lenin's "military organization." [10]

But the success of Lenin's "revolutionary brotherhood" [11] was quickly followed by the downfall and the liquidation of his intellectual co-conspirators. The bureaucrats and economic managers, officially styled "the intelligentsia" in the Soviet constitution, took the place of Trotsky and Bukharin, but they were at best only one of various pressure groups, all held together and bossed by the ruling party. The supreme boss, Stalin, was a master at manipulating men and not a prince of intellect. So was his successor, Khrushchev.

The same fate overtook the German life-worshipping intellectuals. They performed the spadework for a revolution they hoped would be conservative and led by gentlemen. Others, like Spengler, out-nietzsched Nietzsche and proclaimed the coming age of Caesar.

But when he came, their Caesar was a plebeian. Not the intellectuals were unleashed, but the barbarians. Nietzsche's phrase that people in an age of decadence no longer kill with daggers but with words [12] was changed to read that words prepare what daggers will conclude—daggers or their modern equivalents.

Although educated Germans hid their heads in shame and some conspired against the tyrant, the majority adored him. It is not a pleasant story to remember, but those ready to pass judgment would do better to defer it until they can test their own ability to act heroically and, if need be, die a martyr's death.

For the intellectual breed scares easily. Intellectuals are essentially a timid race, and, if act they must, they prefer to act, for better or for worse, vicariously. Hence their frequent, sneaking admiration for the strong, bad guy. His badness makes them feel

9. Hegel, usually claimed for the romantic tradition, deviated from it insofar as he proclaimed the primacy of consciousness as the *primum agens* of the world-historic process.

10. See Lenin's *What Is To Be Done?* (1902).

11. This term of Chalmers Johnson describes "small, secret associations of individuals united by a common sense of grievance that may *or may not* correspond to the objective condition of a social system." See his *Revolution and the Social System* (Stanford, Calif., 1964), pp. 49-50.

12. See *The Joyful Wisdom*, section 23.

good. The house of intellect, inhabited by a disorderly and disputatious lot, seems to some social scientists a house forever fated to remain divided; to others a breeding ground of revolution. "Intellectuals do not constitute a politically homogeneous class in democratic society. . . . *Free-lance intellectuals appear to be more disposed toward mass movements than intellectuals in corporate bodies (especially universities)*." [13] Joseph Schumpeter, although agreeing that "Intellectuals are not a social class," then continued, "they develop group attitudes and group interests sufficiently strong to make large numbers of them behave in the way that is usually associated with the concept of social classes." [14] Raymond Aron reluctantly concurs that "there remains . . . a basis of truth in the hackneyed notion, which has been taken up in a more subtle form by certain sociologists (J. Schumpeter, for example), of the intellectuals as revolutionaries by profession." [15]

In fact, Schumpeter based his estimate of the danger represented by the intellectuals as a quasi-class less on their revolutionary strength than on the weakness of the democratic system. It cannot repress the rebels without doing violence to its own fundamental premises: "In order to do that it would have to change typically bourgeois institutions and drastically reduce the individual freedom of *all* strata of the nation. And such a government is not likely—it would not even be able—to stop short of private enterprise." [16]

In the somnolescent 1950s, the American intellectuals as a whole had no coherence. But their gain in status (during the post-Sputnik scare that benefited many scientists) and accompanying loss in intellectual independence, may have given a minority of them a sense of corporate distinctness. On the other hand, the great majority of those who were not among the elect did not experience in this country the degree of social pressure that compresses outcasts into an unholy union of desperadoes.

If this prologue ended at this point, it might fittingly close with the intellectual angels singing: "Do not force us into unity.

13. William Kornhauser, who wrote this some time ago in his *Politics of Mass Society* (Glencoe, 1959, p. 185), is likely to have changed his mind about the universities by now.

14. Schumpeter, *Capitalism, Socialism, and Democracy*, 2nd ed. (New York and London, 1947), pp. 146, 150.

15. Raymond Aron, *The Opium of the Intellectuals* (Garden City, New York, 1957), p. 209.

16. Schumpeter, *ibid.*

For we would still rather be right than president." Where would that leave the intellectuals? Nowhere, it seems.

But that nowhere is no longer the old utopia. If there is any sense in speaking of the failure of the intellectuals, it is that theirs is the very failure of too much success. Has not their age-old dream become law for our fast-overcrowding world? The rational control of all resources, human and material, has indeed become imperative for large or small, established or emerging nations. But together with this near-fulfillment of the intellectual vision, there has also come, in our part of the world at least, what has been called "the end of ideology." [17]

But has it really? What else is the new pragmatism, the proclamation of the end of ideology, except *another* ideology—of status-quo acceptance, and of second thoughts about the consequences of some European ideologies? If he is still an angry man, the aging intellectual, now a captive of the labyrinth, has an increasingly hard time in making other people angry at him. "Liberal culture has shown its power not so much in the marginal freedom it allows dissenters as in its capacity to absorb—without the slightest indigestion—and even canonize its critics." [18] And indeed, the intellectual rather likes his prison, even if he no longer likes himself. But then, he has been a collector of too many disappointments long enough. "The engine of human progress," Adlai Stevenson remarked once, "has run out of fuel—the fuel of human discontent." He said it after Power, ever wary of the intellectual, had eluded him not once but twice.

In the meantime, new, young rebels have appeared. First those who do not fight the system—they just squat outside Kafka's castle, singing to one another, in a neo-dada way. Then others, ready to attack. New tensions have developed, inside as well as outside American society. The newcomers shun ideologies; they have no use for communism: if anything, they are anarcho-syndicalists and—so far—nonviolent. As they break out of their

17. "Few serious minds believe any longer that one can set down 'blue prints' and through 'social engineering' bring about a new utopia of social harmony." Moreover, "there is today a rough consensus . . . on political issues: the acceptance of a welfare state; the desirability of decentralized power; a system of mixed economy and of political pluralism . . . the ideological age has ended." Daniel Bell, *The End of Ideology* (Glencoe, 1960), p. 373. Henry David Aiken savagely attacked Bell in "The Revolt Against Ideology," *Commentary*, Vol. 37, No. 4 (April, 1964), pp. 29-39.

18. Philip Rieff, *Freud, the Mind of the Moralist* (New York, 1959), p. 303.

underground, their purpose is not to defy the heavens, but on all their battlefields, domestic or foreign, the sky is still their moral limit.

In their determination to bring Presidents to heel, the new professors of the faith and their collegiate cohorts fail to realize that the excrescences of might are those of power structures everywhere, regardless of the social system.

While the young intellectuals are groping toward the New Dispensation, high above them bright new man-made stars glide silently across the skies. What we are seeing today is the merger of two devil images. That of the old rationalistic critic, who has monopolized this study, is now joining with our existential fear of scientific mind. The splitting of the atom and its consequences are our modern version of the Fiend's own handiwork: the devil seen by Martin Luther as telluric demon of the flesh and secularized by Karl Marx as the mystification of the money market, has returned in a new role. The vapors of the ancient Doubter rise today as the big mushroom cloud, our symbol for unmitigated evil.

Do we detect a rainbow in that cloud? Is it too much to hope that the old dualism between mind and body will give way to a reunion of what had been one, before the tree of knowledge yielded its first, deadly fruit? That chastened man would come to terms with death but, in the same breath, elect life?

Mind bloweth where it listeth; one moment it will fancy itself a fiendish despot and the next it will fervently expostulate with the brutality of *1984* and with the absurd rationality of *Brave New World*.

In the shadow of the rising cloud, the old rebellion rages on. Mind's scrutiny of Mind, begun in Heaven, has no end.

Although there may be much truth in saying that the history of human thought is the account of one, continuous revolution, the reverse is not true: The history of revolutions cannot be reduced to intellectual history.

The revolution of the intellectuals, as described in the Prologue, will not be forgotten in the following chapters (it is discussed in chapters 2, 3, 5, 7, 8, 9, and 10). But our principal concern will be with intellectuals not as thinkers but as doers, and with their activities compounded of the multitude of human passions that the intellectual shares with other men.

It remains true, however, that the history of revolutions and the history of human thought converge at some important points. There comes a time when revolutionary thought and action fuse in one tremendous flash of lightning that illuminates broad vistas of the future. But the brightness does not last, and men of coarser fiber thrust the intellectual aside and take over. And just as the rebellion of the intellectuals has been found to reach full circle and turn back upon itself, amounting to an insurrection of mind against mind, so the great social cataclysms too tend to reverse themselves. The revolution terminates in counterrevolution.

But as the rebellion against mind is still an act of mind, however desperate, so counterrevolution likewise may be viewed as still another revolution—as a revolution born of disillusion and despair.

1 The Action and the Actors

REVOLUTIONOLOGY

Even though we know that we should not expect a century to coincide with a historic period, we still tend to do so. We call the eighteenth century the Age of Reason, only to be thrown by the *non sequitur* of the French Revolution; surely it did not turn out to be what the Voltaires and Diderots—and even the Rousseaus—had wanted and expected.[1] To fit that explosive surprise into the scheme of an ordained advance to "higher and higher heights," the latter-day philosophers of history had to resort to Hegelian dialectics and to introduce the laws of contradiction and the concept of the sudden leap.

1. About this sharp hiatus between preparation and result, see Daniel Mornet, *Les origines intellectuelles de la révolution française,* 4th ed. (Paris, 1947). Mornet distinguishes "three kinds of revolutions: revolutions of misery and hunger, the confused uprisings of men tired of suffering . . . these insurrections end in anarchy or bloody repression; revolutions in which an intelligent and audacious minority seizes power, winning over or imposing its rule on indifferent or inert masses; and finally revolutions of a more or less enlightened majority (or at least a very substantial minority) . . . winning over public opinion little by little and coming to power more or less legally. . . . There is no doubt but that, all things considered, the French revolution was of this third type." (Pp. 1-2.)

The nineteenth century is celebrated as the age of liberalism but also known as the epoch of the industrial revolution. Few contemporaries paid attention to the antidemocratic countercurrents which did not emerge until our time. Progress, liberal democracy were the *idées maîtresses;* the intermittent chain reactions of the so-called bourgeois revolution, the upheavals, in the wake of 1789, of 1830, 1848, and 1870, were duly noted. But nevertheless the nineteenth century is not called the age of revolution.

It is the twentieth century—as of 1914—that may receive the title, Age of Revolution, *par excellence.* Not only has the number of successful radical upheavals much increased, but, as the vast, still growing literature on the subject demonstrates, so has our awareness that revolution in our time is not an intermittent break of continuity, not the exception but the rule, our normal condition. Such a term as Helphand-Trotsky's "permanent revolution," originally coined for Marxian use, has now become common currency.

The literature concerned with revolution is of two kinds. One tries to tell the *story* of a revolution. If the account is sympathetic, the "great," epic features of the revolution will emerge; if told with revulsion, as most histories of German or Italian fascism are, it will be a study in pathology. In either case, the narrative will focus on the human cadres, the conspiracies, organizations, revolutionary parties, and above all on the personalities and motivations of the revolutionary *leaders.*[2] Bertram Wolfe's work, *Three Who Made a Revolution*, the pioneer study of Lenin, Trotsky, and Stalin (although Boris Souvarine preceded him with *his* Stalin biography) is a good example of the "cult of personality" dominating the most impressive writings of this school of thought.

The other school, of much more recent date, most of it not older than ten years, although some pilot works go back to World War II and even farther, takes the factual evidence, the revolutionary *story* more or less for granted. Here the purpose is to understand the fundamental nature of *laws* assumed to underlie all revolutions. The sociologist replaces the historian; he is

2. "Such information is of great relevance to the sociology of revolution; and no one would suggest that the determinants of the personalities of Lenin, Atatürk, Hitler, Gandhi, Blanqui, Hung Hsiu-ch'üan, Bakunin, or John Brown are unimportant." Chalmers Johnson, *Revolution and the Social System* (Stanford, Calif., 1964) p. 23.

interested not so much in the psychology of leading men or groups of men as in the social *mechanism* of the revolutionary process. He is looking for the regularities controlling most irregular events.[3]

The dichotomy between "concrete" and "abstract" revolution-ology is only a reflection of the general dichotomy afflicting a civilization of increasingly impersonal relationships for which it tries to compensate by forced repersonalization, to make the dehumanized world bearable again. The Fuehrer, Duce, Vozhd, and, in the democracies, Churchill, Franklin Roosevelt, and Kennedy become the mediators between the collective and the individual, creations rather than creators of the popular imagination.

On this point the Marxist and non-Marxist scientists of revolution are agreed: The great man has his place in history, provided he knows how to keep his place. In fact, the Western theorist will frequently out-Marx his Eastern counterpart in playing down the imprecision of the all-too-human element. Not for him to write of Three Who Made a Revolution, for the Revolution must, by definition, have made *them*.

He will be right, up to a point. For Lenin, Trotsky, and Stalin did not *make* a revolution as one might *make* a cake. They were expecting the upheaval, to be sure, and they prepared and organized *for* it. But when the revolution came, first in 1905, then in 1917, they and the leaders of the other revolutionary parties were surprised by the event and unprepared for its particular demands. They *made* the revolution only in the sense that once the spontaneous combustion of revolution had occurred, they then could try, unsuccessfully in 1905, and successfully in 1917, to channel and control the flow of revolutionary energies. Although their political machines had failed to start the revolution, once it had begun they thrived on its momentum until it was spent.

3. Another possible division would distinguish between "macroscopic" and "microscopic" studies of the subject. In the latter, most recent approach, the use of minute, local data combines the psychological and sociological methods, often, as for instance in the reappraisals of the French revolution now in process, with the most startling results.

FROM INTELLECTUAL MASTERY
TO MASTERMINDING:
COUNTERREVOLUTION

Control does not at first sight seem to be the aim of Western revolutionologists. Crane Brinton's seminal *Anatomy of Revolution* is one of the first contemporary ventures in the field, providing a rough model for a periodization of revolutionary history. His work has both the primitiveness and the sturdiness of a Model-T automobile. Those who followed him, with more sophisticated tools at their disposal, having absorbed both their Parsons *and* their Simmel, concentrated on the interplay of social-equilibrium and social-conflict theories. In this view, revolution is a mere part of a general system of change, which can be closely analyzed and even measured in terms of mass and velocity.

Many writers stop here, satisfied that they are, popularly speaking, "on top of the situation": in intellectual, theoretical control. But from there it is only one more step to thinking about ways and means of actually controlling revolutionary situations. Indeed, much of the writing on guerrilla and "counterinsurgency" warfare, which is pouring from the presses in a seemingly unceasing stream, has the distinctly practical objectives of the manual: It is meant as a guide for action, to instruct political and military specialists how to control, or still better, to arrest, the course of revolution. Most of these studies, directly commissioned or else subsidized by government agencies, have a declared preventive purpose. The authors seem to be aware that a counterrevolution, to be successful, must itself be another revolution; that, distinct from a mere turning back of the historic clock, it partakes of the revolutionary current. Although counterrevolution moves in a different direction, it is fed by the identical hopes and frustrations as the revolution. The counterrevolutionary program competes with the panaceas of the revolutionaries. Although negating their specific means or ends, it cannot afford to be merely negative. The counterrevolution cannot win unless it weakens the hold the competition has on its adherents and presents to them objectives more attractive and—this is important— easier to realize. The counterrevolution cannot, in the age of masses, go against them. Hence the failure of the French to wean the natives of Algeria away from the revolutionary Liberation Front with anything less than the grant of complete independence or, short of that, a radical restructuring of the economy and social system. The irony of the French failure is that it was not due to ignorance. Their military men had studied revolutionary tactics; they were well aware of Mao's "first principle": that the red army should move among the people "like fish in the water" —in other words: the people must be on your side.

The Vietnamese situation too is, at this writing, so unpromising, because the forces trying to arrest the communist rebellion likewise have failed to draw the peasant masses to their side. But then, it is not reasonable to expect the present ruling class of Vietnam to act like revolutionaries, and though our own foreign-policy-makers sometimes seem to endorse democratic socialism abroad, they are not likely to fight a war on two fronts: against the Vietcong *and* the Vietnamese "establishment."

Inasmuch as a counterrevolution usually is a reaction to a revolutionary action already in progress, it is likely to be the result of conscious intent, of a carefully mapped plan. Complete surprise of the opponent, his elimination by a *coup d'état* performed with lightning speed, is the identifying feature of most counterrevolutions, although they do sometimes generate spontaneously. By contrast, revolutions seem to start with what to the contemporary witness looks like a mere accident, and only afterwards comes the realization that it had been "in the cards" for a long time, that the combustible materials had only been waiting for the accidental spark to light the revolutionary pyre. But the explosion cannot be timed in advance: "Revolutions are no conspiracies. They do not erupt because a few men in disguise are plotting in some basement, or because some misguided people agitate among the soldiers at the front or scatter leaflets in the streets. That is the philistine's idea of a revolution. What distinguishes it from a plot and a revolt is its lack of purpose. All contribute to it but without intending to. One cannot agree to make a revolution. Nor is it necessary." [4]

---

4. Eugen Rosenstock-Huessy, *Die europaeischen Revolutionen und der Charakter der Nationen* (Zürich-Wien, 1951), p. 80. Crane Brinton seems to disagree: "To sum the matter up in a metaphor: the school of circumstances regards revolutions as a wild and natural growth . . . outside human planning; the school of plot regards revolutions as a forced and artificial growth. Actually, we must reject both extremes, for they are nonsense, and hold that revolutions do grow from seeds sown by men who want change . . . but that the gardeners are not working against Nature . . . and that the final fruits represent a collaboration between men and Nature." *Anatomy of Revolution* (New York, 1938), pp. 89-90. But Professor Brinton would undoubtedly agree that the collaborators are not always equals, and that revolution (Brinton's Nature) dwarfs conspiracy.

FUSION AND DIFFUSION

In speaking of the "incubation stage" of revolutions, it is hard to avoid thinking of their outcome; the term "revolutionary situation" is fraught with a teleological fallacy. To read into a stage in which the revolutionary forces are still latent the overt form they will take in the future is the wisdom of hindsight.

We commit an even graver error in assuming that the "preconditions" of a revolution could have only *one* result—the one we know to have materialized. But such prediction after the event is patently unjustified. The "revolutionary situation" will, on close inspection, be found to be fraught with many conflicting possibilities. The way in which it finally unfolds is often the one least to be anticipated. Only the historicist fanatic will insist that it had been inevitable.

Shunning labels such as pre-, proto-, or ancillary revolution, let us start simply by saying: Something is going on. Something, or, rather, "a variety of things," threatens the continuity, the orderly performance of the system. What the solution might be, how and by whom it will be found, remains for the time being a moot question. Most contemporaries may not even be aware of the problem.

A variety of things, we said, may underlie the faint malaise or the sporadic and erratic unrest which may already be exploding in such spurts of violence as mass strikes, or public meetings leading to disorders and police repression. But at that stage opposition, criticism of the system, is as yet discordant. That may be because the revolution is already in process, speedily transforming the *status quo*, but it is still a revolution of *things*, not yet of men. The human enemy is still invisible; he cannot as yet be identified. One example is the English industrial revolution in its early stage. It had its Luddites, venting their despair on the demonic new machines, but not until the factory was recognized as a mere part of a distinct political ensemble could the Chartist movement come into existence. Even then class consciousness, in Marx's and Lenin's sense, was still too inchoate to have the one result that would have justified the Marxian expectation: the revolution in the most developed capitalist country did not take place.

Even when "the enemy" has been identified, unification of the groups opposing him cannot be assumed to follow automatically. Peasants will not easily see eye to eye with urban workers; even the same "class" may turn out to be badly split. At an initial stage of an already overt revolution, there is yet no telling which of the contending forces will prevail. The superficial unity of the first days soon wanes, for the removal of the obstacle they all agreed upon marks also the beginning of new discontents, this time directed against their temporary brothers-in-arms. The revolutionary era of good feeling is succeeded by a rough awakening: Behind the hastily erected screen of compromise, the cleavage between ultimate aims widens, soon to reach the breaking point. The revolution now moves from its "open," pluralistic phase into the "closed," or monolithic, stage.[5] Enter the Great Unifier, making an end of diffusion and achieving fusion by either attracting (by persuasion) other revolutionary groups or else eliminating them by force. Sometimes this process of elimination does not result from any purposive activity on the part of the ascending group but from natural erosion, the often noted polarization process that drives the large masses, now apathetic, from the revolutionary stage, and leaves only the extremist few to fight it out. The winning party will attempt to maintain fusion, but a new diffusion is all but inevitable. Now the revolution must be "saved" by terror, all and any opposition is declared dysfunctional, endangering consolidation. The triumphant revolution cannot allow any further revolution—at least none origi-

---

5. In Crane Brinton's classical formulation: "In the society during the generation or so before the outbreak of revolution, in the old regime, there will be found signs of the coming disturbance. . . . Then comes a time when the full symptoms disclose themselves, and when we can say the fever of the revolution has begun. This works up, not regularly but with advances and retreats, to a crisis, frequently accompanied by delirium, the rule of the most violent revolutionists, the Reign of Terror. After the crisis comes a period of convalescence, usually marked by a relapse or two. Finally, the fever is over, and the patient is himself again, perhaps in some respects actually strengthened by the experience. . . ." *op. cit.*, p. 18. Or in Rex D. Hopper's formulation: "Revolutionary movements . . . pass through four stages in their development: the Preliminary Stage of Mass (Individual) Excitement and Unrest, the Popular Stage of Crowd (Collective) Excitement and Unrest, the Formal Stage of Formulation of Issues and Formulation of Publics, and the Institutional Stage of Legalization and Social Organization." Rex D. Hopper, "The Revolutionary Process," *Social Forces*, Vol. 28, No. 3 (March, 1950), p. 270. Clearly, Hopper's four stages do not cover the same time span as Brinton's five. The former stops with the establishment of a revolutionary, the latter with the creation of the postrevolutionary system.

nating from below; to avoid this, it explains the new system as still on the revolutionary move, thus making it palatable to disgruntled old militants, as a revolution directed from above in the name of The Nation, or "the Soviet toilers."

At this point the whole sequence has come full circle. It had started with the alienation of a small minority composed of various groups converging temporarily in order to remove the assumed causes of their discontent. Then, as alienation led to revolution, so the revolution, *via* the polarization and elimination of most revolutionary actors, led again to alienation, this time of the great majority.[6] The alienators of the first part were the representatives of the *ancien régime*, those of the second, the new revolutionary rulers. The trend is from conspiracy to movement, and back to conspiracy again. In the opinion of the new conspirators, the revolution has not solved the problem of dysfunctionality; in fact, it may have aggravated it. This judgment may lead to two opposite conclusions: On the one hand that the revolution was not radical enough, not "carried out"; it was arrested. On the other hand, it might have gone too far, "gone off the rails" and "fallen into the wrong hands." The first view would explain why the French revolution had to continue for another century, until the system finally equilibrated in 1875, when France adopted the constitution of the Third Republic. (Even that date may be wrong, because the system did not really function until the "Republic of the Notables" was displaced by the middle-class regime that came to power through the Dreyfus revolution of the 1890s.) The second view, rejecting the excesses of the Jacobins, confirms the perspective of the permanent French revolution, which could not resolve the problem until the initial claimant to the throne, the middle class, had overcome the thrusts

6. Rex D. Hopper, *op. cit.*, p. 277, lists the following "Causal Characteristics of the Final Stage: (*a*) Psychological exhaustion which undermines the emotional foundations of the revolution. (*b*) Moral let-down and return to old habits (attitudes), including 'escape recreation' and the re-emergence of graft, speculation, and corruption, become deterrents to continued revolutionary behavior. (*c*) Great economic distress, amounting almost to chaos, demands a settling down. Resultant characteristics: (*a*) End of the Reign of Terror; granting of amnesty; return of exiles; repression of extremists; and search for scapegoats. (b) Increase in powers of central government, frequently resulting in dictatorship. (*c*) Social reconstruction along lines of the old social structure but with the new principles (values) essentially intact. (*d*) Dilution of the revolutionary ideal; transformation of evangelistic fervor into the desire for conquest; transformation of the 'revolutionary sect' into a 'political domination.' (*e*) Re-accommodation of church and state."

and counter-thrusts of other groups presenting claims, now premature, now obsolete, and giving France two Bonapartes. (The third one may be Charles de Gaulle, which might be proof that the French revolution still continues.)

All of which is merely saying that a revolution is not necessarily *progressive*. It may very well be regressive, in deliberate reaction to progressive movements of the time or to reforms enacted by the government.

Another example can be found in Martin Luther. His religious revolution was directed against a regime, the Papacy, which in our sense was, if not liberal, then at least enlightened, certainly a far cry from medieval orthodoxy. Luther's protest, like so many others that preceded it, was an attempt not to dismantle or modernize the church but to restore its early Christian purity. His break with Rome was unpremeditated; he was dismayed by the explosion it caused and horrified by the rebellious uproar of the peasants and millenniarists who rushed on where the monk of Wittenberg refused to follow.

Similarly, England's great rebellion of the 1640s had originally been aimed not at establishing Parliament's supremacy but at reversing the trend for absolute royal control; this trend, under way throughout Europe, had existed in England ever since the reign of James I and was there advancing rapidly in the 1630s when Charles I ruled without Parliament. The conscious aim of the rebellious leaders, Pym and Hampden, was the restoration of the—assumed—previous equilibrium between the executive and legislative branches: "King in Parliament." But the rebellion went beyond that, overshooting the limits acceptable to those who had started it.

Conservative revolutions of this kind, intent on bringing back "the good old times," can be so aggressive because they are based on an initial broad consensus. Almost everybody rallies when strong interests (such as, in England, those of London and the landed gentry, reinforced by Puritan dissent) identify themselves with a hallowed tradition. When the consensus fades, the time comes for the Lord Protector to step in. His historic task is twofold: first, he must consolidate the revolutionary gains until a new advance is possible, and second, in order to do this, he must obtain the broadest support possible or at least a pretense of unity. However, once the mass basis is lost beyond recall, the Lord Protector or First Secretary will have to resort to coercion.

Cromwell found himself in that frustrating situation; so did Robespierre. With the difference that Cromwell died in bed while Robespierre met his own lethal "Thermidor," both dictators presided over an "arrested revolution." [7]

The concept, which applies to "progressive" revolutions be they "conservative" or radical, must be used with great discrimination. Revolutions often travel faster than the social traffic of the time will bear; in that case the arresting power will redress the balance between past and future, and the revolution will end because it has "fulfilled its true purpose." Other similar instances are Napoleon III's regime arresting the slow progress of the French Revolution toward the Bourgeois Republic for another twenty years; more recently, on July 1, 1934, Hitler's liquidation of the alleged brownshirt putsch of Captain Roehm contained both the left- and right-wing oppositions, and established the Nazi leader as the Cromwell-Robespierre of the Third Reich. Strange as it sounds, the same is true of Lenin and Stalin: both consistently maintained, within the framework of their radical mandate, a mediating position between the conservative and radical wings of the Party.

The victims of the stabilizer will of course accuse him of betraying the Republic and the Revolution; to the *enragés*, old Bolsheviks, and *alte Kaempfer*, he will merely be the time-server, beneath contempt. He has, however, what the Utopian lacks: a *genius for mediocrity*, pragmatic wisdom before the event, because he is himself a genius *of* mediocrity. Equipped with an unerring instinct for what will be acceptable to most, the great consolidator seems to speak their mind, the median mind of people who reach out for him and find—themselves.

Of course, to such scoffers as Victor Hugo the latter-day Napoleon, wrapping himself in the mantle of the charismatic predecessor, will remain a figure of derision and, worse, not to be trusted. Yet they have no right to say that he does not let his left hand know what his right is doing, for he knows quite well what he is doing all the time—until his time is up. Nor is it his fault that his regime strikes his contemporaries as ambiguous in intent and performance. This is so because the great consolidator is at the same time the representative and creature of a period in transition. The old has not yet entirely passed away, and his notion of the new is hazy. So the young will find him hesitant

7. See below, chapters 4 and 5.

and banal, while the older generation finds him dangerous and unreliable.

CHARACTER AND ROLE

A combination of the sociological and psychological approaches is characteristic of that hybrid literary form, the political biography, in which the actor dominates the scene. This study has the opposite focus; its aim is to illuminate the scene rather than spotlight the actor. The actor's character will be less relevant than his historic role. The individuals selected will not necessarily be figures of prime importance. Second-raters often teach us more about the major problems of revolution than does the Man of Destiny. They are more closely integrated into the whole, complex scheme of things, whereas the outstanding figure literally stands out, above the context, dwarfing it. The hero, it is said, belongs to the ages; for a better understanding of his age, we will do well to turn our attention to less imposing and distracting figures.

In bringing the typology of revolutionary "systems" to bear on selected individuals, we are bound to treat them, more or less, as types, by which we run the risk of pruning away most of their individuality. But by starting with psychological archetypes, we may find out why certain human beings rather than others are attracted to and equipped for revolutionary postures and performances. No harm is done, provided we remind ourselves that this is only a first step toward an understanding of the revolutionary *process*.

It is the revolutionary's functional role, rather than his character endowment, that matters. This is not to say that character is necessarily fixed; quite the contrary: The actor could successfully adapt himself to changing situations with protean flexibility were that all that mattered. Given a broad institutional framework, the most diversified psychological talents may meet the requirements of a function such as the American Presidency, which is generally defined as the power mediating between the various branches of government and between the government and the public. Some of the incumbents of the office have been rather ill endowed for the mediator's function, yet they have made effective or even great presidents. The reason is, of course, that the Presidency demands that the leading man enact more roles than merely the one of honest or dishonest mediator. Failure in one or even several of these roles does not necessarily defeat him.

However, in a revolutionary situation, which not only is extremely fluid but also lacks the familiar props of institutional legality, even the most versatile protagonist may quickly find himself displaced and frequently annihilated if the role by which he has become known changes. No matter how much he may try to change his image, he remains identified with it; the mask his role required can never be torn off.

The downfall of the two Napoleons may serve as an illustration. What at first sight appears to be a failure of nerve, perhaps aggravated by illness, accounts perhaps for the defeats inflicted on them by superior enemies. But Waterloo and Sedan are only the epilogue to the imperial tragedy that has its own internal explanation. Both Napoleon I and III saw, at a point late in their careers (1814 and 1861, respectively) the need for a liberalization of their rule. But although they did find it in themselves —if not easily—to make the necessary adjustment from despotism to constitutionalism, they were not permitted to play a new role that would have seemed false and out of character for them. Their function was to liquidate a revolution, not to continue it, and when they had fulfilled that task, their time was up. Neither would have been creditable as a liberal.

Robespierre's fall too is frequently attributed to some mysterious personal crack-up. His fumbling before Thermidor, his silence when he had only to say the word, his coy withdrawal from the scene of action, seem to indicate a strange paralysis immobilizing the arch plotter. So the plot against him could succeed—miraculously. But it was no miracle. The terror of the guillotine had simply become self-defeating, and the terrorists, afraid of being the next victims, turned upon the head-executioner. Then the same men, Robespierreans all, became the rulers of the *Directoire*. Can anyone imagine Robespierre, alive, as its Director? He could never have lived down his previous role.

Both Mussolini and Khrushchev were in the end outwitted and deposed by their own creatures (although Kremlinologists believe that Stalin's successor never enjoyed unlimited control). Again, it appears as if the two men, aging and not in the best of health, had lost their grip. In fact, when they fell, both were already defeated: Khrushchev by his own mistakes and Mao; Mussolini by the allied armies. Mussolini tried to revert to his initial character of revolutionary socialist, but even without interference by the German army, the "Republic of Salò" and its leader could not return to a played-out stage of fascist history.

In brief, the revolutionary role absorbs and utilizes psychological predispositions but is not determined by them. It derives its character and relevance from the historical process, which is highly unpredictable when history accelerates. True, even revolutions have their archetypical casts of roles to be filled each time; for example, in the prerevolutionary phase, the *idéologues* and plotters; in the springtime of the revolution, the great orators and tribunes of the people; then the harsh taskmasters of the dictatorial climax; and finally the pragmatists of Thermidor. But whether or not all these situations with their quite specific role requirements will occur, which of them, when, and with what results, cannot be predicted. Some revolutions may start with a dictatorship: Castro's in Cuba; or there may not be a Thermidor: has it occurred in Soviet Russia? If so, when? The experts are still arguing about it.[8]

Psychological aptitudes or ineptitudes may to some extent account for success or failure in performing the role function, but they do not create it. Nor does character determine the nature of the role and when it will be performed, if at all.

A last example: Hitler's character was formed by his unhappy home life as a child, by the refusal of the world to recognize his genius as an artist, by his lumpen-proletarian Viennese milieu, and, last but not least, by the experience of the war and the defeat in which it ended. Hitler's so-formed character in turn determined that of the movement he led to victory. Had he died, before or after his accession to power, his successors, lacking his unique appeal, might have governed differently—perhaps less erratically, not necessarily any the less brutally. But the historic role of the Nazi regime, as a destructive force, would not have been different. The uniqueness of the event called Hitler was that character and historic role were so perfectly matched.

We will not deal with him in this study. Even where more admirable heroes are available, our preference, as we said, is for the minor players. Some of them are luckier than the performers with top billing in having the last word. Others fail disastrously.

8. See below, chapter 8.

But study of their failures may more readily help us understand what went wrong on the big stage than study of the hero's downfall, for a failure of heroic proportions holds us spellbound and thus weakens our critical faculty. Still others are not even allowed to speak their piece but remain outcasts, would-be actors, awaiting a cue that never comes or comes only as the curtain is lowered.

This leads us to another major point this study attempts to make.

DECLINE AND FALL

The fade-out time of revolutions cannot vie for close attention with their springs and summers. To be sure, the Thermidorian and post-Thermidorian phases of the English and French revolutions have been studied and recorded in minute detail. It is no less true that the final agony of the Cromwellian interregnum and the death of the First French Republic simply do not and could never be expected to evoke the interest, the passionate excitement aroused by a description of the early, great *journées*. Long before the last chapter our attention begins to flag, and finally we are past caring: not only do we wish the revolution and its men to end, but to end badly, to be swept away into the sewers of historic obloquy. Indeed, if the beginnings of a revolution may be likened to a glorious muddle, and its climax to a wild *extravaganza*, the end seems to be pure persiflage.

As caricatures show up traits of the original we had not noticed before, so the farce of the *finale* is a shortened, if malicious, re-enactment of the revolutionary drama. If we wish to know what it was all about, endurance in studying it to its bitter end will be rewarding. For the epilogue is more than a lament for what might have been, more than a groan of futility. It is all that, but also something else. The funeral pyre of the revolution generates no heat but sheds much light. It has a clarity not apparent when the sun was in its zenith. But it is the clarity of stage-lighting: It magnifies but also oversimplifies the issues and ideals of the ending era, just as the restoration thoughts of a De Maistre or Chateaubriand went back to an austere and yet attractive Old Regime that never was.

Though the temptation to romanticize the end is hardly great, we cannot behold it without feeling something akin to Aristotle's *catharsis:* part horror and part pity, above all relief. We want to laugh and at the same time weep, weep over the passing of greatness. Everything is back to normal; paltry plots and counter-plots are the order of the day. The masses have retired from the scene in bewilderment and apathy. The battle of revolutionary phalanxes has shrunk to the rear-guard actions of platoons, re-peating the old slogans by rote. Cold manipulation takes the place of fuzzy passion. Yet the colors are still flying high, long after the outcome of the battle has been decided. The idea of the revolution refuses to die and continues to assert itself through human agents almost against their will and better judgment. Of conviction there is little left; this is the time of the turncoat and the cynic. Is it still the revolution or already counterrevolution? The dividing line has become blurred, almost invisible. The end of revolution is a time for little men. Gone are the days of a Danton, a Trotsky. But the small stature of the final actors meets the very need of the new situation; the great stage of human passion has contracted to a size accommodating small intrigue. Action no longer *demands* men of gigantic stature; everyday problems are left to be solved by everyday people. If they are given smaller *roles* than their dead or demoted predecessors, it is also true that their tasks are more thankless. If history, in Jacob Burckhardt's phrase, is bound to bring forth the *terrible sim-plificateur,* his favorite hour of appearance is precisely when a revolution nears its end. When the new men, men of mediocrity, take power, luck smiles on them for a short while. They are so sure the worst is over. But it is not. Hardly have they settled down when they are pulled up sharply and contemptuously dis-carded by an underling. The military man appears and puts an end to petty politics. The people, fed up with the new medi-ocrity, hail the return to greatness—under Bonaparte.

COUNTERREVOLUTION IS ANOTHER REVOLUTION

Napoleon I was the son of revolution and the general of counter-revolution. He is the greatest counterrevolutionist of modern history. What obscures the true dimensions of his counterrevolu-tionary role is that he *also* represented and carried into Europe some of the ideas of the revolution. When a revolution stales, the counterrevolution reinvigorates the survivors as fresh air braces congested lungs. The restoration of prerevolutionary "normality" is in most cases the initial aim of counterrevolutionaries, who counter every revolutionary "yes" with their own "no." The strength of counterrevolutionary tendencies is evidence of unresolved antinomies within the revolutionary camp; the opportunity for counterrevolutionary action would seem to be greatest during the first, open, diffused period of the revolution. Such action also may bring this phase to an end by forcing the discordant revolutionary factions to unite against the common, inner enemy. But since the causes of disunity are only driven underground, the counterrevolutionary forces may resurface if the rulers of the day do not at once restore stability—a new stability based on the conquests of the revolution. This result agrees with the objective needs: When he starts out, the revolutionist's subjective aim is change, but once in power he will instantly try to consolidate that power. He will turn "conservative."

Inversely, counterrevolutionaries, wishing to return to the old order, are subjectively in favor of stability. However, inasmuch as that old order no longer exists, they are objectively committed to a fight for change: their target is the new, revolutionary order. Counterrevolutionary action, taking place under conditions of essential instability, tends to increase this order as long as the revolutionary energies remain alive. At the same time, a transformation takes place that deflects the counterrevolutionary dynamism from its original direction to one that, although it still runs counter to the main revolutionary current, does make use of its momentum. Counterrevolution turns into another revolution.

This conversion draws its strength not from the odious victories but from the massive blunders of the opposition. The illusions of utopian rhetoric will be exposed to the advantage of the counterrevolutionist's pragmatic wisdom. His professed aim is identical with that of his opponent: the improvement of the human condition. The counterrevolutionary also knows the price that must be paid for every advance: a price only the Unhappy Few will be prepared to pay. That is the burden of the Grand Inquisitor—the knowledge that the total liberation of mankind is fated to remain a golden myth.

It is this kind of ambiguity that makes all counterrevolutions so suspect and at the same time so alluring. Driven on by his conviction that the revolutionists are bound to fail, the counter-revolutionary is at the same time intensely envious of the revolutionists' historic role. He desperately tries to prove them wrong and himself the better, more authentic revolutionary. He will borrow Lenin's method, without the philosophy; if the result is travesty, it may still work, precisely because imitation often drives out the original.[9] The counterrevolutionary radical is frequently a revolutionist *manqué,* and his success is predicated on the failure of the enterprise without which he would have no justification. This ambivalence may also account for the characteristic guilty sadness of the counterrevolutionary mind: the sadness of the morning after.

If the counterrevolutionist is the gravedigger of freedom, his intentions are most honorable. For he has a mission; history will be his judge. If he should achieve his goal, it would be because the revolution had already reached it. Counterrevolution is not murder, only *devolution.* In their hour of victory, all counter-revolutionaries wear the same mask, expressing nothing. Their own dreams have died, together with the greater vision.[10]

ONE-MAN REVOLUTION

There are two other types of revolutionary leaders. Both are rare, not easily identified or understood. One, the "super-revolutionary," may be the inspiration, founder, and commander of a revolutionary movement, yet he is not bound to it. He is neither its product nor defined by its declared objectives, which are to him merely means to other, greater ends. The normal revolu-

9. "Fascism is anti-Marxism which seeks to destroy the enemy by the evolvement of a radically opposed and yet related ideology and by the use of almost identical and yet typically modified methods, always, however, within the unyielding framework of national self-assertion and autonomy." Ernst Nolte, *Three Faces of Fascism* (New York, Chicago, San Francisco, 1966), pp. 20-21. Nolte also notes: "In its isolated form the definition lays no claim to originality. The basic paradox is already contained in the term 'conservative revolution.' Gustav Adolf Rein, in *Bonapartismus und Faschismus* [Göttingen, 1960], describes fascism as counterrevolution on the soil of revolution." (Nolte, *op. cit.,* p. 466, n. 50). For other definitions of fascism, see chapter 9, note 1 on pp. 133-134, below.

10. The preceding discussion is the outgrowth of some of my remarks in *Makers of Modern Social Science: Pareto and Mosca,* edited and introduced by the present writer (Englewood Cliffs, 1965) pp. 3-4.

tionary leader may, by his explicit orders, cause the ruin of his entire nation, but even so, he will remain convinced of having acted in its higher interest. Our man, however, stands above society; his is a solipsistic universe light-years remote from common mortals and their concerns. As a case in point, Lenin comes to mind, for he looked upon his Russia as a laboratory, transient and expendable. If he was prepared to sacrifice his nation, it was for the sake of something bigger: the world revolution.

Hitler was different. What did he care about Germany? When, finally defeated, she refused to follow him in suicide, he felt betrayed and turned his back on the small-minded Germans as unworthy of him. He was in truth Max Stirner's man: *The Ego and His Own*.[11]

It may seem blasphemous to mention in the same breath all those saintly figures who cared nothing about the plight or even the destruction of their own communities because only God mattered to them. If His chosen people preferred earthly kings and their expensive armies and alliances with heathen nations, then the men of God had to denounce and, if they could, wreck the whole system, even if it meant the end of national existence.[12]

Finally, there is the solitary *displaced* prophet or "the revolutionist without a revolution." He is not to be confused with the now fashionable "rebel without a cause," for he does have a cause. It is his fate to be engaged in revolution at its latent, hidden stage. It may never come to pass, but that does not make it less real to him. His revolution is a genuine response to a need felt instinctively by many, but perhaps repressed by some and heatedly denied by others. The revolution is no mere abstraction or fantasy to him, but a living, lived experience, even though he may never once harangue a crowd or write a manifesto. Being displaced does not prevent him from enjoying or even seeking intimate communion with like-minded souls. His action takes the form of a withdrawal that draws others with him; the withdrawal is the action when no other way seems open. One thinks of D. H. Lawrence and his obdurate attempts to found the new community of the visceral faith in some remote, unspoiled asylum. The supreme example of this genus of man is Nietzsche,

11. *Der Einzige und sein Eigentum*, 1845. Marx and Engels attacked Stirner's monumental egotism in *The German Ideology*.
12. See chapter 2.

possibly the loneliest of all these wanderers. Their withdrawal has the quality of dialectic tension. It combines a maximum of alienation from the system with a maximum of agonizing for it. The conjoined force of rejection and attraction makes the displaced prophet hesitant to act, and he risks losing sight of his own revolutionary vision, but his hesitation to act in no way diminishes his revolutionary zeal. He will seem to move in a circle, trying one thing after another. His biography seems to consist of hopeless repetition, of retreat and lunge, lunge and retreat. His own momentum (revolutionary) and what blocks it (the nonrevolutionary situation) is internalized as self-mocking nostalgia—"Irony," as Thomas Mann has said, "is a parting with love"—and externalized in a pretense of "playing ball," of not fighting the system, except from within. In fact, this type of rebel will frequently be an insider, the intimate of those in power; at the same time he will try to spoil their game by playing it according to their stupid rules. The figure of existential protest, the other British Lawrence, T. E., of Arabian fame, comes here to mind.[13]

13. See below, chapter 10.

As this is being written, the Buddhist leaders of Saigon are threatening the military masters of South Vietnam with rebellion—this for the second time in a few years. The holy men propose to overthrow the government not by the mere use of their prayer wheels; they threaten to call out the masses. Their declared purpose is to give the country a civilian, democratic government. They revile the warlords as the enemies of God, their God, and of his people.

It is an old, old story, as old as our Bible. It tells the same tale clearly: once there was a nation unto God; it did not need a King with armed men and tax collectors; for that was the way of slavery. Yahweh was the war lord of free men, led by his servants and spokesmen, the judges and prophets. The issue was clear cut: Kingship was blasphemy, the aberration that led to perdition, conquest by the foreigner. The Chosen People must not, cannot, ever become a nation like the others; it was unique, the issue of a pact between men and their creator. In our modern terminology we would speak of a confrontation between the advocates of an archaic, pastoral theocracy and the progressive forces of bureaucracy, of power politics.

Who won? In the short run the progressives: those who wanted a strong monarchy capable of standing up to the invaders of the little country, Israel. But in the long run, the holy ones triumphed; the nation conceived as a spiritual body survived the bondage of Egypt and the exile of Babylon. Translated into modern language again: The counterrevolutionary ideology of the prophets prevailed over the revolutionary innovations of military monarchy. The old proved to be younger than the new.

2 Prophets in Revolt

SACRAL COMMUNITY AND
NATION STATE

The first recorded revolution—and counterrevolution—in the Western world occurred at its easternmost fringe in what is now called Israel. Our source is the Old Testament.

It has become the fashion to compare the ideologists and leaders of contemporary social movements to the ancient Hebrew prophets (and this study will be no exception).[1] Such assertions as "the revolutionary tradition which has found so many of its leading recipients and exponents among intellectuals . . . . orig- inates in the apocalyptic outlook of the prophets of the Old Testament," throw into high relief the normative and therefore frequently utopian character of intellectual politics. As one soci- ologist has observed, "The disposition to distinguish sharply be-

1. A recent example of this tendency is Louis J. Halle's essay, "Marx's Religious Drama," *Encounter*, Vol. 25, No. 4 (October, 1965), pp. 29, 37: "Marx . . . had more of St. Paul in him than of the social scientist, or the empirical scholar. . . . Marxism . . . met the need for a religion of the industrial age." The tendency to see Marxism as a secularized version of Hebrew eschatology has found its most extreme expression in Arnold Künzli's recent study, *Karl Marx*, Eine Psychographie (Wien, Frankfurt, Zürich: Europa Verlag, 1966).

tween good and evil . . . the insistence that justice be done though the heavens fall, the obstinate refusal to compromise or to tolerate compromise"—all these features "must be attributed in some measure at least to this tradition." [2]

This school of thought stresses the mythical, nonfalsifiable content of a social message.[3] The opposite tendency to reduce the ancient prophets to the level of contemporary ideologists, which also has impressive though fewer advocates, may be defined as the endeavor to sociologize the myth. The task is harder the farther back in time the sociological imagination roams. The difficulties in distinguishing between fact and myth are disheartening; Max Weber speaks of "the hopeless unclarity in which figures such as Balaam, Samuel, Nathan, also Elijah, today appear to us." [4] Clarification of the mythical penumbra would, however, only worsen the predicament: Our penetration of the "truth" experienced by a prophet may destroy it, because for him reality was not only organized *a priori* but also expressed in terms of mythical configuration. Truth is blinding; stared at too much, it becomes a lie.

So much as an excuse for our attempt here at two imaginary and entirely hypothetical reconstructions of the clash between myth and reality in Hebrew history, a clash not susceptible to a solution, much as Hebrew myth and history remain inseparable. The first reconstruction deals with the origins of Hebrew statehood, and the second reflects an early phase of its prolonged decline.

A PROPOSAL FROM A FELLOW TRAVELER

To: Achis, Lord of Gath
From: His Liege Man, the Dawidūm *of Ziklag*

May the mighty Baal grant you long life and health! Your humble servant has received your message and he hastens to comply with your request. You wish to know the truth about the mountain men, to wit: the savage people who dared descend into your realm from their bare hills, a hapless lot whom you and

2. Edward A. Shils, "The Traditions of Intellectuals" in *The Intellectuals*, George B. de Huszar, editor (Glencoe, 1960), pp. 59, 60.
3. George Sorel's mythicization of the Marxian heritage comes to mind.
4. *Ancient Judaism*, transl. and ed. by Hans H. Gerth and Don Martindale (Glencoe, 1952), p. 105.

your confederates, the mighty sea lords, smote not once but twice. Yes, you have taught them who are the true masters of the plain and its walled cities; you have driven them back into their dank lairs where they now lick their wounds and wail, bewail him whom you slew on Mount Gilboah, the man Saul who called himself King of the Hebrews. I lament him? Do not, oh my Lord, trust those who try to poison your ear, carrying tales about your good servant. How could I feel sorrow about Saul who drove me from his presence, threatening to take my life so that I had to flee to the hills? And still, he pursued me, driving me from cave to cave, and once it was I who surprised him sleeping and I did not touch him, for the love I once had for his son Jonathan.

No, you came to the right man. Having lived so long among the mountain men and knowing their ways well, I am the one to tell you how to deal with them. But let me first dispose of an old slander, to wit: that it was I who slew your good knight, Goliath. Let them sing their song: it is not true. Another man, not your obedient servant, overcame that noble lord in knightly combat, his name, Elhanahan, the Bethlehemite. Trust them to falsify the record, but the truth they dare not suppress altogether, so in their small cunning they named both of us as slayers, hoping nobody would find them out. Such is the way of scribes. Let me tell you what they did to Saul.

They did not like him from the first, the headmen who had ruled the mountain men for ages in the name of their God, Zebaoth, or as some call him: Yahweh—a small god compared with the almighty Baal, but in the hills they knew no other than Him who had led them as a fiery column out of Egypt's bondage and then had spoken to them through Moses, His servant, from the fiery mountain, Sinai. So they came to Canaan and prospered. And they fought in the old ways, led into battle by their headmen, Yahwe's prophets. Armor, chariots they knew not, and so You vanquished them. The Ark in which they kept their holy scrolls you carried off into captivity. That should have been the end, but no: They kept on fighting. So you took away their spears and swords and you forbade them to forge their own plowshares; they had to come down into the plain to you for their tools. And still they kept plotting against You, and some would say: Our headmen know not how to fight against the Sea Lords, we must find one who will teach us, we must have a

King! An old man, Samuel, first would have none of it, but when he saw that many of the people wanted a strong war lord who would be their King and leader of armed bands like yours, he finally gave in and made it seem as if it was his, Samuel's, own wish. So he anointed Saul, a valiant fighter who towered above the crowd. And things went well for a short while: Saul won some skirmishes against your outposts. You thought little of it at first. But then you gathered your whole strength and that was poor Saul's end.

But let me tell you how Saul was betrayed by them while he was still locked in battle with Your might. For You must know, my Lord, the secret of the mountain men: they are forever of two minds and he who knows it will become their master. Here is the answer that your faithful servant will reveal to you alone, for You showed him mercy when he came to you as a poor fugitive from his own people: now has come the time for him to give you proof of his eternal gratitude.

The mountain men are ruled not by one master but by two. One is their God, their Yahweh, who once made a covenant with them: as long as they would recognize and worship Him as their true, only ruler, He would hold His hand forever over them.

But when the ark was lost, they wavered in their faith and said: Who will protect us now? Let us choose a master as the other nations have and be like them. And that was how they came to ask Saul to be their king. I related how old Samuel gave in to their demands. But then he pondered deeply and he recognized that once the mountain men became a nation like the others, Yahweh would no longer be their king and those who had long judged the people would no longer judge them. Instead, the new king would have his judges and his hundreds, and the people would be taxed and ground into the dust. So ran his warning and the people knew not whom to follow—their old leaders who had lost the ark or the new king who would impose his yoke upon free men. And so the mountain men split into two camps, one proclaiming the old overlord beyond the clouds who had vouchsafed them mastery over their enemies if only they would remain faithful to Him; the other, made up of fighting men who put their faith in swords, not miracles.

My Lord and Benefactor: if you want to keep the mountain men at bay, you must act wisely. It is not enough to occupy and guard the passes against their marauders; that would be a thankless and endless undertaking. For the mountain men are a stiff-necked lot: Do not expect them to surrender ever to Your mighty sword. They will not render homage even to their own, anointed kings, if these kings encroach, as they must do, on Yahweh's claims. He who wants to be master of these people must know how to serve both masters: the earthly lord certainly, for without him they will become slaves of other nations, but that earthly lord under their heavenly King of Kings. The human king will be your friend and he will take your daughters into marriage and give his as hostages to You. But you must find the man who will know how to please the King above, so that He will not be jealous and strike his servant, the anointed king, with madness, as He struck down Saul.

How to find that man, Your man, you ask me? I will tell you. I will tell you what I did, and what, if it please you, I can further do on your behalf.

I came to you, an outcast and a beggar, and your guards would not unlock the gate for me. And I was truly at the end of my wits and frothing at the mouth, and they reported to you that there was a madman at the gate, and were there not already enough madmen in your city? And You answered in your wisdom: Forsooth, I am indeed supplied with madmen! Yet you did not send away the supplicant. You gave him shelter, and you fed him, and you trusted him to govern, in your name, the town of Ziklag. And I gathered around me the men who had not left me in my times of trial, a hardy lot, of whom a captain of men could be proud. And so I built Your force and led it into battle, and when you gathered all your levies to crush Saul, I offered You my men and myself, to fight with you. I will avow that I was hurt when Your war council turned down my offer and told me to stay in the rear; I did not then well understand why you refused me. Could it be that you distrusted me, your bondsman? I know now that in the kindness of your heart you did not wish that I should have to face my old liege lord in battle.

But I am not one to bear grudges. Here then is my plan: I am not without influence in my own native Southland, in the mountain fastnesses of Judah. I even have some ties with tribes that are not members of the mountain men's confederacy. Altogether six of them are willing to have me as their king. I would accept

*their offer as your confederate and liege man, if the Lords so
order me. Thus you would be master of six of the twelve Hebraic
tribes!*

*Under your suzerainty, I would be king, first of one half and,
with divine help, then of the entire confederation. Do not worry
about Yahweh and His men. They hold me in esteem. Was I not
the sworn foe of their foe, Saul? Their emissaries came to see
me in the desert, to enlist me on their side. Then I could do
but little for them. Now, with your consent, I can become their
King—as Yahweh's servant. And as your good friend and ally,
keeping peace, as faithfully as I was*

Your Dawidūm of Ziklag who calls himself

D a v i d

COMMENT

The David image sketched in the preceding pages is not pretty,
but most of the facts narrated can be found in the official text;[5]
others can be reconstructed: "The northern Israelite peasants
and the Judaic mountain herdsmen . . . made common cause
against the Philistines only at a late date. At first the herdsmen
abstained altogether from the struggle and remained loyal to the
Philistines. . . . David began as leader of a mountaineer following
of the usual conspirational nature. He was a vassal of the
Philistines and made himself independent only when he became
city-prince of Jerusalem. . . ."[6]

By blending David's story into that of King Saul's northern
resistance movement, the official tradition makes its hero actually
appear in a most dubious role: as deserting from the national

---

5. The first book of Samuel tells the story of Saul's elevation (10);
Samuel's warning against kingship, and the people's reaction: "We will
have a king over us; that we also may be like all the nations" (8) already
states the basic objection of the old religious leadership to the new trend
toward a nation state: Yahweh's people were not meant to become just
"another nation." Sam. 21:19 has the name of David's knight who slew
Goliath (in our story the event occurs, as it does in the Bible, in Saul's
time). According to Martin Noth, *Geschichte Israels,* 2nd ed. (Goettingen,
1954), p. 165 n. 2, David was apparently not his original name but derived
from Dawidum, meaning commander, troop leader, indicating David's rise
as a chief of trained soldiers rather than tribal levies. The term "mountain
men" is used here to identify the Hebrews clinging to the fastnesses of the
Judaean hills as seen through the eyes of the Philistines, the inhabitants of
the coastal cities.

6. Max Weber, *op. cit.,* p. 55.

leader and becoming a collaborator of the occupying alien power. The sociological imagination can explain how the deserter finally succeeded, by sheer diplomatic cunning, where the upright hero, King Saul, tragically failed. It also must do justice to the other David who was able to appease the strong, religious opposition to a Hebrew monarchy because he was himself a genuine religious leader. By making the old center of the Yahweh cult, Jerusalem, his capital, the renegade emerges as the great reconciliator of the two opposing camps, the *Henri IV* of the Hebrews who could say that Jerusalem *vaut bien une messe* if Israel was to be unified against the conquerors. Some fissures still remained, and it is not quite clear to which side David gave offense when he accompanied the ark into Jerusalem as an ecstatic royal hierophant: "Michal, Saul's daughter, . . . saw King David leaping and dancing before the Lord; and she despised him in her heart." [7] Now Michal had been taken into David's harem, as a token of the new reunion of the northern and the southern tribes; does her disapproval, faithfully retained by the recording scribes, hint as some resentment of the northern element against the sly usurper from the South or at the religionists' objection to the new king's priestly affectation? [8]

When all is said, the David legend justly triumphs over the historic fact. It does not matter that the professional military man is retransformed into the first *guerrillero* in history to overcome advanced war technology, just as later, at Crécy, the crossbow would humble the medieval equivalent of the modern tank, the armor-plated mounted knight. Hebrew popular imagination was right in attributing to David all the glory of the liberator; it was more right than it knew because the liberation of the country presupposed the end, by David's almost Augustean compromise, of the preceding civil war between the Hebrew past and the new era of the nation state:

The destiny of Israel: Here was a people that began its existence with a radical leap in being; and only after the people had been constituted by that initial experience did it acquire, in the course of centuries, a mundane body of organization to sustain itself in existence. This sequence, reversing the ordinary course of social evolution, is unique in history. . . . A society

7. 2 Sam., 6:16.
8. The same distrust was voiced against his predecessor: "Is Saul also among the prophets?" I Sam., 10, 11.

is supposed to start from primitive rites and myths, and thence to advance gradually, if at all, to the spirituality of a transcendent religion; it is not supposed to start where a respectable society has difficulties even ending. . . .[9]

For a brief historic moment Israel's theodicy and history remained in equilibrium: the Davidian monarchy outlasted its founder; but after Solomon, and already during his great reign, the conflict between Hebrew character (that of a community of worshippers) and Hebrew role (within the context of near-eastern history) was renewed:

> In the ninth century, the exigencies of the power game brought the experiment to an end. The diplomacy of the Omrides [886-841; the Northern kingdom after the break-up of the united Solomonic empire] had to compromise with the cosmological order of the surrounding powers to such a degree that solution to the problem could no longer be found within the range of Yahwist symbols. At the risk of destroying the conditions of Israel's mundane existence, the response had to be a revolutionary return to the origins. The archaic Israel reasserted itself in the political revolt of Elijah, Elisha, and the Rechabites [a tribal sect of "true believers"]. On the level of pragmatic history the movement was a ruinous reaction that broke all hope for a recovery of Israelite power. On the spiritual level, however, it preserved Israel from sinking insignificantly into a morass of ephemeral success.[10]

The author of this passage, Eric Voegelin, seems to view that great revolt as an attempt to arrest and undo the results of Israel's mundane adjustment to the technological and administrative requirements of the more advanced societies surrounding the new nation. In modern terminology, he would seem to describe a counterrevolution, whereas Max Weber, as interpreted by Talcott Parsons (correctly, we believe), saw the emergence of free prophecy as a twofold advance beyond the limitations of traditionalist Nabism: the tribal type of holy men and seers, comparable to dervishes and fakirs, who led the nomadic tribes and later the peasant levies of the Hebrew immigration into battle against Canaan. In contrast, the great prophets replaced ecstasy by reasoned argument. They also broke away from the established

---

9. Eric Voegelin, *Order and History*, Vol. I, *Israel and Revelation* (Baton Rouge, 1956), p. 315.
10. *Ibid.*, p. 316.

order, to proclaim their God as super-national, hence immune to the mundane indignities that Israel was to suffer at the hand of the new super-power, Assur, later Babylon. The God of tribal conquest now ordained the conquest of His chosen people as the World God, using Assurbanipal and Sennacherib as the executioners of His inscrutable command. Thus, in Max Weber's view, the prophets were agents of the process of rationalization that transformed a tribal cult into a world religion. In this sense they were the leaders of a revolution, not, as Voegelin would insist, of counterrevolution.[11]

The conflict between the two views, however, is more apparent than real. For the prophetic protest, while signifying a rationalizing advance and breakthrough (hence a revolution), was also a traditionalist protest against the technological-bureaucratic rationalization that transformed the tribal confederacy of Yahweh worshippers into the Davidian nation-state and its successors, Israel and Judah—a process so dear to the student of what Weber termed the "routinization of charisma."

There is no harm in seeing the great conflict between revolution and tradition as a clash between utopian and pragmatic needs, without expressing preferences. The emergence of that self-styled dynasty of prophets [12] is in itself such a tremendous fact that the attempt to understand it has not slackened even in our day. Quite on the contrary, the rise in our time of a new type of apocalyptic prophecy has done much to rekindle our curiosity about these semi-mythical foretellers of destruction and redemption. And if so, the figure of him who came first, the Lenin, as it were, of that tradition, tempts us to lift, disrespectfully, the sacred veil of secrecy, for a short peek at the gestation of great leadership. Not daring to approach too closely precincts closed to secular curiosity, the observer will avail himself of a safe witness: safe because twice removed from the original. The sociological imagination will use the perspective of one close to the successor. More fortunate than Lenin, prophet Elijah could transmit his mission to Elisha, and Elisha had *his* eye on a most talented disciple

11. See Talcott Parsons' Introduction to Max Weber, *The Sociology of Religion* (London, 1965), pp. xxvii ff.

12. Weber's thesis of a disestablished, independent prophecy is not borne out by more recent research. See Peter L. Berger, "Charisma and Religious Innovation: The Social Location of Israelite Prophecy," *American Sociological Review*, Vol. 28, No. 6 (December, 1963), pp. 940-50. See also the conclusion of this chapter.

whose name is recorded in the sacred text. The problem of succession as an aspect of all revolutionary or counterrevolutionary leadership deserves close attention. The relationship between the initiator and the heir is more than just a question of ambivalence, of veneration fraught with envy, of the irresistible compulsion to outstrip the giant who came first, the old man who, because of the historic accident that had him appear earlier, had forced the second man into a role for which his character may have been ill-fitted. In this sense, the dialectics of succession may affect decisively the course of the whole revolution or counterrevolution. The very unity of opposites is already contained in the two names, Elijah and Elisha; a latter-day philologist may even establish that both are mere variations of one and the same fantastic prototype.

A PROPOSAL FROM A DOUBLE AGENT

To: Naaman, Captain of the host of Benhadad, the Syrian King
From: Gehazi, First Secretary to Elisha, Man of God

Greetings.   Your servant has received your contribution on behalf of his master as a token of your gratitude for successful treatment. You realize that he is not permitted to charge fees. Your contribution will accordingly be used for distribution among needy waifs and widows. In the future, should my Lord come back for more checkups, may I recommend that you address all further remittances to the Shunemmite female known to you, noting that they are meant for Izaheg, which name is like a coat reversed.

Your servant's heart is gladdened by my Lord's words—that he has found favor with his master, the great King, and that I am to carry on my humble work, to wit: as far as my devotion and allegiance to my master will permit, to serve the common interest of our two nations by submitting to Your Excellency all and sundry information that may throw light on the intentions of my master who is a great power among our people.

You keep asking me: What kind of man is he? How can one who commands no hosts intimidate a mighty kingdom? Who is really behind him? My Lord, you sadden me. Your questions only prove that it is difficult for even such distinguished and enlightened gentlemen as yourself to fathom Him who has endowed my Lord, Elisha, with the might and fury of the unnamed God,

*against whom all the hosts of certain kings are like weak reeds.
I am of course here speaking only of domestic matters—far be it
from me to question and belittle Your great King, my Lord.
But a word to the wise: It might be well to be in the good graces
of that unnamed God who, needless to remind You, was the One
who cured my Lord Naaman from his ailment through the
agency of his great servant, Elisha. And since a change of dynasty may well be in the interests of our two nations, may I say
that I have some intelligence worth a great deal to Your great
master: to wit, that a certain captain, Jehu by name, has visited
my master twice within the last month, and this secretly, at
night. I was unfortunately detained by other duties, but I have
good reason to believe that Jehu is my master's man, in case
the unnamed God should wish to have done with the present
King and his whole household, for this King is a wicked man
who does not walk in the ways of the Lord. But I beseech you,
my most gracious Lord, not to reveal my name in this connection; should there be any questions as to how this information
reached you, I shall have to deny everything.*

*You understand my master has powerful connections; he is not
a lone man crying in the wilderness. Many listen to him, and
the King is mortally afraid of what he might say. And it is true
that my master is a man of wrath who will not suffer fools
gladly. One time he passed through a village where he was a
stranger, and the village youths ran after him, with shouts of
'Baldhead! Baldhead!' which my master indeed was, for though
bushy-haired once, his hair has fallen out of late, no longer
covering his brow. He did not like to be reminded of his loss,
and to my horror, he called down upon the heads of harmless
babes the vengeance of the Lord! Soon after, he calmed down
and, I am sure, repented his rash words. But the next day word
came that bears had come down from the hills into that village
and devoured some of those children. It was a most unfortunate
event.*

*That is how it is with my great master. He is a veritable
column of fire. Of divine fire, to be sure, but even divine fire
is a thing that needs most careful watching! Those are the very
words he uses, and they are the words of his late master, of Him
who was called heavenwards in God's own chariot: the great
Elijah. And so are many other words that he left as a precious
legacy to his disciple, Elisha. It is not easy to walk in the foot-*

steps of one who was God's own darling. Often, at night, I can hear my master turn in his bed, sleepless, speaking to the dear removed: "Why? Why hast thou forsaken me and left me alone to carry the burden much too heavy for my shoulders? Let me go! Let your son go! It is the one thing I ask of you, but you remain silent, safe up there, secure in your great glory! Do you or do you not wish me to handle things? You do? Then let me handle them in my own way. Don't meddle. Stop advising, only to withdraw behind your clouds when I make a mistake and cry for help. I do not need you, do you hear me?" And so he clamors, and I can hear him through the wall.

But again, when he feels well, he will drop hints that Elijah too had made mistakes in his own time. That he had done some great things, to be sure, and some of them had been suggested to him by his humble servant, Elisha. And that the old man had been too timid. He said that Elijah had not known his own strength, but that he, Elisha, would not make the same mistake!

I am speaking of the miracles he works. It is no use denying that he works them, for with our own eyes we have seen them done. And such is the intoxication of great feats accomplished that there cannot ever be an end to them; each miracle calls for the next and greater one. And he ended by working magic with a woman who was barren. That was in the town of Shunem, and said woman vexed him for she would not readily believe that he possessed that kind of strength.

So came to pass what makes Your servant flush with shame and anger even now: He was so bent on helping that poor woman that he made the child himself, appearing to her in the dark of night. And she, believing that an angel from the Lord had come at the behest of the great prophet, lay with him, the silent one, and got with child. Should we condemn him for it? Not so. For the Shunemmite is happy now. Her boy is growing up and is a joy. Why spoil it? I shall never tell her. And yet, for she is my woman now, whenever I lie with her, I think of him who betrayed her trust, and I hate him, hate him, may the Lord forgive me!

My Captain, burn this letter, as I shall burn yours. There is a certain doorkeeper I don't trust; he covets my position and tries to incite the master against me. Already the great kindness You showed me during your last visit made my master angry, and when, after having shown you on your way, I came back to the

*house, he shouted at me: "If ever I catch you at unclean dealings
with the Syrian, unclean shallst thou be thyself!" This greatly
worries me, for in our close neighborhood there have been some
fresh cases of leprosy. I must be careful. It is evil magic with
that man. When I think of him, I can already feel it coming over
me: first one white spot, then more, then my whole body being
covered as if by a sheet, a shroud! So burn this, and bring a
burnt offering to Baal for Your too faithful servant, poor*

G e h a z i

COMMENT

If imagination has, in the preceding, run away from sociology, amends are now in order. The essential difference that
separates Elisha from Elijah a close reading of the texts (1 Kings,
17–21; 2 Kings, 2–19) will certainly bear out; the story merely
translates these objective data into subjectivities. Elisha's fury
has a very human cast and his irascibility is close to being peev-
ish, he is vain and vindictive. These characteristics are not present in the portrait of Elijah left to us. We must conclude that he
is indeed more a mythical than an historic figure, while Elisha's
picture shows the brush strokes of historical veracity. In the
comparison, the first man sets the pattern and the second man
appears as the great executor of a semi-mythical design, less
blemished by the harshness of reality. Elijah can be loved; Elisha
hardly. Had Lenin lived until, say 1936, we would today blame
him for Stalin's deeds.[13] Not only is Elijah finally withdrawn
from earthly judgment, literally "lifted up" but throughout his
life he remains detached from social ties, the One against the
Mighty of the earth, whereas Elisha is enmeshed in many social
and political relations. True, Elijah also mightily affects the
polity, but as a solitary power in his own right, whereas Elisha
comes much closer to our notion of the master *politician*,
credited by most scholars with having been the real mastermind
behind the Jehu "revolution" of the orthodox against the sinful
Omri dynasty, although the biblical legend still attributes it to
Elijah's instigation. Elijah is the solitary who comes *to* society.
Elisha, coming from Elijah, belongs to society but acts the solitary

13. See below, chapter 8.

in the great tradition founded by his predecessor and continued by their classical successors in the pre- and postexilic eras.

Is this individualistic emphasis of the tradition a mere literary device used to enhance the stature of the men of God, or is there any evidence to make it an historic fact? The modern mind has difficulty in believing that the prophets stood alone; it wishes them to represent a class, a movement, if not an institution. The scholars are divided on this point. Even Weber, who as a sociologist would rather see the prophets as the leaders of some social force, is not quite sure whether the categories of sociology apply and whether their projection onto the Hebraic scene might not reintroduce a crypto-Marxian heresy into his own new reading of religion as another independent variable. The facts themselves are not in question: Israel is called up to revert to the religion it had been taught by Moses. That in turn implied a longing for the simpler ways of life which had once existed for the nomadic ancestors but which were rendered impracticable by urban life and central monarchy, taxation, exploitation of the poor in the towns and in the country by the greedy rich, foreign entangle-intermarriage of the dynasty, the foreign wives being accom-ments with their alliances, which in those days meant foreign panied by their own heathen priests. (So at a much later time, Henrietta Marie, the French princess, would bring her priests to the court of Charles I of England, to the horror of the Calvinist divines.) These conditions amounted to depravity, and Yahweh would not stand for them: only He could save his people from perdition.

But who said so? Were the gloomy warners speaking only for themselves, out of the certitude of sacred inspiration? Or were they the spokesmen of the premonarchic, tribal hierarchy, now out of power? That was Max Weber's view in writing of the new "seers and prophets independent of the king, the popular heirs of the military Nebiim, now without commission" as the opposition hallowing "the time when Yahweh himself as war leader led the peasant army, when the ass-riding prince did not rely on horses and wagons and alliances, but solely on the god of the covenant and his help." [14]

Yet Weber makes a sharp distinction between the old seers

14. Weber, op. cit., p. 111. "The prophets . . . were no longer military dervishes and ecstatic therapeutics and rainmakers, but a stratum of literati and political ideologists." Ibid., p. 112.

and the new prophets: "Elijah differed from the old 'man of god' in that he addressed his oracles, at least in part, to the politically interested 'public' and not alone to the authorities: kings or elders. Elijah is the first specifically 'clerical' figure of Israelite history." In this connection Weber has some harsh things to say about the second prophet: "Elijah had been made into a magician of the type of Elisha only by legend and by the endeavor of this epigonus of the ancient Nebiim to pose as Elijah's successor, an endeavor which even in the tradition shows as ambitious 'straining.' " [15] His characterization of the later prophets reads like a description of the party struggles in the old Greek polis or in medieval Florence. In a colorful passage Weber conjures up the figure of the religious "demagogue" whose "oracles highlighted obscure fates of the future like lightning out of somber clouds. Such prophecy was authoritarian in character and averse to all orderly procedure. Formally, the prophet was strictly a private citizen. . . ." But "whether the prophets wished it or not they actually always worked in the direction of one or the other furiously inner-political cliques, which at the same time promoted definite policies. . . . Hence the prophets were considered party members." [16] The struggle was between the pro-Egyptian and the pro-Assyrian-Babylonian factions. Yet Weber is loath to relinquish his idea of the prophet as an isolated individual:

> In solitude did the prophetic spirit come. . . . The prophets did not think of themselves as members of a supporting spiritual community. On the contrary, misunderstood and hated by the mass of their listeners they never felt themselves to be supported and protected. . . . The pathos of solitude overshadows the mood of the prophets . . . [Their] sacred states . . . were . . . truly personal and were thus experienced by them and their audiences, and not as the product of an emotional mass influence.[17]

It is difficult to reconcile this statement with the notion, also held by Weber, that the prophets "were considered party members," but again the difficulty may be overcome. It has been overcome by post-Weberian scholarship, which finds the thesis of the prophet as a solitary individual untenable and holds in-

15. *Ibid.*, p. 108.
16. *Ibid.*, pp. 271, 274.
17. *Ibid.*, pp. 292, 293.

stead "that the prophet emerges from a traditionally defined office, exercising his charismatic activity in terms of this office." With this modification, Weber's findings are accepted. In the contemporary view, the genius of the prophets, although rooted in nonindividualistic, institutionalized forms, grows beyond these forms. Thus "Weber's insistence on the autonomy of religious ideas" is vindicated: "The new interpretation of prophecy, as located socially not on some solitary margin but within the religious institutions of ancient Israel, does not weaken the Weberian notion on the innovative power of charisma. On the contrary, it strengthened it." [18]

There were no winners in the struggle between ancient Hebrew "modernists" and the religious opposition. "Under the pressure of the Empires, Israel would assimilate itself to the culture of the more powerful neighbors, and then suffer a revival of Yahwist nationalism which precipitated a political disaster." [19] That disaster may have been inevitable in any case. The revival of postexile Israel as a small province of the Persian empire with autonomy in matters of religion made it possible for Judaism to survive, if at a price. So perhaps in the long run the utopians proved to be the better pragmatists.

18. Peter L. Berger, op. cit., p. 950. But Gerhard von Rad, in Old Testament Theology, The Theology of Israel's Prophetic Traditions, Vol. II (London, 1965), although recognizing "that there were in Israel cultic prophets, with a definite place in the cultus," rejects the view "pressed by some to the point of dissolving all tension between the canonical prophets and the priests." The author "recognizes that Nahum may have had a function within the framework of the cult, but dismisses the possibility for all the others, though he thinks there may be some imitation of cultic liturgies in the prophetic books." The [London] Times Literary Supplement (November 4, 1965), p. 987.

19. Eric Voegelin, op. cit., p. 356.

The civil war recounted in the Bible was a preview of the end of revolution, of unworldly victory through secular defeat. The next selection posed a problem. After Judaea, should not Athens be the next station in our search for meaningful examples of important revolutions? The idea of probing into the problems of Athenian democracy, successfully evolving out of primitive conditions but ultimately defeated by the oligarchic Spartan power, was a tempting one. Nor was there any lack of representative figures: Pericles, the uncrowned democratic king; and as the end approaches, those towering intellectuals, Socrates between the extreme factions, prototype of all moderate victims of political polarization, and Plato looking for his Sicilian philosopher-king and ending as a prisoner sold into slavery. . . .

But none of them summed up so well the great aims and great defects of middle-class democracy, no Greek figure represented perfectly the juncture of an old revolution and a brutal counter-revolution as did the man from another Mediterranean culture, a culture so inferior in intellectual accomplishment to Athens, so infinitely more pedestrian, but also so much more solid and modern, in the sense that we moderns can feel instantly at home in it and recognize its men and women as our contemporaries. That place is Rome, and the man Cicero, who, like the artillery officer N. Buonaparte in Stephen Vincent Benét's story, was born at the wrong time. Unhappy the man born for greatness who appears either too early or too late. Cicero meant to save the Republic and he had to see it die. An intellectual in politics, he proved to be an astute politician at a time when political astuteness met its match in a new type; the politician in control of an army. Caesar, and after him Augustus, presaged the advent of Bonapartism—a demagogic power of the sword, which will haunt the rest of this study.

3 Cicero, Father of the Republic: An Epitaph

"Victrix causa deis placuit
Sed victa Catoni."

All the world loves a winner, but it does not love all winners equally; some it loves only grudgingly. As for the losers, there are far too many to keep track of. Moreover, they are an embarrassing reminder of what might be in store for us. So it is better to forget about the losers, unless we decide the loser should by rights have been the winner. In that rare case, we will side with him and weep for him and his lost cause, for pity and self-pity are twins.

Marcus Tullius Cicero was such a loser, but in his posthumous life he was not always treated fairly. Because he harped incessantly on his own greatness, the suspicion of posterity was easily aroused. But his demotion from his self-built pedestal, the merciless exposure of his flawed character, led to the underestimation of the role that pitted him against the greatest personalities and forces of his time.

Between revival and eclipse, his figure has assumed an ambiguity that well mirrors that of the age in which he lived. The very label usually affixed to that age sums up all the confusions that so stubbornly persist: The End of the Republic. The great names of Caesar and Augustus seem inseparable from our notion of a Roman revolution that came to a head when Cicero was consul and declaimed *ad nauseam* *"Quousque tandem, Catilina."*

But surely it was an odd revolution to have started centuries ago and still be in progress? Normally, we would reserve the term revolution for a sociopolitical cataclysm running its course in a matter of days, weeks, or months—a few years at the utmost.

We might save the term by speaking of a basic, never-ending revolutionary situation or condition, comparable to a geological fault in the earth, erupting off and on in revolutionary tremors. That would be the same as saying that the social system in question suffers from a lasting instability. But in the Roman case that instability outlasted centuries without disrupting the continuous evolution of the system—proof of a truly paradoxical stability of instability.

If revolution means a radical recasting of the social structure, then the last installment of the Roman revolution was enacted almost a hundred years before Cicero's time when the two Gracchi tried to halt the expropriation of the peasant class. The conservative design of their reforms was easily obscured by the political extremism of the Gracchian means; by trying to enlist the moneyed bourgeoisie against the landed aristocracy, they brought the concentrated fury of the threatened interests upon themselves, and in the end the financiers broke ranks, preferring the security of their own interests to the uncertainties of political power.[1]

After that the history of Rome was no longer the clear-cut contest between social classes it had been since her early days but a mere struggle for control within the ruling group, brought into being through a fusion of plebeian and patrician elites. Although the factions still appealed to the old social interests, the contest was no longer one between democratic claims and oligarchic privilege but, or so it would seem, exclusively a struggle for pre-eminence among the leading figures.

But that appearance is deceptive. The contenders were still fighting over issues, but no longer the old issues. Class was not pitted against class, since all Romans, rich and poor, had now become exploiters of a conquered world. (The followers of

1. See chapter 6, below.

Catiline came from both the lumpen-proletariat and the lumpen-aristocracy.)

Marius could still look like the protagonist of populism and Sulla (the only dictator in all history who abdicated of his own free will) could still pose as the Lord Protector of patrician interests, because their time had as yet no awareness of the problem facing Rome: how to adapt the constitution and administration of a market town to the dimensions of a vast, tricontinental empire.

This task, the reconstruction of the ancient model on a worldwide scale, taxed the ingenuity of the best minds beyond endurance. It was not an undertaking suited to the Roman genius, so much like that of the English, with their love of precedent and compromise, their preference for gradual advance. The revolution now in progress was of a new type, demanding a new order for which there was but a single precedent: a return to one-man rule. A hated king?

It was Rome's tragedy that it enacted that new revolution as if it were a mere re-enactment of the older ones. It was the only way Rome knew: to fight within the narrow pale of The Republic. In the end, its institutions, emptied of all social and political significance, were taken over by the new regime, to serve it as the ceremonial monuments of a tradition now in ruins.

That was the devolution, called The Fall of The Republic (which had given up the ghost long before). The new, imperial revolution did not take shape all at once. It came in stages. First to be affected was the hard core of the Roman state: the structure of the army. The old citizen militia, which had fought supremely well in short local campaigns, had to make room for standing armies of professionals, divorced from their communities and utterly dependent on the plunder of victorious generals. Characteristically, that reform, the logical response to the now continental scope of war, was carried out by the same Marius whose name stands for populist resistance to conservative reaction. But it was he who created the foundations for a system based almost exclusively on military force.

PRAETORIANISM

The Praetorian Guard developed out of the traditional praetorian cohort of the Roman legion. It was only as the large-scale body-guard of their imperial masters that this corps of hand-picked soldiers was transformed, first into an elite police force and then into a political force of considerable, frequently decisive, influence. One of the major flaws of the imperial system lay in the absence of a clearly defined mechanism of succession. Since the only other organ that could claim authority, the Senate, had become nothing more than an imperial creature, representing no one, a third force had to step in to close the power gap. Thus it came about that the Praetorian camp became the market place in which the crown was huckstered to the highest bidder. Frequently the turn-over was accelerated by the removal of an incumbent: Succession by praetorian violence became a regular tradition of irregularity.[2]

Praetorian power has one deadly flaw: its holders, forced to play the role of political decision-makers, as a rule are utterly deficient in political ability. It simply is not in the military character. The sooner the military man can find a shrewd civilian to tell him what to do, the better; and better still to turn over to him entirely the detested task. Rare is the professional army man who is an able statesman. Napoleon was that exceptional man, although his rule could never deny its military origins. Marius and Caesar, on the other hand, were both civilians who turned out to be good generals, although Caesar's military genius has been questioned by some. What gives the careers of these two men the "proto-praetorian" character was their ability to translate the political power first into a military fief enlarged by conquest, and then, starting from that basis, back into a lever for political control. The army, led by the civilian-become-general, returned home to take its place as the decisive social force. It became the instrument of the charismatic leader, who gave back to his soldiers, former rural proletarians, what they had lost, long ago, as mem-

2. Emperors murdered by the Praetorian Guard were Nymphidius Sabinus, A.D. 68; Servius Suplicius Galba, A.D. 69; Flavius Sabinus Vespasianus, A.D. 69; Helvius Pertinax, A.D. 193; Didius Julianus, A.D. 193; Ulpianus (praetorian Prefect), A.D. 228; M. Clodius Pupienus and D. Caecilus Balbinus, joint emperors, A.D. 238; See M. Gary, *A History of Rome* (London, 1949), p. 795.

bers of a social *class*. Later, as the uniformed proletariat of the ruined countryside, they carried out what Rostovtzeff called the great Severian revolution against the predominantly urban culture of the Empire.[3]

The temptation is great to explain the civil wars between the Roman factions as a process of recoiling of the nation's energies that until then had found an outlet in external action; with the boundaries of conquest stretched almost beyond the point of endurance, all the internal problems left unsolved clamored for attention. Their repression was no longer necessary or possible. So internal war internalized once more those social conflicts that external war had both repressed and at the same time, by transforming and destroying the old Roman system, aggravated.

Seductive though the theory may be, it violates the known facts—that wars of conquest and domestic unrest coincide. Each fed on the other; they were linked in a concatenation in which cause and effect became indistinguishable elements of a dialectical tension expressing itself simultaneously as war *and* revolution, moving horizontally and vertically, until The Republic could no longer stand the strain. War had made Rome the mistress over other nations; now the new force that she had herself created, in turn conquered Rome. The conquest, formalized after a time of troubles as the Augustean Compromise, replaced the now impossible social revolution from below by the new war-like revolution from above.

THE MIDDLE MAN

Into that time of troubles Cicero was born. His letters, which reveal more of the man than all his famous books or speeches, show the deep bewilderment of one whose personality goes to extremes of hopes and fears, of vanity and self-abasement. He longed for quiet, moderation, normality, but could not find them in his time. He was the intellectual with a mission: as a *homo novus*, representative of the Italian middle class demanding to be recognized as Roman, the young lawyer had a master plan for the solution of all problems: the reconciliation of the classes, his *concordia ordinum*.[4] How could it fail when compromise was

---

3. See Michael Rostovtzeff, *Social and Economic History of the Roman Empire*, chapters X–XII. But *cf.* Cary's reservations in *op. cit.*, p. 782.

4. See José Ortega y Gasset, *Concord and Liberty* (New York, 1946).

indicated as the only way to steer between extremes? What Cicero, the moderator, could not understand was that The Republic of his time was breathing its last, that abnormality had become normality. So he continued to climb up the ladder of honors until he was Consul, Father of the Fatherland, an alternately splendid and pathetic, ruthless and procrastinating figure, saving Rome from Catiline: nervously postponing the decisive showdown and then violating the rules of due process, a mistake that his enemies later used to hound him into exile. He had crushed a desperado from whom greater gamblers had withdrawn protection. Cicero's short triumph blinded him to the true danger coming from The Three Men: Pompey, Crassus, and Caesar. He would never understand that Cicero, the Roman patriot, was acting in a shadow play before an audience that dutifully applauded his performance while waiting for the curtain to come down.

But to describe the temper of the Roman public as fatigued and resigned would be wrong. It was a time of decadence, but Nietzsche taught us that it also was the time when "the old national energy and national passion . . . has now transferred itself into innumerable private passions, and has merely become less visible: indeed in periods of 'corruption' the quantity and quality of the expended energy of a people is probably greater than ever. . . . It is when 'morals decay' that those beings whom one calls tyrants first make their appearance." [5] Cicero's Rome was not very different from the great capitals of our day: The gossip of the hostesses and diplomats in mansions overlooking the Potomac faithfully echoes that from the hills above the Tiber. Thornton Wilder caught Rome's sinuous elegance in all its splendid wickedness: the coming tyrants and the advocate of yesterday who to the last remained convinced that he was in their league, that they would play the game according to the rules, and that he was the man to beat them.[6]

The Catilinarian tragi-comedy was followed by the tragedy of Cicero, the middleman of the Republic. Having saved it once, how could he fail with Pompey and with Caesar? Were they not his great, good friends; was he not their most valued confidant? Himself, he trusted neither man; when he discovered that they

5. Nietzsche, *The Joyful Wisdom* (New York, 1924), section 23.
6. Wilder, *The Ides of March* (New York, 1948). For another imaginative reconstruction of the period, see Rex Warner, *The Young Caesar* (Boston, 1958), and *Imperial Caesar* (Boston, 1960).

did not trust him either, he was hurt. But never once was his conviction shaken that they needed him and could not do without his counsel. Trading not so much on his forensic gifts as on his established public wisdom and authority, he acted unwisely and lost whatever yet remained of his authority. It is the fatal self-deception of the intellectual in politics that he confounds his minor role as an auxiliary of the political practitioner with that of a director of affairs; that he considers himself the equal if not the superior of the man whose ear he has; and finally, that he anticipates intimacy with the great will buy him immunity, if there should be a parting of the ways. And a parting there always is, because the powerful will cease to listen to the wise, and their vindictiveness is deadly.[7]

In the end, the middleman found himself in the cross fire of the factions, sincerely hated by all. The awful moment arrived when Cicero had to take sides. He could no longer stay above the battle; he had to join it.

Joining Pompey, he chose badly. At the mercy of the winner, Cicero came close to looking like a trimmer. But these were mere moments of despondency, of existential *Angst*. Then he would flatter and demean himself: the exile wanted to come home, retire to his beloved Tusculum to write—goodbye to politics! Yet, at the same time, he was, in a feline way, quite fond of Caesar. The two men had much in common. They were supremely sensitive to each other: Cicero knew Caesar; Caesar, Cicero. Perhaps they knew too much about each other to remain good friends. But Caesar was spared, by the daggers of Republican romantics, from becoming Cicero's destroyer. That legacy he left to his young nephew. It was fitting that Augustus should proscribe the old man who had been the self-imagined father of the lost Republic.[8]

7. "The sternest axiom which a politician must obey is that he must not be tempted into seizing imaginary initiatives: the intellectual temperamentally believes that the opportunity for them is always there. . . . The sternest rule which a politician must observe is that he is not acting for the future, for history, but simply for today: the intellectual does not as a general rule care for the untidiness—the intractability—of the present. . . . Unless, then, the intellectual submerges himself in politics, and in so doing ceases to be an intellectual, he will go on misapprehending the political process, expecting both too much of it and too little. . . ." Henry Fairlie, "Johnson and the Intellectuals, A British View," *Commentary*, Vol. 40, No. 4 (October, 1965), p. 52. In the original the last sentence precedes the passage quoted.

8. To be exact, Augustus yielded to Marc Antony's insistence to put Cicero to death.

The end of Cicero's Republic and of the long democratic revolution was a process here defined as *devolution*. The term denotes literally a rolling back, as for example in the, slow or fast, unwinding of a tautly wound cable, and thus connotes the relaxation of strains that have become unendurable. This task requires surprisingly little strength, for to remain within the metaphor, the cable is more than ready to snap back. Still, some force has to be available to do the job of devolution. It will either be a force that has survived intact the general decomposition, or a combination of new forces generated by the crisis.

The next chapter gives another illustration of the devolutionary process typical of ending revolutions. Its central figure, the Cromwellian General, George Monk, is a product of the Great Rebellion that shook England during the two decades between 1640 and 1660. It was Monk, the commander of the Commonwealth army in Scotland, who restored Charles II to the British throne. A turncoat? A reactionary in disguise? If so challenged, he would have answered that there were, in his time, quite a few governments in power, but that he, Monk, had been able to serve all of them quite loyally. He was that rarest of all animals, a military professional with the political flair of a Machiavelli. What he did, he did because it was the thing to do. Like Caesar, he did not destroy the Commonwealth; he merely buried what was already defunct.

A word about the technique used in this chapter. It is, first of all, a narrative, based on contemporary sources. But telling the story was only a means, not the end. It is the only chapter in this study in which microscopic closeness was deliberately attempted. One result, this also deliberately sought, was the obliteration of the great, dramatic line; another the obfuscation of the real issues. This, it is hoped, yields a picture as it must have looked to Monk's contemporaries. What looks like stupidity or criminality on a man's part, may be explained by his inability to see the larger context of the events in which he is so closely involved. Rather, he sees only the immediate needs. The same myopic lack of a perspective shows in the contemporary testimonials we have about Monk. But that lack has its advantages, the greatest being that we know so much about the man, his every word or silence, frown or laughter. Being in the center of the dénouement, he was more closely watched by friends and foes than was good for him. His fleeting moment of historic eminence was mercifully followed by oblivion.

4 The Kingmaker: General Monk

The King knew what was brewing. He had tried to stop the evil at its source. For more than ten years (1629–39) he had managed without Parliament. Then the mad men in Edinburgh made war on him, and he had to call a new Parliament to vote him subsidies. That was the end of his last chance to make the royal power absolute. The men of the new Parliament saw their opportunity to cut the royal power back to size. The Stuart had dreamt of becoming as strong as his cousin, the French Louis, but in England it had always been "the King in Parliament." The time to stop Charles and his French wife with her papist priests was now. But they overplayed their hand. They thought they had him by the throat, and the temptation to shear *all* his power was too great. It looked as if it would soon be: "the Parliament above the King." At that the moderates took fright; the Commons split, and the King suddenly acquired a royal party (1641).

The civil war broke out (1642), and it did not go well for Parliament, which had to fight a man who still remained the English King. The politicians who had challenged but did not wish to destroy him, were now themselves challenged by new men who meant to see the war through to the bitter end. The Lords, who had conducted lackadaisical campaigns against the King's professionals, had to make room for the dissenters who marched into battle singing psalms of Israel. Oliver Cromwell was part of that second revolutionary wave, and he rode into power on its crest. He had recruited his own men from among the yeomen of the Independent congregations, while the House of Commons, master of the army, was controlled by Presbyterians.

Throughout history, armed forces intervened in politics, but Cromwell's Ironsides became the first *political army* with an ideology apparently all its own. However, this impression is deceptive, because Cromwell's political soldiers had been militants as civilians before joining. In fact they had joined precisely because, like their leader, who had been a backbencher in Parliament, they were already dedicated to the cause; it was that cause that had made them into soldiers. As soldiers they were able to infuse the military institution with their own brand of religiously inspired political and social ideology. The result was a New Model of fighting efficiency as well as a new revolutionary army that refused to be the tool of politicians because it had its own program, its own vision of the Christian Commonwealth.

So far the English revolution had gone through three stages: Multiform in its inception, the convergence of the gentry, city, and sectarian interests had given Parliament a passing semblance of united force. It was a spurious unity that broke apart. The revolution now entered its second phase: the struggle for control was shifted from the law courts and the Commons to the battlefields of civil war. The deadlock in that war led to the radicalization of the parliamentary campaign effort and to the creation of the military instrument to reinforce, in turn, the radicalization of the revolutionary ends. Now, with the King eliminated as a power factor by defeat and capture (1645), a new split developed, this time between the civilian and the military wing of the rebellion. The victorious army found itself, ironically, thrust into the King's position: Parliament, still prevalently Presbyterian, faced a new contender for supremacy, one against whom its only weapon seemed to be to sit tight when it came to voting subsidies (1648).

The crisis was resolved, first by the sudden, and illegal, purge of Parliament (1648), and one year later, by the execution of the

King, who had been wooed by Parliament and Army High Command alike. The revolution now seemed to have reached the fusion stage, with the Cromwellian army left in full control. But once again the impression is deceptive. The execution of the King was an attempt to maintain army unity, with Cromwell himself unwilling to face the issue but yielding to pressure from the army radicals. They were the English Jacobins, in some respects even more radical than their French counterparts. Oliver Cromwell was not one of them. A country gentleman, he looked askance at the Heads of Proposals of the Army Levellers. Demands for equal suffrage, overhaul of the judiciary—these people went too far too fast!

The moment of decision had arrived: Unless the revolution were arrested on the spot, it would soon reach the point of no return. Cromwell turned around and smashed the Left. From then on it no longer represented any threat to him. It could be argued that, inasmuch as he had never been a radical himself, he could not betray radical ideals. Cromwell merely returned to the center of the scene. But with this difference: He found himself now in the place of chief executive, triumphant where the Stuart king had failed. He now represented precisely what he had been fighting.

Cromwell spent the rest of his life in efforts to restore some kind of equilibrium between Parliament and the chief steward of the government, himself. He was willing to surrender all prerogatives but one, control over the army. But a strange thing happened: his own creatures in the Commons, in one parliament after the other, stubbornly refused to humor him. They, like their predecessors, claimed that ultimate authority should be with Parliament. It was too late for Cromwell to call on the Left for help; moreover, the move would not have been creditable. Without "mass basis" and, as a regicide, unable to turn to the Right, he had to rule with what was left, a center group made up of two discordant coteries—Cromwellians and Republicans (the latter hoping to convert him to their constitutional designs). The rest was simply army rule.

The revolution lay at dead center. It remained there until the Protector's life came to a peaceful end, in 1658.

AN UNKNOWN QUANTITY

At that time, the general in charge of Scotland was George Monk. As generals of the period went, Monk was exceptional: He took no part in politics. That alone made him suspect to other generals.

When at last Cromwell died in his caesarian residence at Whitehall, while a thunderstorm outside provided a symbolical accompaniment, many people felt relief. With Richard, his son and successor, life would be much easier. The generals in any case believed it would be easier for them to run things—not too much disturbed by Parliament and even less so by the City. The moneyed men of London were quite willing to let Whitehall and Westminster have free rein—as long as business was good and it was. If only the army were not so frightfully expensive, much more so than under the late, increasingly lamented King. . . .

In the Commons certain members who had not been heard of while Cromwell lived, now quite audibly demanded the Republic. They were rebuffed, not so much by those who not quite as audibly demanded the return of the King's son from exile, as by the late Lord Protector's faction. It was one of the new men in power who rose to speak his mind: "I say that not all the authority rests with the people. Moses was not elected by them. Neither were Samuel and Saul." The King's men heard it gladly. The debate about the new Protector's confirmation dragged on for seven full days. On the eighth the wearied members shifted to the problem, vexing to Republicans, of the Upper House, where the new Cromwellian aristocracy had entrenched themselves. Some people with long memories recalled that the *old* Lords had been far less liberal in granting their King money to fatten the army. . . . The Republicans were joining forces with radical sectarians such as the Fifth Monarchists, who recognized no authority except the Bible, demanded land allotments for all poor, and the abolition of all courts. The popular chorus was not missing: Deputations (from the poor) knocked at the door of Parliament in order to present their Humble Petitions and Remonstrances, as they had been accustomed to throughout those stormy years. But they were in for a surprise, for Parliament enjoined the deputations sternly to go home, refused to hear their pleas. The revolution had been driven from the street.

The sovereign body was discussing the late Lord Protector's foreign policy. It asked for an accounting. Heavily Secretary Thurloe under whom Oliver had placed his name to state papers, rose and lectured the assembled members about the concatenations of diplomacy. He spoke softly, in a tone deliberately dry, but not dissimulating his distress that something which, to his mind, was a science, should become a political football. Unctuously, he ended on the line, "Of course, your wisdom must decide." They would gladly have wrung his neck. But Cromwell's foreign policy was unassailable.

So was the Army; it remained above discussion. There were, to be sure, some isolated instances of arbitrary treatment of civilians by the military, some of them high-ranking individuals. Would the party of the Lord Protector cover up malfeasance? It would not. The Commons voted overwhelmingly to issue half a dozen summons. This amused the Army. But the warrants did get published, and the officers were ordered to present themselves before the bar of Parliament to be harassed and humiliated by bewigged advocates. The Army trembled with rage. Not a single word in their defense came from the young Protector. He did not care for their company, preferred to do his drinking with the atheistic Ingoldsby. No time to answer complaints; too busy writing to the Netherlands; ingratiating himself with the young Stuart runaway.

Eight hundred officers convened at Wallingford House to deliberate. A Humble Petition to the Lord Protector was drawn up and presently dispatched to him, demanding full immunity for officers from the tribunals of the undercover Stuart-lovers. Richard kept the document for a few days, then sent it to the Commons. They duly took notice, with some kindly words for the Beloved Army. But the eight hundred stayed together, ominously, and in Parliament the temper also rose. It was resolved that no member be permitted to leave before the vote. The General Council of the Army could meet only with the consent of the Lord Protector and both Houses. There were a few voices of protest on the Left, which earlier had been loud in denouncing military misdemeanor. Now the same men pleaded with the House: do not estrange the Army. The majority, however, remained firm. Resolved: Nobody could hold a commission without pledging himself to uphold and protect Parliament. Also resolved: to pay the army arrears forthwith.

In Whitehall Palace, Richard Cromwell wrote a letter to George Monk in Scotland asking whether he could count on him? He offered the old man twenty-thousand pounds for his support. Support was forthcoming from other quarters: Members of the House called him the fountainhead of freedom (from the military); generals called to reminisce with him about his blessed father. The son's honor, bound up with that of the army, called for dissolution of the odious Parliament and new elections. A reply from Edinburgh suggested that the Lord Protector keep his twenty-thousand: "They will be more useful to you than yours respectfully, George Monk."

The Whitehall councilors worked late into the night. They scanned the regimental lists: Who could be and who could not be counted on? Lord Howard bristled: Never mind the regiments! Take care of the troublemakers, and there would be peace. Young Cromwell answered, "I am no man of violence." "Then," the reply, "they will do violence to you!" And Cromwell's last word, "I dare them!" he retorted. Lord Howard bowed and took his leave. Soon he was working for Charles Stuart. That son knew what he wanted.

The officers came back, politely asking to see the dissolution order. In vain Secretary of State Thurloe tried to reassure them. They remained cold and were soon gone. Throughout the night the noise of drums and fifes could clearly be heard in Whitehall Palace. Urgently the Lord Protector asked the Lieutenant-General of the Army, Fleetwood, to present himself. But the great Lord failed to appear. Richard ordered his guards to produce him. Much embarrassed, the guard officers begged off. Their master, speechless, withdrew to his chambers. Soon the news arrived; an order of the day from Lord Fleetwood to the Army: meeting place St. James's Palace; counter-order of the Lord Protector: the Army to meet at Whitehall.

A sole squadron answered Richard's call, and some of his guards left him. Until noon the Palace remained all but deserted. At noon, the Lieutenant-General appeared with a small retinue and chatted with the Lord Protector. He did not insist that Richard personally sign the dissolution order; nor did he tell Oliver's son in so many words that he was through, but Richard understood.

He lingered on for many weeks in Whitehall Palace. When he finally left for his country seat, taking with him many wagon loads of possessions, Richard remained convinced that they would call him back. He died, an old man, on his property, and few people would remember him, Oliver's boy without Oliver's strength.

THE EMBARRASSED PRAETORIANS

So one more Parliament had been dismissed, and soon the officers were asking themselves the old question: what to do with the now empty House. Somebody had to tend the shop. Not they! Their trade was not to bandy words but to command; they were professionals, not sectarians. Only civilians need apply. But no one did. The City went on minding its own business, which was doing business. Who held power? Nobody knew who was friend, who enemy. This was the time to look for allies. What about old Monk, up there in Scotland? Under Oliver he had been nothing much, but now he was a power to be reckoned with. The mail that came to him from London was voluminous. The General read and answered all. Wherever officers and politicians met in London, one of them was likely to produce a friendly letter, likewise signed George Monk. The General employed three clergymen to carry on this mounting correspondence: one to answer army letters, while the other two took care of ex-M.P.'s and Royalists abroad, respectively. The three divines detested one another, gossiped to strangers, and had visitors a General of the Commonwealth was not supposed to meet. From time to time Monk would give the three a tongue-lashing and end the lecture by inviting them to dinner. He was a great trencherman, fond of the bottle. At table he would be exuberant one moment and relapse into a sulky silence the next, studying his guests with mocking eyes. Nobody knew what went on in his mind. He was, though a stiff disciplinarian, popular with officers and men alike. For monarchists he had no use and would not suffer royalist talk at his table (at one occasion, when somebody started to speak on the subject, he rose and left the room).

Word came from London that the Army and the Left had joined in proclaiming the Republic and that moderates and monarchists had offered no resistance. When all the reports were

in, Monk nodded and said nothing. But it was not long before
another spate of messages arrived: All hell had broken loose in
London—Sons of Israel, Fifth Monarchy men were on a rampage,
the City was fed up, and the Army tired of serving a small
clique. And again Monk nodded, saying nothing. However, when
sounded out on what he would do if in his neighborhood a certain Colonel Booth, a Royalist, were to raise his standard, Monk
loudly answered: "I should march against him."

Colonel Booth did rise, and the new masters sent their great,
swashbuckling Lambert to put the rebellion down. He did so
with dispatch before Monk had a chance to move, and the
Republic, once more saved by its good army, stood triumphant.
Rumor had it that the savior, Lambert, coveted the office of the
Lord Protector. Meanwhile, the New House of Commons, which
was the old Rump, recalled,[1] debated the renewed demands the
Army had presented: military self-rule, with no interference on
the part of Parliament, stern punishment of defamators. When
the House arrived at no decision, the long-suffering High Command had its Petition printed and distributed among the people.
It was a declaration of war, and Parliament reacted promptly
by deposing all the generals and by naming seven commissioners,
one of them far from London, named George Monk.

Again the drums sounded; two conflicting orders pitted regiments against one another; Lambert moved to the attack. Some
Members of the House sneaked through the siege lines circling
Westminster. Inside, they joined the Council of State in its heated
session. Colonel Sydenham spoke for the Army, "Destiny has
forced our hands." Old, ailing Bradshaw rose to answer him,
"Prepared to meet my maker, I shan't tolerate these blasphemies."
A fortnight later, the old radical was dead. It ended in the now
familiar vein: The Parliament of the Republic yielded and ceased
to exist. The people watched the outcome calmly; few knew
what was at stake. Life in the London streets continued as usual.

---

1. The remnant of the purged Long Parliament of 1640. The purge of
Presbyterian members, which took from the officer in charge the name of
"Pride's Purge," took place in 1648.

ARMY RULE

The English Army was in sole command. But the commander of the Scottish garrison declared for the civilian power. Monk stood firmly on the platform of legality. He had just lived through a great crisis of his own. He had almost shown his hand and ruined his career. When Colonel Booth rose against London for the exiled Stuart, Monk was ready to send off a letter asking Parliament to quit and order new elections. Booth had made the same demand. But at the last moment Monk had had second thoughts and stopped the letter. When the news came that Booth was finished, there was jubilation in Monk's army. At the dinner table, officers agreed: Today would be a weeping day for Charlie Stuart. Whereupon Monk commented, "There ought to be a law: Whoever mentions the name of Charles Stuart, ought to hang." But when one captain shouted, "There will be no peace 'til we get rid of all the preachers!" Monk got up and answered in an ominously quiet voice, "All right! If you have not your fill of overturning yet, I too shall do some overturning."

Later on, his intimates congratulated him for having been so patient; otherwise they would now all have become guilty of high treason. Someone asked him: What if Booth had not risen? "Then," Monk answered, "I'd have done it without Booth. A few people would have followed me." And with a smile, "That blockhead. He deserves the rope." The chaplains thought: The General is sorry that it was not he who captured Booth.

It had been a narrow escape for Monk. But his relief soon gave way to despondency. He locked himself in his room and worked long hours at a letter of resignation to Parliament. But the letter, although sent, failed to reach Parliament, and after a few days Monk urgently requested that it be returned. Again, his luck held: Lenthall, Speaker of the Commons, had not passed it on. His hope of using Monk against the Lambert faction seemed, for the time being, dashed; he was delighted when a messenger appeared to ask for the return of Monk's disastrous letter.

One of the last measures of the dying Parliament, to make Monk, with six others, commissioners for army matters, also looked like a dead letter. But the General had heard the call and took the new commission very seriously, announced it to his army, and had some young officers write a gazette expounding the authority of government and everybody's duty to obey it. Officers of known republican allegiance, more than one hundred and forty in all, were discreetly shunted to the sidelines and replaced by apolitical professionals. Monk hastened to establish contact with the officers' committee now controlling London and sent emissaries to the capital. While they were on their way, the news reached Edinburgh that Lambert was in York assembling a force of twelve-thousand men against the Scottish army. That was more than Monk could mobilize at the moment. But at the same time he received his patent as supreme commander over all the forces in the British Isles. It was signed by a committee of the expelled Parliament. At once Monk began to concentrate strong detachments in the border town of Berwick.

His officers were laying bets: Was old Monk for or against Stuart? One of his own chaplains, Price, was so disturbed by the whole question that he could not bear it any longer and, not able to find sleep, went into Monk's room where he found his master sleeping on two chairs in front of the fireplace. Monk woke and listened patiently to the Divine who questioned him: How could he, who had always stood against a Parliament that overreached itself, now serve as Supreme Commander of a Parliament that did not even exist! Monk heard him out. At last he said, "Oh well, I must not make them angry. They don't trust me." Taking the man's hand, "With the Lord's help I shall accomplish it." "What? What?" "That which you have in mind."

By now he had six-thousand men in Berwick. Lambert did not budge from York. Confusion reigned in London. There was only one man who had kept his head: the Keeper of the Great Seal, Whitelocke. He was arguing with them: The country's grievances are many. Let us beware lest it confide them one day to a single man. The country is against these many Parliaments. So is our man. We do not want the Stuart, for that would mean war. That man, Monk, does not ever speak of Stuart, so he has on his side all those anxious to bury the axe. Once it is buried, it will be all right for the Stuart to come back. He won't defeat us. But if we destroy one another he will be the one who is left. Monk does not look for him. Monk goes along with everybody. He is for that which is possible, and much seems possible today; yes, even the Fifth Monarchy. George Monk would serve it well; indeed, he seems to mind them less than Cromwell did.

Monk dislikes making enemies. If it is God's will that the Stuart rule us, Monk will bring him. It must not be done against our will. So let *us* do it. Then Monk will be with us. Take your time in dealing with the Stuart; make conditions. We shall all remain, it is the lesser evil.

Nobody silenced Whitelocke. Fleetwood was won over instantly, and he had the respect of all. Desborough and Vane both joined him. Then at the last moment Fleetwood had a change of heart. Whitelocke was waiting for him in an anteroom, and Fleetwood, in a fever, turned on him, "I cannot do it; we can't do it. Yet it has to be. Yes, but *we* cannot do it." What else *could* they do? Call still another Parliament. The soldiers were paid very rarely now, the City being most unwilling to disgorge the funds. The rank and file began to requisition, sword in hand, and Cromwell's Saints were threatening their officers. At night, in drunken rage, they would engage in gunfights. Not even a Parliament left for them to disperse; how could they get one, quickly? They could not wait for new elections.[2]

So they went to find the former members of the Parliament that Cromwell had dissolved—the great Long Parliament of the first civil-war years. Those whom they found were terrified, and some even denied that they had ever sat in the old body, so much did they distrust the soldiers who so suddenly had found "religion." Those parliamentarians who agreed to serve assembled slowly at the home of their old Speaker, who had outlasted so many Parliaments. It was the same man who had suppressed Monk's letter of resignation: Lenthall. He proposed at once to call out the London garrison. The group agreed, and to their great surprise, the garrison obeyed. It was glad to obey somebody.

That was the end of government by generals.

2. "The fundamental cause of the Restoration was that the rank and file of the English army deserted their officers . . . so that generals without an army found themselves as helpless as the politicians they had bullied. The lower ranks . . . grew less and less eager to endanger their lives and to incur popular hatred and legal penalties for the selfish aims of their leaders. They realized that Parliament alone could provide for their arrears of pay and indemnify their many illegal acts." I. Deane Jones, *The English Revolution* (London, 1931), pp. 109-10.

MONK'S MOVE

It was the moment for which Monk had waited. In the name of Parliament, he crossed the English border on the first day of the new year, 1660. The new masters rushed a message to him which was full of praise but did not summon him to London. Monk had the dispatch read to his troops, and when the soldiers cried, "We want to see this Parliament!" he shrugged his shoulders and gave in.

He did not stop at York. When it was clear that he intended to continue straight for London, Parliament decided to invite him. It was just debating a new oath of loyalty, which read: For the Republic, Against Stuart. In the version finally adopted the reference against the Stuart was omitted. It was common talk in London that George Monk intended to proclaim the monarchy. At his next stop, another message from the Commons reached him; it was an official letter notifying him that an annuity of a thousand pounds was his reward for faithful service. He continued on his way, occasionally stopping to receive the delegations of the country people sent to greet him. They were for the most part moderates who in the past had fought against the King, but only to defend their rights, not to destroy his. Now they came to see The Man.

The General received them coldly, saying either nothing or, "It's up to the civilian power; I am only executing orders." Information reaching Parliament failed to provide a single clue to Monk's intentions. The man was uncanny.

From St. Albans, Monk requested Parliament to disband the London garrison. It would be dangerous, he argued, to let soldiers who had once rebelled against them "intermingle with those whose loyalty we tested." Parliament was still considering this when Monk, one month to the day after he had crossed the Tweed, reached Barnet, a mere four hours from London. Upon his arrival he went to bed but was soon aroused by one of Parliament's delegates accompanying him on the last stages of his march with the news that the London garrison refused to leave and that the City was in plain revolt. "You must march in at once; this is an official request." Monk, however, was not to be rushed: "What? Parliament in danger?" he asked. "Oh, well, it will hold out till tomorrow."

Parliament held out. The mutineers were pacified by a pay raise. Cavalry dispersed crowds of apprentices and journeymen. A few radical officers were cashiered. The Army of England, properly speaking, had ceased to exist. The columns entering and leaving London did not meet; the General had seen to that. He rode in with a stately entourage. The Speaker of the House and he met in the street; the two embraced and kissed. The people looked on in deep apathy. The newcomers were said to be friends. But they were soldiers, and the people were fed up with soldiers, all of them.

INTO THE CITY

London swallowed Monk's army and digested it as it digested any other crowd. The General himself was carried away by the whirlpools of publicity: formal receptions by the public bodies, followed by intimate encounters in the clubs and private homes. As seen from Scotland, everything had looked so simple—as simple as he described it, one day after his arrival, in the House of Commons: "The people wish to see the government of this country settled. The fewer oaths of loyalty, the better. Keep both the Stuart's Cavaliers and the Fanatics out."

To the Republicans it smacked of demagogery. But that same evening the same man was overheard to say, this time not for the record but in private conversation, "We must live and die for the Republic." Had they done him an injustice? One of them exclaimed, "The Levite and the Priest have passed us by and given us no succor; perhaps we have found the Samaritan who helps us." The Monarchists were dumbfounded. Monk a Republican! Another pint-size general who had been hoodwinked by the mystics and romancers of the perfect commonweal, the Overtons and Harringtons. But in the Commons some were haunted by the vision of another Cromwell. It was high time to make clear to all and sundry that the Cromwells were no longer needed. Warrants of arrest were issued against Left and Right.

Then suddenly the unexpected happened: London rebelled. For the first time since the outbreak of the civil war, the City, the fountainhead of all financial strength, openly defied the government. It was intolerable. London must be brought to heel without delay. A council of war was convened to plan the necessary measures. There was unanimity: They had the means—an army able to subdue the city. And they had the man to do the job. They called the man and told him what they wanted: London occupied, its chains and gateposts razed. What did he think? It was the acid test. If Monk obeyed, he would be tied hand and foot to the regime forever after, utterly discredited in the eyes of all its enemies. They watched him closely.

Monk obeyed. At six o'clock next morning he marched into London. At the last moment his wife tried to talk him out of it; he rudely silenced her. Through London's narrow lanes the cavalcade advanced at a canter, past the lines of long-faced citizens into the inner City. At the Three Tons he set up headquarters, convened his officers, and, marching up and down the chamber, chewing tobacco, he issued orders: against chains, posts, and barriers. The officers looked sullen. "So you won't obey Parliament?" he asked. "No, General," said one of them. Monk shouted, "Must I do it myself?" and moved to the door. Then they rushed after him. While the dismantling was proceeding, City emissaries came with an official invitation for the General to dine at Guildhall. He refused. Soon they were back to bring this message: To receive blows from one who is a friend, not an enemy, makes us more sad than angry. We know it is not your doing; we would not refuse *you* anything. "Let's see," Monk said and had the razing of the gates delayed, while waiting for the answer to a letter he had dispatched to Parliament. It was a compromise proposal, with a postscript: Hurry the elections, let it be your contribution to the general pacification.

Having conquered the City of London, Parliament indignantly requested Monk to stick to his assignment. He obeyed again and issued orders to complete the wrecking of the gates. He was informed that entire companies refused to do their part, and that Republicans were forming cells in all the regiments to fight the "bailiff of Parliament." His aides named the most dangerous subverter; it was Haslerig, a member of the House. They also told him what the talk was in the Commons: after London, Monk. They urged him to reconcile the City and drew up a letter, which amounted to an ultimatum, to the Commons. After some delay, he signed it.

But at six o'clock next morning, his troops once more moved into the City. "Any posts you overlooked?" the apprentices called. But Monk's emissary, Clargis, warmly assured the Lord Mayor: "We are no longer as we were the day before yesterday." The Aldermen remained distrustful until Monk arrived in person. He seemed a new man, talkative, almost affectionate. They settled down to dine, exchanging toasts. Just when the mood had become cordial, two plenipotentiaries arrived from Parliament with a cold message thanking him for his good services. As for the rest, the House proposed to carry on its consultations at the proper time. Wordlessly, Monk passed the letter to his aides. They did not remain silent. The emissaries of the House suggested that the General pull his troops out of the infectious City. His answer was evasive: "If the House takes my advice, all will be well." With that he went to meet the city fathers.

They gave him an ovation. When he left, he was their and London's general. All he had done to win them over was to read the letter he had sent to Parliament, with its demand for dissolution, new elections. Parliament was through. The bells were tolling, bonfires lit, and many drank His Majesty's health.

Not Monk. Was he not now the country's master? What prevented him from making himself the new Lord Protector, from aspiring to even higher dignity? This was Monk's trying hour. It passed. For days he looked like a sick man. But when he went before the House, now dominated by the Presbyterian moderates he had brought back, his voice was firm, and what he said reminded them of Whitelocke's shrewd advice: The old foundations of the state are gone for good. If you recall the King, first you will have to crush the people, and then he, the King, will have you at his mercy.

That they understood, and in the secret negotiations following in due course they exacted many safeguards from the Stuart who was still in Holland. Their aim: the restoration of a *captive* King, a King who would be at their mercy, seemed to suit the temper of the nation. While the Royalists still kept their peace, the House was able to turn its full energy to the reform and purging of the state administration. Hundreds of Justices of the Peace and other officials too devoted to the radical Republic were removed; the local militia was restored to the command of the old gentry. Already there was interference with Monk's own command. He thought: How times have changed. First he had sided with the House against the little Cromwells; later with the City against Parliament. Did they now think they could get rid of him? No matter who had power, Monk intended to be with it. Having held out for the longest time against the only ally still available to him, now he was forced to listen to his envoy. They would obey the King, backed by Monk. "Tell your master," he informed the emissary, "I have always been his humble servant." His voice was heavy with emotion.

THE END

When the young Stuart landed, George Monk greeted him respectfully. The two embraced and kissed. A long list of recommendations that the General submitted the next day, caused the new monarch some embarrassment, for it contained the names of many outspoken Republicans. But then Monk informed him: I had to enter into all kinds of connections, but that cannot bind you. And the King breathed easier. He showered Monk with honors, then and later.

As the General rode through the streets of London in the company of many Cavaliers, his old campaigners called him: "You did not have those with you before." He waved to them in great good humor.

On Blackheath Heights Oliver Cromwell's army, a long, black front of thirty thousand men was lined up to be inspected by the King. The war was over. During all that time, they had seen many leaders come and go, too many. Now it was over. When their own Monk appeared with the young, smiling master, they stood, watching them in rigid silence.

It was the end. But only the end of the Great Rebellion. Twenty-eight years later, after a resumption of the royal drive for absolute control, the question of supremacy was again raised and this time settled. The event was called the Glorious Revolution—glorious because it was brought about by peaceful means, but glorious also because the ruling classes settled matters without any interference from "the street." It was a revolution from above.

The Great Rebellion, a conservative attempt in its inception, aiming at a redress of the imbalance between Crown and Parliament, soon went beyond the purely constitutional concerns to raise the wider issues of religious and political group interest. By mobilizing and uniting previously distinct and smothered energies, the Great Rebellion changed in character: The revolutionary elements, now in the lead and no longer satisfied with the return to constitutional propriety, forged far ahead into political and social no-man's land. If, by arresting that advance, the Lord Protector stabilized the revolution in accordance with the given disposition of his class, it was his tragedy to leave the revolution in its constitutional predicament. While trying to find a solution that would satisfy the necessities of legality, he could not provide legitimacy, and it stood waiting in the wings.

Seen in this context, Monk, at first sight nothing better than the complete turncoat, was in fact a providential figure. He appeared at the right moment to perform a necessary and inevitable task. He only buried what was already dead. He was not an attractive figure, but then actors of a dying revolution seldom are. The villainy of Monk was in his role much more than in his character, which was no worse than that of the majority of human beings in a time of moral chaos and bewilderment. If he was above average, it was in his capacity for self-deception and survival. *Honi soit qui mal y pense.*

If Cicero was the victim and George Monk the executor of the devolutionary process, the French clergyman, Sieyès, has the unique distinction of uniting in his person both the role of executioner and victim: He brought Napoleon to power and thus caused his own undoing as the intellectual statesman of the French Republic. And he was unique in still another sense, as the man who gave the rising middle class its stirring slogan and who lived to become the destroyer of the revolution. Yet, by initiating devolution, he did not, in his own mind, betray the revolution. It had destroyed itself. Like Alexander Kerensky in our time, Sieyès managed to survive the Lenins and the Stalins of his day. Perhaps, if he had been a man of greater caliber, he would have shared their fate. However, he was inconspicuous enough to grow old peacefully and yet sufficiently significant to sum up in his flawed career the entire tragedy of the French revolution.

5 The Survivor: Sieyès

"But no particular class in Germany has . . . that revolutionary daring which flings at the adversary the defiant words: I am nothing, but I must be everything. . . ."

KARL MARX[1]

When Marx wrote the passage above, more than half a century had passed since a forty-year-old clergyman had asked and answered, in a pamphlet published under his own name, Emanuel-Joseph Sieyès, these three questions:

What is the Third Estate? Everything.

What has it been? Nothing.

What does it ask? To become something.

That was enough to make the author immediately famous as the foremost champion of the bourgeoisie.[2]

1. *Toward the Critique of Hegel's Philosophy of Right,* 1844.
2. The punchline, *"Qu'est-ce que le Tiers Etat?"* was claimed, as *his* intellectual property, by Nicholas Champfort, who "had supplied 'his Puritan Sieyès' with the formula" and had "wondered what Sieyès, 'with that ill-cut iron pen of his,' would make of it." J. H. Clapham, *The Abbé Sieyès* (London, 1912), p. 54. The author cites his source with reservations.

Today, Sieyès—or, as his name was sometimes spelled, Sieys—is one of the forgotten men of the French Revolution, although he not only gave the signal for the first attack but also played the final taps. Nicknamed "the mole of the revolution" by his great opponent, Robespierre,[3] Sieyès became one of the liquidators of the revolution and, together with Barras,[4] the man to help Napoleon Bonaparte into the saddle as First Consul of the French Republic.[5]

He was the first of the *idéologues,* so feared and persecuted later by Napoleon. Madame de Staël called him, in 1791, the "Newton of politics." [6] If not exactly that, he was the architect in residence of almost all the constitutional construction work done in that decade. None of his proposals was adopted without changes he considered stupid; still he left his mark on the new tablets of the revolution.

Between its dawn and dusk, where was he? During the worst terror, Sieyès was indeed a mole gone underground to wait in safety for the storms above to die. Asked later what he had been *doing* at the time, he gave his famous answer: "*J'ai vécu,*" "I lived," or, in effect, "Survival was my business." He might have gone on to say, as one commentator imagined: "People continually wonder how one survived those times, how I survived. What is there to say? It was like a lottery. And some of us held winning tickets. Those who held them are here today. And there is no one of whom we can ask the question 'Why?' " [7]

Sainte-Beuve claimed that he had seen all the papers the old man left behind: "philosophic essays, drafts of constitutions, above all intimate letters. . . . In one word, I have uncovered

3. Georges Lefebvre, *The French Revolution From 1793 to 1799* (London and New York, 1964), p. 243.

4. "An observer of the French political scene in 1794 would no doubt have written off Barras as a staunch supporter of the Jacobins. After all, Barras had voted for the execution of the king and excelled in the suppression of the counterrevolutionary rising at Toulon. Clearly a most unlikely man to liquidate the French revolution?" Walter Laqueur, "Russian Roulette," *The New York Review,* Vol. 5, No. 1 (August 5, 1965), p. 18. The same could have been said about Sieyès.

5. "His was the unique destiny to be the man both of the beginning and the end, and to perform a leading role on the first day as well as on the last." Charles-Augustin Sainte-Beuve, "Sieyès," *Causeries du Lundi,* December 9, 1851, translated from the 3rd edition (Paris, 1869), Vol. 5, p. 203.

6. Sainte-Beuve, *op. cit.,* p. 196.

7. Ilya Ehrenburg, remarks made at a recent public reading of his memoirs dealing with the years of Stalin's terror, as reported by Ralph Blum in "Freeze and Thaw. The Artist in Russia—I," *The New Yorker,* August 28, 1965, p. 94.

Sieyès' secret. . . ." He feared that the death of the friend who held those documents in trust had ended all hope that the collected works of Emanuel-Joseph Sieyès would ever see publication: "Once more he has re-entered, possibly forever, the silence which he loved so much." [8]

It might be tempting but perhaps misleading to write history in terms of the "grey eminences" who have prompted or claimed to have prompted the performers on the stage. One could imagine an account of the Wilsonian age, with all attention centered on his Colonel House, or an appraisal of the second Roosevelt by focusing exclusively on Louis Howe and Harry Hopkins. This temptation had better be resisted.

Moreover the case of Sieyès is another matter. He was more than a mere prompter. He was one of the main actors, representing continuity, amid change and turmoil. He never changed; what changed were not Sieyès' convictions but the circumstances. From beginning to end, Sieyès remained "a central Republican," [9] equidistant both from radical democracy and Caesarism. If the revolution had not, in its middle phase, "gone off the rails," Sieyès would have remained, behind the scenes or out in front, the ideologist of the French bourgeoisie; intent on keeping out the mob, "cooling down" the lava of the revolution, holding fast to the initial principles that—after two more revolutions, two more kings, and one more Bonaparte—at last prevailed, in 1875.

It is in his capacity as the true "anchor man" of the Republic that Sieyès is worthy of attention, and it is a matter of regret that he has, to this day, remained an object of not more than intermittent and oblique curiosity. Suppose he had not been so reticent about his own share in those great events and suppose he had written down his comments about the men he tried to lead —what would Sieyès have said? Something like this, perhaps.

A MEMOIR TO POSTERITY

Today, I had a most annoying conversation with a fellow who I am sure must have bribed my man to be admitted. I do not recall his name—something like de Valzac or Balzac; I am convinced the "de" is fraudulent, for his gross physique betrayed the

8. Sainte-Beuve, *op. cit.,* pp. 190, 216, n. 1.
9. Clapham, *op. cit.,* p. 161.

roturier *(plebeian)*. In any case, the fellow penetrated into my cold study, which I cannot warm, although a fire burns in it, claiming that he was a novelist. *"Are you quite sure,"* I asked, *"that you are not a journalist to interview me? And why, may I ask? How could one with my record as a Jacobin be of the slightest interest to your contemporaries?"* "But, Sir," he expostulated, *"you are an historic monument!"* "A monument?" I asked. *"But monuments are of the dead, and I am still, so I believe, alive."* "A monument in your own lifetime," he answered glibly and sat down in my own chaise longue, *making himself comfortable, pen in hand. I did not ask for his credentials, but I could tell from his porcine face that he was from the police, an agent sent to ferret out my sentiments and discover whether I approved of Charles X.* "Go, tell your masters that I am a loyal subject of whatever majesty sits on the throne, no matter for how long or short. A Louis, is he? The eighteenth, if I remember correctly. A good man, but not well served by his advisors. What? Deceased! Is he now?"*(The sooner he believed in my senility, I thought, the sooner would he take himself out of my sight. I was mistaken, though.)* "You say it's Charles now? Well, so be it. Tell him that I have a plan for him, just as I had a plan for all his predecessors. The details? They are his if he would receive me without witnesses. Impossible? My good man, I have talked to the great Bonaparte in confidence. He asked me if I would stay on with him as one of the Consuls. I replied, No, Sir. I do not choose to be your handyman!* [10] *Stop gaping and take this down! Do you doubt the words of one who made him Consul, ergo Emperor? But I forgot, you said you were a novelist, and in a novel it would not sound true, would it? Ah, truth is not for the likes of you!"*

But that was not what Fouché was after. *"Is it true, Sir, that you voted for the death of our late, martyred King, with the additional remark,* sans phrase?" I answered drily, *"For the last time: I did not make that additional remark, which would have been in extremely poor taste. The execution of Capet was a political necessity, not something I would gloat over. What happened was this: All the others made long speeches when their vote was taken. I was satisfied to speak the necessary words, 'La mort.' But the record later read, 'Sieyès, death, by all means.'* [11]

10. Sainte-Beuve, *op. cit.*, p. 215.
11. *Ibid.*

*Those were wild days. As your De Maistre put it long ago, 'It
has been said . . .' how did it go? Ah, 'that the revolution
manages men rather than being managed by them.'* [12] *Yes, he was
always the clever one, De Maistre was. A terrible reactionary
though. Is he still alive? I doubt it. They're all dead, the clever
ones. They never know when to speak out and when to be
silent. I was silent, that's why I'm still here to talk to you. That
big fool Danton, he had to go and make speeches, getting himself
killed!* Well, chacun à son goût: *That woman chaser, he loved
to hear the boom of his own voice. Thank God, mine never went
beyond a squeak. No, sir, I did not laugh. It is the smoke from
the defective chimney that makes me cough. If you would be so
good as to call my servant?"*

*That's how I got rid of him. Or else he might have gone on
to ask me:* "Remember, Sir, when Doctor Guillotin's machine was
working at top speed? And when the men of the Convention
offered you important posts? How wise of you, Sir, to beg off,
contenting yourself with such menial tasks as the reform of
education, saying, 'I'm a good hack for light work, but I would
make a bad coach horse.' " [13]

*Would they not love to make me look, a coward first, a
trimmer afterwards! What do they know! I always was most
frail in my body, as a child. I wanted to become an officer in
the King's army; instead they made me enter Saint Sulpice, from
which I was—no, not expelled as a subversive—merely asked to
transfer to another place of sacred studies. I was already a
philosopher in my own right. But not of the sort flying through
the empyrean. I was fond of music, and what is the secret of
that art form if not mathematical precision expressing itself with
the sweet sublimity of sound! So also it would seem to me that
the philosopher's task is to be an artist, fashioning society just as
a sculptor fashions the correct dimensions of his statue.* L'art
social, *the art of the sociality, I called my philosophy. Alas! Men
refused to be reasonable, and their republican assemblies during
the "great days" reminded me of monkeys with the larynxes of
parrots!* [14] *Asked for my views, I remained silent, thinking: What*

12. Joseph de Maistre, *Considérations sur la France* (1797), pp. 5-6, cited
by Daniel Guérin in *La Lutte de classes sous la première république* (2nd
ed., Paris, 1946), Vol. 2, p. 406.
13. Clapham, *op. cit.*, p. 177.
14. Sainte-Beuve, *op. cit.*, p. 207.

would be the use of adding my wine to this flood of rotgut? [15]

Wasted time. But when it mattered, I was always ready to stand up for my convictions. When that miserable creature, Poulle, tried to assassinate me on the twenty-third of Germinal, Year V, was I a coward then? Shot through the hand, I still disarmed the scoundrel and had him arrested.[16]

It is true: I do not like the stage. I do not like to face the sweating masses, I feel ill if forced to bully my inferiors. The creator wanted me to use my brains, not my emotions, which are easily fatigued. He chose me to become the guide, not the commander or tribune of the people but the one who whispers into his ears. And when the time came to look for a sword, I knew where to seek it. I found my trusted soldier, my Joubert— and lost him when he got himself killed in the battle he lost at Novi. And I had to turn to a replacement: Bonaparte.

I made him, not Barras. Why did I do it? Had I changed sides? Betrayed the revolution? More of the same rotgut!

Ah, those early glorious days! My days! It looked as if the art of sociality had finally come into its own! They listened, but they did not understand. It was a happy babble of many voices, and my own was never strong enough to outshout Mirabeau. The love letters he wrote me: that I was "the master of his thought, whether I liked it or not." I did not like it. Begging me for interviews: "If only my audacity would act in unison with your great courage, and my verve together with your admirable logic!" [17]

Him I kept at arm's length, aware of his most questionable reputation. Later, when it was established as a certainty, that he had been in the Court's pay, I was glad my "great courage" had been in abeyance. Too many incorruptibles were watching me distrustfully—one in particular.

Our Maximilien never trusted me, and, I confess, he frightened me. Still, for a while, he looked like the man who could save France from itself. There is in all revolutions a beginning when the most diverse groups join hands to pull the historic chariot forward; the mirage of fast and simple solutions fires them on. It is a precious moment but it does not last. Dissent ensues, and the wild men appear and drag the chariot off into their wilder-

15. *Ibid.* In the original: *rogomme,* cheap liquor.
16. Armand Bigeon, *Sieyès. L'Homme—Le Constituant* (Paris, 1893), p. 49.
17. Sainte-Beuve, *op. cit.,* p. 207.

ness. They must be spotted early and must be dispersed at once —if necessary with a whiff of grapeshot. Maximilien seemed just the right oppressor of those who would oppress the Republic. Like another Cromwell, he stamped out the Hébertistes and Enragés, cutting off the vines threatening to choke the great freedom tree.

But then Maximilien too went mad and plotted to destroy his own associates, to whom, fortunately, I did not belong. Came Thermidor and Maximilien's end, and with it renewed hope of putting the Revolution back on the right track. Did I refuse my help? Was I not ready with another plan?

I was. But once again, they heard and did not understand. They told me my new chariot had too many wheels, wheels within wheels. Precisely! My intention was to filter the will of the sovereign people, tempering its righteous fury in the service of judicious moderation.

They thought they knew better. So the new state soon had to resort to force to save itself from the still restless Jacobins and Royalists. We rulers needed a Monk. I can no longer recall how many times the army had to be called in to safeguard the Republic.[18]

Who were those saviors? Hoche was one and Augereau another. It matters not. They did their work well. But it was not enough. That strange compulsion of weak rulers to repeat forever their own failures was never demonstrated more convincingly. And so the Corsican became our last resort. It came to that.

He started quite a promising young man, almost another Mirabeau. What flattering dispatches he sent me from his battlefields! I thought it might be worthwhile to take him in hand. The truth is that I had his number all along. When he returned to Paris from his Pharaonic misadventure, he had coarsened, but we all do as we grow older. I will confess that I did not much care for his Italian cunning. My distaste for once got the better of my caution. When I asked him, "Do you want to be a king?" he was furious. Soon I was informed that "he began to think of throwing Sieyès over altogether." [19]

I found myself deserted by my friends and blamed for every-

18. Five times between 1795 and 1799, on the historic days of *Vendémiaire, Fructidor, Floréal, Prairial,* and *Brumaire.*
19. Clapham, *op. cit.,* pp. 248–49.

thing. The man who was my creature assumed patronizing airs. He dared tell me to my face: "Ruined as you are in the eyes of all parties, I shall soon be your only defender." [20] That was his revenge for my refusal to serve under him. I was reported to have said after Brumaire: *"Messieurs, we have a master. This young man knows everything, he can do everything, and he wants everything." [21] Well said, but not by me, and my denial was, of course, reported back to him at once, by some good "friends."*

The truth is that I no longer had any choice. It was Napoleon or chaos. Yes, it was the end of the Republic, long before he proclaimed himself emperor. The Caesars never cause but merely advertise and consummate the Fall of the Republic. As if I did not know it!

So with open eyes I made my leonine pact with the man. The revolutionaries, not I, had betrayed the Revolution. Even my plan for the Consulate was nothing if not a return to the sound principles of '89, for crude democracy was patently absurd.[22] The separation of the legislative function, equally distributed among three houses, the distinction of constituent and constituted powers, whatever they did with it: by this I stood. I held the line. Let them consult; let them compare my constitutions: they would certify my constancy.

I asked for nothing. They had, of course, to make me one of the Directors; under Bonaparte, I was content to be a member of the Senate. What went with it, I accepted: the emoluments and an estate; it was no more than I had justly earned. They called me venal, his kept man, but Bonaparte knew better, his memoirs bear it out, "He was fond of money, but he also was a man of severe probity, which pleased Napoleon well, it being what he deemed to be the foremost quality of any public figure." [23]

Always true to type, however, he did not exonerate me until his career had ended, literally on the rocks, the rocks of St. Helena. His great ambition had been to be Caesar and Augustus in one. Starting as Caesar, he had crowned himself as Augustus, only to be forced to revert back to being Caesar, and his end was almost that of Catiline.

All this I remember. It did happen, I was there. But thinking of

20. *Ibid.,* p. 254.
21. Sainte-Beuve, *op. cit.,* p. 214.
22. Clapham, *op. cit.* p. 241.
23. Sainte-Beuve, *op. cit.,* p. 215.

it now, I can feel nothing. It is over, and I am still alive. I told them: "I no longer see, I no longer hear, I no longer speak; I have become entirely negative." They wanted me to write my recollections, and I answered them: "Cui bono?" What indeed would be the purpose? So I said, "Our work is great enough to need no commentary. Our acts will teach those who care to understand our thoughts, and all our warnings would not save from our errors successors who will only earn our wisdom at the price of misfortunes like ours." [24]

So much for the record, but it does not quite convey my real thought. I meant to say that men such as I must be resigned to being bested by men such as Bonaparte. I comfort myself with the thought that long after their short and tawdry triumphs are forgotten, we will still be there to carry on. The price is high. But no regrets. I never compromised, but I was always prudent. Neither was it in me to disdain intrigue if it was in the service of the Truth. Where is the line that separates the probity of ends from the hypocrisy of means?

I told them to stop asking me, "I no longer find the word; it hides in some dark corner." [25]

Let it be. One thing they cannot take away from Sieyès: He survived. Yes, I outlived them all—Louis XVI and XVIII, Danton, Robespierre, St. Just; but it is Bonaparte's end that gives me the greatest satisfaction, even now.

I can no longer see what I am writing; I must call the man to light the candles. Also, I must not forget to tell him, "If Monsieur de Robespierre should call, tell him I am not at home." To think how close I came to perdition when they questioned my old shoemaker about the loyalty of Citizen Sieyès, and the good man responded in his innocence, "Oh, that one I know well, he takes no interest in politics at all but only in his books. I ought to know: I shod him!" [26]

Who goes there? No answer. Maximilien, is it you? Help! Keep the scoundrel out! [27] *What have I done to deserve so much punishment? I wish it were all over for me. How old am I? I lost track long ago, but I am at least eighty-five now, perhaps older. Never mind. I am the conscience of the Revolution; so I*

24. Clapham, *op. cit.*, p. 260. His source is Sainte-Beuve.
25. Sainte-Beuve, *op. cit.*, p. 214.
26. *Ibid.*, p. 216.
27. *Ibid.*

must live on until the great betrayers, all of them, have been destroyed. I, Sieyès, shall be prosecutor and judge in one. There shall be no Thermidor for me.

COMMENT

"The revolution manages men rather than being managed by them," wrote De Maistre.[28] And Tolstoy, observed about Napoleon's *Brumaire*, "He has no sort of plan; he is afraid of everything; but all parties clutch at him and insist on his support. . . . He is needed for the place that awaits him, and so, almost apart from his own volition, and in spite of his uncertainty . . . he is drawn into a conspiracy that aims at seizing power; and that conspiracy is crowned by success." In Tolstoy's view, Napoleon's power was not original with him but rather—like all power—an accumulation of effects: "*Chance* circumstances create the characters of the [Republican] rulers of France, who cringe before him. . . . *Chance* and *genius* give him the victory at Austerlitz. . . . We have found that historical characters and their commands are dependent on the events. . . . However many commands may be given, the event does not take place if there is no other cause to produce it." [29]

Tolstoy's "chances" and "events" dictate to the historic actors what has here been called their *role*. Their triumphs and defeats may be conditioned by their character. In Bonaparte's case, military genius and historic constellation (chance) conjoined gave him the victory of Austerlitz. But ultimately triumph or defeat depend on the events; they circumscribe the roles for which the actor brings or fails to bring the proper character equipment. When Napoleon, back from Elba, tried to introduce a liberal regime, we say that his move was out of character, whereas in fact we mean that he adopted a new role that could not possibly be creditable.

Insofar as the French Revolution was a movement toward rational organization of the social system, Sieyès' genius as a model builder cast him for a great if not decisive role. His character, his personality disqualified him. He simply was not an attractive man. His razor-sharp intelligence made others, par-

---

28. De Maistre, *op. cit.,* p. 406.
29. *War and Peace* (Modern Library Edition), pp. 1067, 1131.

ticularly Robespierre, resentful; he was never one to hide his light under a bushel. And with all his power of perception, Sieyès never understood what made him so unpopular. He seemed quite unaware of the massive resentment his haughty intellectualism generated. To remove that obstacle, he would have needed, in addition to the politician's skill, the iron energy of a Napoleon. He had neither. His perfectionism, his mental tidiness made Sieyès the ideal spokesman of a temporarily united nation, the clear voice proclaiming the consensus that concealed the pluralistic nature of incipient revolutionary movements.[30] Later, when the situation called for plain, uncomplicated stratagems, that same perfectionism defeated him.

The first phase ended when the King ceased to cooperate with the reformers who tried to create a liberal but still monarchic constitution. This alone might not have been decisive in deflecting the course of the revolution from a moderate solution. It was the external factor or, in Tolstoy's language, the "event" of foreign intervention that made the French Revolution swerve so radically to the Left, resulting in the Jacobin, mass-based dictatorship of national resistance and the eclipse of moderation. During that stage, Sieyès' role was minimal; his viewpoint did not meet the needs of the historic moment for centralization of all powers (which Sieyès abhorred) and for their ruthless use against the foreign and domestic, real or imaginary, enemies of the Republic. It is the moment in the history of revolutions when the intellectual recoils in horror from the unexpected consequences of his own ideas.

When the danger has passed, the mole deserts his secret place and sniffs the air. It is still not the air of freedom; yet the very man whose name has been a synonym for terrorism is now trying to rid his camp of the extremists. Within his generally radical location, Robespierre has turned conservative, perhaps only asserting what he had been all along. A risky business, this attempt of Robespierre's to change his image from that of a Stalin to that of Khrushchev. By liquidating the Left opposition, Robespierre destroyed the power equilibrium that had enabled him to keep the Right in check, just as another Russian, Kerensky, de-

30. Alfred Cobban in *Historians and the Causes of the French Revolution* (London, 1958), p. 39, uses the term "multilithic" (contrary to monolithic), but does not limit it to the early phase of revolutions. Cited by Charles Tilly in his valuable study of the Vendée rising, "The Analysis of a Counter-Revolution," *Theory and History*, Vol. 3, No. 1 (1963) p. 58.

stroyed his own precarious hold on the Republic when he was finally forced to opt between Kornilov and the Bolsheviks (as a good Socialist, he had to opt against Kornilov, thus putting himself into Lenin's "helpful" hands). The more determined Frenchman kept the lid on for a while by tightening the screws of terror, and the mole had to return to his hole.

It ended in the macabre confusion of the Thermidor events. Confusion, because Thermidor is *not* the turning point that legend made it. The revolution was still far from being liquidated, Jacobin strength far from being spent.[31]

However, the distinction between ante- and post-Thermidorian France remains significant in two respects. For one, the revolutionary scene contracted severely after Robespierre's fall: The play was no longer enacted in an amphitheater but on a narrow stage in front of the initial public, the bourgeoisie. The hour for the revival of old constitutional devices seemed propitious, and we will not be surprised to see Sieyès restored to influence and office.

But stability remained as unattainable as ever. While reflecting faithfully the cultural ambience of a middle class at long last come into its own, the new Directory ruled over a French nation deeply alienated from its government. At this point the second change, not immediately apparent but in process since the fall of Robespierre, became a decisive factor: the Directory had to rely repeatedly on armed force to repress the opposition, now of the Left, now of the Right. The generals, although nominally still the servants, were in fact already the obliging major-domos of their feeble overlords:

> The 9th Thermidor marks the ruin of the military system established by the Convention and the beginning of the end of civilian control over the army. The term of service of the roving delegates [political commissioners] is shortened: they can now only suspend, but no longer dismiss a military officer. To this reduction of the civil power corresponds the increase in the power of the generals. Their intervention in the making of political decisions is facilitated by the attitude of the Convention, which appeals to them for protection.[32]

31. This point has been most vigorously made by Daniel Guérin, *op. cit.*, Vol. 2, pp. 297ff. The author makes the most of Robespierre's essentially conservative predispositions.

32. G. Chevrier, "Les Rapports du pouvoir civil et du pouvoir militaire, de la chute de l'empire romain à la fin du 1er empire," *La Défense Nationale* (Paris, 1958), p. 83. Already cited by the present author in *The Fall of the Republic, Military Revolt in France* (Ann Arbor, 1962), p. 149.

The army, in short, had to play the role that the civilian forces were no longer able to perform: the hour had struck for the Praetorian to look for a politician to do his thinking for him, while the politicians fell over one another vying for the favors of the general who would oblige them.

It so happened that one general was capable of doing his own thinking.

If Sieyès, the initiator of the revolution, may be said to have been too much of a doctrinarian, that charge cannot be upheld against him who wrote *finis* to the revolution when he deeded it to Bonaparte. But it is not unusual that the man of intellect, when placed in a position of responsibility, will become more pragmatic than the most pragmatic politician. Hamlet playing Fortinbras would rather be called wrong than indecisive. If the people were incapable of reasoning, so much the worse for them: now Sieyès would pay them back in their own coin. He would give them what they seemed to understand best: force and cunning.

"Truth," the old man might have reasoned, sitting half-blind, alone, forgotten in his chamber in the rue St. Honoré, "all our truths are bound to turn into untruths unless they comprehend, include our lies, all our pretensions, all our subterfuges; as La Rochefoucauld put it, 'No one deserves to be called good unless he has the strength to commit evil; any other goodness is more often than not only laziness and lack of will power. . . .' We would often be ashamed of our best actions, if the world knew all our reasons for them.[33] Truth, if looked at closely, will be found to be a compound of the noblest and the basest metals. Truth is what is found in nature, and what is more natural to us than lying? Why, it is the very stuff of which our choicest dreams are made."

Is that the secret which explains the power of survival in a hostile world? Had he surrendered to what he continued to despise, no matter how hard he tried not to remember? To remember how it started, how he started, bold and clean, but also how it became sordid, and how he had been so clever and so masterful. But had the game been worth the effort? Would it have been better for him not to have survived the Revolution? Any regrets, Citizen Sieyès?

He has no answer.

---

33. *Maximes*, Nos. 237, 409.

In the following, the greatest of all revolutionary intellectuals, Marx, takes to task the man who was the liquidator of another French revolution; that man happened to be Napoleon the Great's nephew, Louis Bonaparte. But Napoleon the Little, as the greatest French poet of the period called him, was a dangerous opponent for the revolutionary intellectual, because his power defied the social theory of the critic. Bonapartism heralded something that did not come to full fruition until our day. Marx, with uncanny insight, grasped the secret that made possible the Mussolinis and the Hitlers. He lifted the veil, but then, dismayed by what he found, dropped it again and kept the secret from his followers.

6 A Premature Totalitarian: Louis Bonaparte

The praetorian, as defined before,[1] is not the servant but the temporary master of the situation. He not merely lends his force to politics; he makes politics. The praetorian may or may not have a program of his own. He may procure it from some source and thereby run the risk of being taken over by the interests the program promotes and being demoted to the role of policeman. Or in the rare case that a praetorian army has developed its own ideology, it is likely to change from a praetorian to a political army, capable of acting as a social force in its own right for those who are too weak to act or have not at that time an independent existence.[2]

There is no point in speaking of "praetorian guards" in normal times. External and internal peace are not conducive to praetorianism; it is a phenomenon of crisis. In the absence of great social tensions, the police will be sufficient to keep order. In addition, modern armies, based on mass conscription, lend them-

1. See above, chapter 3, pp. 58–59. See also below, pp. 174–175.
2. See below, chapter 12.

selves with difficulty to political indoctrination, much less to intervention in political disputes. The most a military leadership opposed to the regime is able to achieve is to seal off the army from the nation, to transform the army into an apolity.

In times of crisis that army may become a force of intervention not in spite of but because of its political vacuity. The order to disperse a crowd, to shoot to kill, if necessary, will be executed by a troop of men turned into a well-functioning machine. As long as they do not "get ideas," they will not fraternize with whoever has been pointed out to them as the internal enemy. This is the harvest time for the ambitious general or for the man who knows how to use the generals. It is the situation for a Bonaparte or for the Bonapartist schemer; and his time to act, the eighteenth of Brumaire.

In 1851, the French adventurer was not a general or military man at all. The nephew of the great Napoleon was as unrelated to the uncle as Octavian had been to the murdered Caesar.[3] But he had inherited the glorious name, had added a touch of Saint-Simonian socialism. Thus equipped, he had begun to woo the army; he had been expelled once, and a second time imprisoned. Though not bold by nature, he did have tenacity. No charmer of crowds, he was a past master of intrigue: Not revolution, but infiltration was his game. He also had a gifted *alter ego*, likewise illegitimate, who did his dirty work for him, constructing his political machine.

Still, in 1848, when the revolution came, the name of Louis Bonaparte was not among those thought most likely to succeed. When the new Republic was beginning to look for a savior from the revolutionary proletariat, it called on its generals, and they obliged. First Cavaignac, then Changarnier, Bugeaud, Lamoricière, all from Algeria, the newly conquered colony. They detested the Republic. To destroy a regime of civilians "who dared to give orders to the heroes of Africa" was for these intrepid officers "a chance to stage another glorious raid." [4] One hundred and ten years later, the historic scene would be repeated.

Both the Second and Fourth Republics found their end through army intervention. Whether Charles de Gaulle is the fourth Bonaparte, as some believe, remains to be seen. Napoleon III,

3. Louis Napoleon was the son of Joseph Bonaparte's wife and a Dutch admiral; Octavian had been adopted by the Roman dictator.
4. Henri Guillemin, *Le Coup du 2 décembre* (Paris, 1951), p. 310.

unlike de Gaulle no general, also made use of the generals, and they, unlike de Gaulle's competitors, gave the civilian Prince no trouble after he had been elected President of the Republic. Getting ready for his *coup d'état*, he could address them: "Soldiers! Both in 1830 and in 1848 you have been treated like defeated men, though you are the elite of the nation. Be proud of your mission; you will save the fatherland!" [5] Before, they had propped up one or the other faction of Republicans. Now they had found their master, who addressed them on his eighteenth of Brumaire with these words: "I won't say to you: 'March, I shall follow you,' but: 'I shall march, you follow me.' " [6]

It is therefore correct to say with Raoul Girardet that "the advent of the Second Republic marks the beginning of an exceptional period of three to four years, during which the army . . . intervenes decisively in the struggles of the parties. It is a time when the military leaders sample the temptations of public life and end by holding in their hands the fate of the regime." Yet it is equally correct to say, as does the same author, that, "though of military origin, the government of the Second Empire was in no sense the government of the military." [7]

But if not praetorian, what was Louis Bonaparte's regime? Who ruled? Or rather, inasmuch as the Emperor seemed to be very much in charge, whom did he represent, what social interests, or, to use the obnoxious term, which class?

The answer would appear to be that he represented no class in particular, but all the classes; the evidence for it was the plebiscite by which the great majority of the French people legalized Napoleon III's *coup d'état*. If there was any opposition, it was powerless and easily repressed. The bourgeoisie, entrenched in Parliament, was paralyzed; the split between progressives and conservatives was beyond repair. But the true reason why the restoration of the Empire could succeed was that the revolution had, in three years, run its course. It had already reached the stage of counterrevolution during its first year, when Parliament called in the army to repress the second, social revolution of the proletarian unemployed. Since then the European bourgeoisie would fight a two-war front: not only still battling and advancing against the entrenched precapitalist classes but also on the

5. *Ibid.*, p. 359.
6. *Ibid.*, p. 348.
7. Raoul Girardet, *La Société militaire* (Paris, 1953), pp. 133, 143.

defensive against the new masses spawned by the industrial revolution. The bourgeois Republic, having conquered for a moment, was in full retreat; appalled by the emerging logic of its own demands, the liberals took fright and turned for help to the appointed chief of the Republic, only to discover that they were now at his mercy.

ENTER THE OBSERVER

All this was confusion compounded. The mere repetitiousness of moves and countermoves characteristic of all revolutions made this one particularly difficult to understand. Later generations too continued to be baffled by the hybrid nature of the Bonapartist system. Marxists or not, historians tend to identify the source of power, preferably in one class or in a coalition of two or more classes. Even if no direct class rule can be ascertained, the expectation of detecting the class interest behind the rule is habit-forming.

Fortunately for us, an observer happened to be on the scene who insisted that he was no Marxist and proved it by dispensing with a major tenet of the Marxist canon that declares the state to be an organ of class domination. When he investigated the Napoleonic state, the evidence did not bear out that theory. The Emperor, so the observer found, did not *reflect* the interest of any class. At best, he might be said to *benefit* that interest: the peasants' for example, or that of the bourgeoisie. But it was not correct to say that Louis Bonaparte's regime was the creation and the creature of the bourgeois or the peasant class. So the main Marxist notion of the state had to be abandoned, or at least modified to fit the case. The operation was successfully performed, and to this day the subtle sharpness of the final diagnosis has not ceased to be exciting.

The name of the observer was Karl Marx. The title of his piece, *The 18th Brumaire of Louis Bonaparte*, is to remind the reader of the fate awaiting all successors: "Hegel remarks somewhere that all facts and personages of great importance in world history occur, as it were, twice. He forgot to add: the first time as tragedy, the second as farce." [8]

8. Karl Marx, *The 18th Brumaire of Louis Bonaparte* (New York, 1963), p. 15.

This is the beginning, and it sets the tone of savage irony pervading the whole work. He wrote it in white heat, while the impression of events was still fresh; he also wrote with the black rage of the defeated, but not for a moment did he let his sovereign contempt for the Napoleonic upstart interfere with the objective of the icily dispassionate historian, to unearth the facts. His findings have held up well, considering his lack of scholarly resources; they become still more impressive for demonstrating how a great mind can triumph over its own bias. For it is in this work that Marx restates once more succinctly his main definition of the state, though he does not yet name it in this passage:

> Upon the different forms of property, upon the social conditions of existence, rises an entire superstructure of distinct and peculiarly formed sentiments, illusions, modes of thought, and views of life. The entire class creates and forms them out of its material foundations and out of the corresponding social relations.[9]

When does the state as a phenomenon of class control arise? Before the first French revolution the class character of statehood was apparently obscured by the enormous growth of bureaucratic centralism, which "sprang up in the feudal days of the absolute monarchy, with the decay of the feudal system, which it helped to hasten." Marx obviously considers the authoritarian Bourbon state as a transitional, progressive force which, by a revolution from above, deprived the feudal class of the possession of the state that rightfully, according to Marx's definition of the superstructure, should have been a feudal state, albeit by then in full decay.

The revolution ought to have propelled the bourgeoisie into the driver's seat. Instead, the process of centralization went right on. "All revolutions perfected this machine instead of smashing it." Napoleon I made himself its master, but his episodic rule was "only the means of preparing the class rule of the bourgeoisie. Under the Restoration, under Louis Philippe, under the parliamentary [second] republic, it was the instrument of the ruling class, however much [bureaucracy] strove for power on its own."

The state had finally become the bourgeois state. But not for long, because "under the second Bonaparte . . . the state seem[s]

9. *Ibid.*, p. 47.

to have made itself completely independent," under "an adventurer blown in from abroad, raised on the shield by a drunken soldiery, which he has bought with liquor and sausages, and which he must continually ply with sausages anew." [10]

Too many sausages here, and the analyst must shut his eyes and hold his nose. But truth will out: "France, therefore, seems to have escaped the despotism of a class"—the bourgeoisie—"only to fall back under the despotism of an individual, and, what is more, under the authority of an individual without authority. The struggle seems to be settled in such a way that all classes, equally impotent and equally mute, fall on their knees before the rifle butt." [11]

But were the soldiers not recruited from the peasantry, and could it not therefore be said that Bonaparte, elected and protected by that class, was nothing but its representative, and that the peasantry, availing itself of the democratic franchise, was in fact the new ruling class?

Not so. First, peasants "do not form a class," for "there is merely a local interconnection among [them], and the identity of their interests begets no community, no national bond and no political organization among them. . . . They cannot represent themselves, they must be represented. Their representative must at the same time appear as their master. . . . The political influence of the small-holding peasants therefore finds its final expression in the executive power subordinating society to itself." [12] In only slightly different circumstances Trotsky was to say the same thing about the Russian peasantry of 1905.

Nor was the army really a peasant army: It was recruited from "the peasant *lumpen-proletariat*," [13] which is Marxian for elements of a society that have become dysfunctional or, as Marx put it, are no longer playing a direct and active part in the productive process.

But the Bonapartist ruler did not depend only on the armed forces. He had his own mass organization which, in Marx's colorful description, instantly reminds us of contemporary mass formations. Bonaparte's Benevolent Society of December 10th anticipates the para-military units of a Mussolini and a Hitler. Re-

10. *Ibid.*, pp. 121–23, *passim.*
11. *Ibid.*, p. 121.
12. *Ibid.*, p. 124.
13. *Ibid.*, p. 130.

cruited from the slums of Paris, it was "organized into secret sections, each section led by Bonapartist agents, with a Bonapartist general at the head of the whole." It was a fearsome crowd of social rejects, part underworld, part *lumpen-bourgeoisie:*

> Alongside decayed roués with dubious means of subsistence and of dubious origin, alongside ruined and adventurous offshoots of the bourgeoisie were vagabonds, discharged soldiers, discharged jailbirds, escaped galley slaves, swindlers, mountebanks, *lazzaroni*, pickpockets, tricksters, gamblers, *maquereaus* [procurers], brothel keepers, porters, *literati*, organ-grinders, ragpickers, knife grinders, tinkers, beggars—in short, the whole indefinite, disintegrated mass, thrown hither and thither, which the French term *la bohème.* . . ." [14]

Or as we would say, the whole ensemble of the *Three Penny Opera*. But then the entire nation had by now become a congeries of atoms, an "indefinite, disintegrated mass," a mass of maneuver and manipulation, the material for the system not yet called, but in effect, totalitarian.

AN OPPORTUNITY LOST

At this point Marx began to feel uneasy. He had almost but not quite discovered the French prototype of Fascism—a ruling power representing no class in particular but claiming to be representative of all. It was a model flatly contradicting, at first sight, the Marxian postulate that all political regimes are, by their very nature, class regimes.

The contradiction could have been avoided if Marx had made allowance in his general theory of the state for a pseudo-independent ruling power growing in strength with the intensification of the class struggle. So Marx could easily have found a place for his new "fascist" type within the context of his main, class scheme of domination, at the very end of a continuum stretching from complete cooperation to complete deadlock between all the classes—a situation that makes possible the intervention of a man, a group, a movement representing no class in particular. But the resulting new consensus would not be the one assumed by "general will" theories but, on the contrary, an

14. *Ibid.*, p. 75.

imposition in the double meaning of the word: an order imposed from above; also, a fraud.

To the great detriment of later Marxists, Marx shied away from this conclusion, leaving them to cope with the phenomenon of Fascism without the benefit of his almost disclosed discovery. So they explain the Brumaires of the new Bonapartes as "the last-ditch stand of bourgeois imperialism." [15]

Retracing his steps, Marx searched for some class other than the temporarily incapacitated bourgeoisie with which the Emperor's regime could be identified. His first choice was the same French peasantry to which he had a short while before denied the title of a class. Now he reviewed the case. Some of the peasants did apparently regret their earlier enthusiasm for Bonaparte because they rioted against the government—poor peasants who did not partake of the prosperity so providentially coincidental with the Second Empire's initiation. Then, as now under de Gaulle, France made sharp economic gains, but gains unequally distributed among the branches of production. The unrest caused by this disparity might generate revolts of sinking expectations, as distinguished from revolutions made by a rising class.[16]

Those poor peasants in rebellion against Bonaparte's government were obviously not his ruling class. The real explanation was close at hand, and Marx's eagerness to pounce on it shows the intensity of his relief:

> Let there be no misunderstanding. The Bonaparte dynasty represents not the revolutionary, but the conservative peasant; not the peasant who strikes out beyond the condition of his social existence, the small holding, but rather the peasant who wants to consolidate this holding. . . . It represents not the enlightenment, but the superstition of the peasant; not his judgment, but his prejudice; not his future, but his past. . . .[17]

15. The Yugoslav "revisionists" came closest to an understanding of totalitarianism when they declared that "fascism occurs when the bourgeoisie as a class is no longer capable of retaining power, while the proletariat is still too weak to capture it." Alfred Sherman, "Tito—A Reluctant Revisionist" in *Revisionism*, ed. by Leopold Labedz (London, 1962), p. 260.

16. For the debate about the British gentry in the Great Rebellion, on the question whether it was rising or sinking as a class, see H. R. Trevor-Roper, "The Social Causes of the Great Rebellion," in *Historical Essays* (London, 1957), pp. 195ff., and J. H. Hexter, "Storm over the Gentry," in *Reappraisals in History* (New York and Evanston, 1961), pp. 117ff.

17. Marx, *op. cit.*, p. 125. See also Raymond Aron, *Main Currents in Sociological Thought* (New York, 1965), pp. 248–60.

But even that conservative part of the peasantry was actually, as Marx showed, victimized by the new dynasty, exploited to provide the surplus value eaten up by the giant, parasitic bureaucracy. However, Marx did not depend on the conservative wing of the peasantry to make his point. His *pièce de résistance* was the same bourgeoisie that had lost its ruling class position to Napoleon I.

Not for long, however, we are now informed. The argument has two ingenious twists—the abdication of the bourgeoisie was *voluntary* rather than enforced, and Louis Bonaparte's rule would, in turn, promote the bourgeoisie's *return* to power. By placing the events from 1848 to 1851 into the larger context of French history, Karl Marx ended with another version of the long-range revolution that he had proclaimed in 1850 when he told the members of his Communist League that the proletarian battle cry must be "The Revolution in Permanence," thereby anticipating Trotsky's term by more than half a century.[18]

FREEDOM FROM RESPONSIBILITY

Generally, the first French revolution is referred to as the triumph of the bourgeois system over the last vestiges of feudalism. Although some recent studies of that revolution tend to denigrate its bourgeois character, some of them going so far as to speak of it as a revolt against at least part of the bourgeoisie,[19] the bourgeois label will most likely stick to 1789 and all that. If so, all one can say is that this revolution and its 1848 succession were defeated. In both instances, the bourgeois institutions of the revolution were replaced by dictatorial systems.

Yet the socioeconomic gains made by the bourgeoisie remained intact under both Napoleons. What accounts for this disparity between political effectiveness and economic strength? Marx found the explanation in the very nature of bourgeois ideology: Revolution hurts the bourgeois interest. If economic power is endangered by exposure to the limitless demands bound

18. Karl Marx and Frederick Engels, *Selected Works*, Vol. I (London, 1950), p. 108. Trotsky's thesis of the Permanent Revolution was first developed in *Itogi i Perspektivy* (1906), while the book of that title is of 1930.

19. See Norman Hampson, *A Social History of the French Revolution* (London and Toronto, 1963), and Alfred Cobban, *The Social Interpretation of the French Revolution* (Cambridge, 1964).

to be made upon political democracy, then democratic power must be sacrificed. As he finally saw it, the economic role of the French bourgeoisie required abdication of and freedom from political responsibility:

> As long as the rule of the bourgeois class had not been organized completely, . . . the antagonism of the other classes, likewise, could not appear in pure form, and . . . take the dangerous turn that transforms every struggle against the state power into a struggle against capital. . . . The parliamentary regime lives by discussion; how shall it forbid discussion?

Once in political control, the capitalist class discovers that the case is altered:

> By now stigmatizing as *"socialistic"* what it had previously extolled as "liberal," the bourgeoisie confesses that its own interests dictate that it should be delivered from the danger of its *own rule;* that in order to restore tranquillity in the country, its bourgeois parliament must, first of all, be given its quietus; that in order to preserve its social power intact, its political power must be broken . . . that in order to save its purse, it must forfeit the crown. . . .[20]

The Bonapartist ruler who picks up the crown "feels it to be his mission to safeguard 'bourgeois order.'" Nevertheless, he is somebody solely due to the fact that he has broken the political power of this middle class and daily breaks it anew. Consequently he looks on himself as the adversary of the political and literary power of that middle class. "But," Marx goes on, "by protecting its material power, he generates its political power anew." [21]

In other words, the mediator who resolved the temporary deadlock between the antagonistic classes by interposing himself as the ruling power has fulfilled his mission. He has normalized the working of the system; in due time the superstructure will once more express the hierarchy of class relation. At long last, the bourgeois revolution will be fully consummated.

Marx predicted well: The Emperor was forced to make concessions at least to the literary power of the middle class by relaxing censorship and by restoring Parliament to some significance when he inaugurated his "liberal empire" in the early

20. Marx, *op. cit.,* pp. 66, 67.
21. *Ibid.,* p. 131.

1860s. But historic roles are never changed at will: The liberalization of a dictatorial system is at best half-hearted, therefore unconvincing, and will only whet the revolutionary appetite.

THE TIMING OF SALVATION

So it would seem that Marx grants to political "adventurism" a decisive function in the revolutionary process. In his text the interloper is a providential villain; his assignment is to arrest each revolutionary spurt, so that the larger revolution may continue, with the dialectic leading *via* multiple negation (failure) to the final affirmation, victory.

In turn, each revolutionary upsurge is an indication that the long-range revolution has been stalled. The intervention of the providential agent thus assumes a meaning that is likewise dialectical: It has to be both brake and prod, a breakthrough and a hindrance, but as much a hindrance to regression as a passion of and for the past. Without the renaissance of the Napoleonic legend in the early 1840s Louis Bonaparte would have remained in limbo.

Ultimately, the success or failure of the interloper will depend on perfect or defective timing. He must come when the contestants, temporarily exhausted, have stopped fighting. If he appears before the fighting has begun, he may succeed, but it is much more likely that he will not get a hearing. Neither must he come too late, after the worst is over, because then his help will no longer be needed. Yet were he to appear while fighting is already going on but still has a long way to go, his fate might be that of a Catiline or a Cicero.

Napoleon III, no longer a well man but still a clever schemer, lasted until taken prisoner, not by French revolutionaries but in battle against a superior schemer, Bismarck, and his Germany. The Emperor was finally replaced by the bourgeois republic, and Karl Marx was vindicated, though the outcome of the Franco-Prussian war made him unhappy.

If intellectuals are people who exalt the conquests of the mind over all other satisfactions, then their concerns were never very far from those thus far discussed in this study. But it is true that, with the exception of intellectuals who for religious reasons wanted to arrest their nation's drift into modernity, intellectuals have played auxiliary rather than decisive roles in the history of political revolution and counterrevolution. At best they were, like Cicero and Sieyès, intellectuals who had come to grief in politics.

The next chapter resumes the theme, first sounded in the Prologue, of the intellectual revolution proper. It deals with the breaking away of an elite of social theorists from their own, middle class tradition. These men tried to exorcise the Marxian spectre, principally by scholarship rather than by polemic. Their findings, which amounted to an intellectual counterrevolution against Marx, soon led them to conclusions equally suspect to Marxists and the orthodox defenders of the liberal faith. The counterrevolution proved to be more radical than the tradition of the new, the Marxist revolution, while the liberals felt about the new school the same way the exiled English royalists in Cromwell's time had felt about their champion, Hobbes. Protect us from such defenders!

The confrontation between Marxists and the bourgeois innovators underwent a subtle change as time went on: It turned into an undeclared convergence. Without officially deserting their camps, some doubting Marxists and some doubting liberals met in the no-man's land between the front lines: theorists of power based on economic class and theorists of the elite that governs by authority were unable to find the line dividing them. Marxist defectors and middle-class rebels jointly happened on the master institution of our time, bureaucratic collectivism: the meeting place of East and West, Bonapartism brought up to date, totalitarian in character even where it can dispense with terrorism.

7 A Major Defection

Toward the end of the last century a constellation of great social scientists who had much in common appeared on the horizon; so much did they have in common that Talcott Parsons saw the convergence and essential unity of their ideas as informing what he called "a major revolution in the scientific analysis of social phenomena." [1]

That group was composed of Freud, an Austrian; Weber, a German; Durkheim, a Frenchman; and Pareto, an Italian. Their "crucial concern was the irrational, virtually unchanging nature of human sentiments—what Freud usually referred to as 'drives' and what Pareto rather awkwardly termed 'residues.' However radically these thinkers differed from Marx, they at least agreed with him that what was 'deepest' in human conduct for the most part fell into a pattern of mere repetitions." As human thoughts

An earlier, rather different version of this chapter appeared under the title "A Question of Affinities" in *Cahiers Vilfredo Pareto,* 5 (1965), pp. 165–174. Reproduced by permission.
1. T. Parsons, *The Structure of Social Action,* 2nd ed. (Glencoe, 1949), p. B.

were now reduced to rationalizations, myths, or ideologies, the problem of *consciousness* became central. "It was no longer what actually existed that seemed important: it was what people thought existed." [2]

It was "a revolution of such magnitude in the prevailing empirical interpretation of human society," that Talcott Parsons found it difficult to answer the question: "What is to account for it?" [3] For the second time within one century the bourgeois camp of thought had seen a mass defection, with the difference that the new revolutionaries were no Marxists and in fact opposed to Marx. This does not prevent Talcott Parsons, who is not a Marxist either, from toying for a moment with an explanation along Marxian lines, when he considers it "very probable that this change is . . . an ideological reflection of certain basic social changes." There he stops, because "to deal adequately with this problem would far transcend [his] study." [4] He prefers to assume "that a considerable part has been played by [a] development within the body of social theory and knowledge of empirical fact itself" and he proposes to show "that scientific theory—most generally defined as a body of *logically interrelated* 'general concepts' of empirical reference—is not a dependent but an *independent* variable in the development of science. . . ." Theory and factual knowledge interact: "Neither is the 'cause' of the other. Both are in a state of *close mutual interdependence.*" This rehabilitation of Mind also opened up the possibility for a new "voluntary theory of action." [5]

The anti-Marxian thrust of the whole argument, ascribed to the new school, is obvious. But its representatives knew only the mature, the standard Marx. The publication of the early manuscripts of 1844 and 1845 still lay ahead. Even the much younger Talcott Parsons was familiar only with Marx as economic writer, not as the philosopher who postulated the same interaction and "close mutual interdependence" between theory and factual insights, which is the burden of the Parsonian demands. If the determinist element seems to favor the preponderance of the material "basis" in Marx's best-known writings, Frederick Engels'

2. H. Stuart Hughes, *Consciousness and Society* (New York, 1958), pp. 4, 66.

3. Parsons, *op. cit.,* p. 5.

4. *Ibid.*

5. *Ibid.,* pp. 15, 6, 11, 14, respectively. Our italics.

rehabilitation of the "superstructure" in his well-known letter [6] qualifies the force, if not the final prevalence of the material variable to the extent that an element of indeterminacy may be said to have replaced the iron-clad persistence of the Marxist primer.[7] The road was opened for Lenin's party, which *imported* political class consciousness to a still dormant proletariat, and for Stalin's "active superstructure," which not merely mastered but actually *created* the economic basis, in short, for the ascendancy of the activist over the determinist Marx. The distance to Professors Parsons' "voluntary theory of action" would seem almost negligible.

Almost, but not quite. Communist voluntaristic theory kept hurtling itself against Lenin's "stubborn facts," and Stalin, in his very last *ex-cathedra* pronouncement, felt obliged to warn his planners against underestimating the persistent power of the economic laws.[8]

Economic determinism becomes biological determinism in Pareto's inversion: "Marx believed domination to be simple 'superstructure,' or 'reflex,' or consequence of economic differentiation, but closer research has shown that political rule has an existence of its own, independent of economics. Pareto, for his part, takes domination as a simple 'superstructure,' or 'reflex,' or consequence of natural differentiation among men, and his view is exposed to the same doubt and criticism as Marxism in this respect." [9] But in contrast to Marx's historical determinism, Pareto's determinism is essentially anti-historic. From his notion of a psychological antipathy existing between socio-biological types, he derived his theory of cycles, which is indebted to Plato and Vico but emptied of their idealistic and rationalistic contents, retaining only "a psychological formalism that permits him to link the undulatory process to an alternation of the two main resi-

6. Engels to Starkenburg, in Karl Marx and Frederick Engels, *Selected Works, op. cit.*, Vol. II, p. 458. But *cf.* Eugene Kamenka, *The Ethical Foundations of Marxism* (London, 1961) p. 164: "It was Engels, with his blindness for alienation, with his crude evolutionism, his utilitarian concern with economic *satisfaction*, who became the 'ideologue'—the propagandist and populariser—of Marxism." For a more restrained version of this view, typical of recent Western Marxicology, see George Lichtheim, *Marxism* (London, 1961), pp. 237ff.

7. See Robert K. Merton, *Social Theory and Social Structure*, Rev. Ed. (Glencoe, 1957), pp. 462–63.

8. J. V. Stalin, *Economic Problems of Socialism in the USSR* (Moscow, 1952), pp. 5–6.

9. Franz Borkenau, *Pareto* (New York, 1936), pp. 110–11.

dues." [10] History thus is reduced to eternal recurrence, change to mere, if long-range, oscillations. The social equilibrium is bound to be restored to its old order, strength to prevail over cunning; the "circulation of elites" takes care of that. But none of the two archetypes ever prevails in the long run: The indefinite predominance of Residue I, which accounts for rationalization, namely, progress, cannot be conceded by Pareto, for it would disrupt the predetermined balance of the two psychological constants. The ideology of violence, a Residue II property, assumes the function of an absolute *necessity*.[11]

There is then a considerable amount of ambivalence at work in both the Marxian and the Paretian systems. If the former blends deterministic and voluntaristic elements, Pareto's "logico-experimental" science is "in all respects relative, contingent" and it offers "no conclusions as 'certain,' 'necessary' . . . 'absolute.' " [12] Yet it contains a built-in, "absolutist" bias. It is a convergence of impurities—which may account for the great passion of the East-West controversy around Pareto and Marx.

Bourgeois sociologists never accepted Marx as one of their own, and the Marxists retaliated in kind. To them, the "intellectual revolution," which so puzzled Talcott Parsons, was no problem: those philosophies of self-doubt and sociologies of pessimism simply reflected the "heightening contradictions of monopoly capitalism." Once a "progressive" ferment of decomposition (the negation of the feudal past), the bourgeoisie, about to come into its own, recoiled before the new industrial proletariat and became defensive, unsure of itself, reactionary. Social change now had a decomposing effect on the former decomposers. As the cornered scorpion is supposed to turn its deadly sting upon itself, so the aging bourgeoisie will voice its fears more or less candidly. Freud's Eros pales before the death instinct; in a world increasingly bureaucratized, the talk is no longer of the advent of Superman but of the "routinization of charisma," suggesting by his very absence the need for a charismatic leader. After long abuse by the financial foxes, it will be the turn of leonine elites to restore order.

All this has been said more learnedly, and with obsessive single-

10. Guy Perrin, "Thèmes pour une philosophie de l'histoire dans le traité de sociologie générale," *Cahiers Vilfredo Pareto*, 1 (1963), p. 31.
11. *Ibid.*, pp. 32–33, 35.
12. Pareto, *The Mind and Society* (New York, 1935), IV, p. 1924, ii-m.

mindedness, by the man acclaimed by many as the greatest Marxist thinker of this generation, Georg Lukacs.[13] In a study written before Stalin's death and liberally sprinkled with the ritual tributes to his genius, Georg Lukacs savagely abjured the intellectual gods of his pre-Marxist youth as the destroyers of Reason; or rather, because the devil theory of history is unacceptable to Marxist historiography, Freud, Durkheim, Weber, and Pareto are indicted as the leaders of the school that tried hard to conceal but actually unmasked the bourgeois failure of nerve. Lukacs traced it through a series of retreats from a reality that refused to conform to bourgeois wishes. So reality, the primacy of social being, of objective truth as given independently from consciousness, had to be questioned. "Pre-war imperialist sociology" thus was condemned to turn inward, toward subjectivism. "The indefinable, irrationalist character of *Fuehrertum* is already in evidence." This is what Lukacs had to say about Max Weber's postulate of a value-free social science: "What was intended to be a purge of sociology of all irrational components only serves to point up the irrationality of the historical and social process." No wonder then that the theories of leadership and the elite were formulated in two countries in which the tradition of democracy was weakest: in Germany, by Weber, and in Italy, by Pareto.[14]

End of convergence? Again, almost, but not quite. What there was of convergence had to go underground. One may observe a gradual breaking away from fixed positions on both sides of the divide. There was some deviation in the East which was officially repressed, such as the late Professor Varga's heresy when in the 1940s he suggested that monopoly capitalism was capable, at least in war time, of transcending the narrow limits of class interest. Others took their lead from the Master's words themselves; they would point to certain passages in the *Communist Manifesto*, where the nonproletarian class origin of the "vanguard" is clearly established; they would cite those lines from Lenin's *What Is To Be Done?* distinguishing between the proletariat, "able to develop only trade union consciousness," and the *classless* party of social-

---

13. Not by George Lichtheim, who calls him "An Intellectual Disaster" in *Encounter*, No. 116 (May, 1963), pp. 74–80.

14. *Die Zerstoerung der Vernunft* (Berlin, 1955), pp. 478–79, 485, 496–97. But in his most recent work, *Realism in Our Time* (New York, 1964), Lukacs contemplates a possible synthesis of the "bourgeois-democratic and proletarian revolutions."

ism. Such deviants as Machaisky, a Pole, openly asserted the nonsocialist, elitist character of Lenin's "machine" long before October, and Ciliga, a Yugoslav, lost his faith in the regime soon afterwards. These theorists of "bureaucratic collectivism" were driven into inner or external exile. Worse, they found themselves assaulted by the prince of heretics, himself in exile, Leon Trotsky. One who called upon himself the wrath of the Old Man was Bruno Rizzi, while his fellow countryman, Antonio Gramsci, ventured to declare that Machiavelli's Prince was in our time bound to assume the form of organized minorities. His formula applied to Lenin as well as to Mussolini, who kept him in prison for eleven years, releasing him to die before he could become suspect of heresy in Moscow. Another Yugoslav, Djilas, very late in the day discovered the Soviet regime as a New Class of collective exploiters. He is, at this writing, still jailed by the Tito government.[15]

While these Eastern Marxists veered toward elitist notions, Western liberals, disturbed by the accelerating bureaucratization, followed suit. The pioneer work done by Weber was their starting point. The promptings of Pareto and the other great elitist, Gaetano Mosca, combined with the influence of Eastern deviationists to give the Western syncretism its peculiar character. For instance, the American who more than any other writer made *The Managerial Revolution* a byword, James Burnham, was indebted to the two Italians *and* to the rebellious Marxist, Rizzi, with whom he had to share the censure of his former master, Trotsky.[16]

The new formula still showed the traces of Marxian influence, but with the substitution of the concept of authority for that of class. Elitism had to be toned down somewhat, so as to adapt that formula, the suspected proto-fascist dogma, to the demo-

---

15. About Waclav Machaisky, see Max Nomad, *Aspects of Revolt* (New York, 1959), pp. 96–117; Anton Ciliga is the author of *Au pays du grand mensonge* (Paris, 1937). About Bruno Rizzi, author of *La bureaucratisation du monde* (Paris, 1939), see also Leon Trotsky, *In Defense of Marxism* (New York, 1942), p. 10. About Antonio Gramsci see the essay by Neil McInnes in *Survey*, No. 53 (October, 1964), pp. 3–15; also George Lichtheim, *op. cit.*, p. 368 and n. 1, and James H. Meisel, *The Myth of the Ruling Class* (Ann Arbor, 1958, 1962), p. 295 and n. 22 and 23. Milovan Djilas, *The New Class* (New York, 1957), pp. 37ff.

16. See Trotsky, *op. cit.*, pp. 72–94, and Burnham's reply, *ibid.*, pp. 187–211.

cratic scene. Thus Joseph Schumpeter, who tried to blend the democratic and elitist recipes, did so without once mentioning Pareto or Mosca.[17]

C. Wright Mills, rejecting both as spokesmen of the past, still showed the traces of their influence in his *Power Elite*. The preparatory notes he took from Mosca [18] prove that he still took him seriously, although perhaps not quite so seriously as did Burnham, who followed his *Managerial Revolution* for the benefit of Western readers with a presentation of four "Defenders of Freedom," two of whom were Mosca and Pareto.[19]

If their acceptance in the democratic West, as far as it went, was achieved by indirection and at the expense of authenticity, there was nothing coy or furtive about the attempt by other Westerners to extricate Marx from his Muscovite entrapment. It was no accident that the discovery of the young humanist Marx coincided with the Stalinist freeze: "Objectively," to use that hieratic Marxist term, the lively interest in the author of *The German Ideology*, *The Holy Family*, and last but not least, *The Economic-Philosophic Manuscripts*, amounted to an ideological counteroffensive against the Kremlin. There, the re-Hegelianization of Marx could only be regarded as another symptom of the recurrent, revisionist disease. That it also meant the at least partial rehabilitation of Marx in the West, could only increase orthodox uneasiness. For a rehabilitated Marx, but a Marx minus the *Manifesto*, was condemned to the fate of Unarmed Prophets: to be swallowed up by the tradition. The alacrity with which the bourgeois scholars pounced on the convenient Marxian theory of *alienation* was suspicious; so was the attempt of certain Freudians to assimilate Marx, or worse, to revert to the pre-Marxian idylls of an Owen or Fourier.[20]

17. Joseph A. Schumpeter, *Capitalism, Socialism, and Democracy* (New York, 1942, 1947), chapter XXII: "Another Theory of Democracy." But Schumpeter knew his Pareto; see his *Ten Great Economists: From Marx to Keynes* (New York, 1951), pp. 110–42.
18. Reproduced in *The Sociological Imagination* (New York, 1959), pp. 203–4.
19. *The Machiavellians: Defenders of Freedom* (New York, 1943). The two other freedom-fighters are Sorel and Michels.
20. *The nouvelle vague*, which understands Marx above all as the philosopher of alienation, did not remain uncontested. See Sidney Hook's attack (in the new, paperback edition of his *From Hegel to Marx*, Ann Arbor, 1962) on Erich Fromm's *Marx's Concept of Man* (New York, 1961) and on Robert Tucker's *Philosophy and Myth in Karl Marx* (Cambridge, 1961);

"Marx is dead—long live Karl Marx!" seemed to be the cry of C. Wright Mills, who in his Marxian primer paid grudging homage to the thinker of a "period . . . that is ending . . . ," while George Lichtheim, in a study of Marx that is anything but an obituary, remarked ironically "that a new doctrine becomes academically respectable only after it has petrified." [21]

There is certainly no evidence of *rigor mortis* in the use to which some independent Marxists put historical materialism, applying it, like Lucien Goldmann, to a period (the baroque) and subject matter (Pascal, Racine's tragedies) not usually investigated by the orthodox. And the last word has not yet been said about Jean-Paul Sartre's self-denying ordinance; the work purporting to reintegrate his existentialist philosophy into the framework of a revived Marxism. With equal right it may be claimed that Sartre is trying to bring home the great expatriate from a self-chosen exile that has lasted a whole century.[22]

Ever since Marx had contracted out of the bourgeois establishment, its intellectual champions had been looking for a counter-ideology as militant and virulent as his. It turned out to be not democracy, congenitally unfit for the purpose, but her step-son Fascism. And Pareto became "the bourgeois Karl Marx," the "Marx of Fascism," or even "an old man who aspired to be the Machiavelli of the middle classes."

These epithets do not bear serious scrutiny. "Marx" has become the synonym for an exploited class. But who in Pareto's time exploited the bourgeoisie? Or—to return to Talcott Parsons' question—was the intellectual revolution of that time indicative of important social changes fissuring the middle class establishment?

But what was meant was, of course, merely that Paretianism was the long-sought answer to the proletarian surge, along the

---

see also Richard Pipes, "Marx and Alienation," in *Encounter*, Vol. 23, No. 2 (August, 1964), p. 94, and the ensuing debate; *cf.* further Edmund Demaitre's "The New Treason of the Clerks," in *Problems of Communism*, Vol. 8, No. 5 (September-October, 1964), pp. 21–28. For the most recent contributions of Sidney Hook and Edmund Demaitre to the alienation debate, see *Problems of Communism*, Vol. 15, No. 4 (July-August, 1966), pp. 26-35.

21. C. Wright Mills, *The Marxists* (New York, 1962), p. 12. Liberalism is another creed that Mills considered to be out of date. Lichtheim, *op. cit.*, p. 394.

22. Goldmann: *Le dieu caché* (Paris, 1955); *Recherches dialectiques* (Paris 1959). Sartre: *Critique de la raison dialectique* (Paris, 1960).

lines suggested by Pareto's friend, Sorel: that proletarian violence would provoke bourgeois counter-violence, thereby restoring the old vigor of the Western world. It was the Marxist theory of class conflict, but turned around, against the proletariat, with Pareto as the Marx of counterrevolution.

There is some truth in that, provided it is understood that counterrevolution, unable to restore the past, may turn into another revolution, sometimes much more radical in scope than the original.

In that connection a fact must be noted which does not agree too well with the impression that Pareto was a bourgeois Fascist. It so happens that Pareto loathed the bourgeoisie with all the passion of a Marxist and, while rejecting socialism as utopian, showed much understanding for its causes. He agreed with Durkheim's "sharp distinction between the logical values of socialist doctrines—which he found virtually nil—and the social reality they reflected." In his study of contemporary socialisms (1902) Pareto wrote: "There is in Marx . . . a sociological part, which is superior to the other parts . . . and has all the characteristics of a scientific theory." Marx "has one very clear idea—that of class conflict; it is this idea that inspires all his practical action, and he subordinates to it all his theoretical researches." [23]

It is no exaggeration to say that Pareto was closer in spirit to Karl Marx than to the bourgeoisie considered as a *class*. Accordingly, H. Stuart Hughes, who cites Pareto's eulogy of Marx, refrains from emulating Lukacs. He does not try to confine Pareto in the narrow cage of vulgar-Marxist class analysis. True, he refers to him as "the great rationalizer of authoritarian conservatism in our time." But the student of society knows also that he is "confronted with more than a simple struggle between 'bourgeois' and 'proletarians.'" In Hughes' view, "one of the great virtues of Pareto's schema is that it cuts across the conventional left-right cleavage." [24]

Pareto, Weber, Durkheim, Freud: All four were looking into the not necessarily better future of post-Marxian man. If we insist on linking their appearance to some basic transformation of the bourgeoisie, we may get help from C. Wright Mills, who

23. Hughes, *op. cit.*, pp. 79–80, citing from Pareto's *Les systèmes socialistes*, II, pp. 338, 402.
24. Hughes, *op. cit.*, pp. 82, 81, 269.

analyzed the transient character of a specific phase of capitalist evolution: In most European countries, "established cultural workmen have often been held in high esteem. During Stage Two, they remained somewhat in tension with the commercial ethos of capitalism, and with the expanded authority of the modern state. They have been based upon pre-capitalist (often anti-capitalist) traditions and institutions, and they have themselves constituted one such basis. . . . Closely related to political authorities, at the same time they have been autonomous from them. In both these respects, of course, the European cultural agencies and cultural workmen are undergoing decisive change." [25]

The protest of that cultural elite, working within, but at the same time independently from, the Establishment, is directed against both the bourgeois state and at the visibly evolving proletarian counter-state—democratic liberalism and Marxism become twin targets. In its methodology and scientific insights the work of Weber and Pareto, starting as the counterrevolution of two insiders, leaves the intellectual achievement of their own class far behind. But they also advanced beyond Marx who threatened their world. From defenders they turned into radical aggressors, fitting neither into the bourgeois theme nor into the proletarian pattern. No wonder they have been accused of having given an assist to the hybrid movement that likewise fought that two-front battle against Mill and Marx: fascism.

The differences between Marx and the four bourgeois rebels remain real. They are also complementary. Together, these men made the only revolution that is truly permanent: the revolution of the man of genius against the dictatorship, not of the proletariat or the bourgeoisie, but of stagnation and mediocrity. It shows in the cartoons of a Daumier or a Hogarth; it is the unending catalogue of human idiocy compiled by Flaubert in his *Bouvard et Pécuchet,* and by Pareto in his *Treatise.* In this civil war, no quarter is given, fratricide is the order of the day, and every Proudhon with his *Philosophy of Poverty* will have his Marx, exposing the whole poverty of that philosophy. And if, in turn, "Pareto turned Marx on his head," [26] perhaps avenging

25. C. Wright Mills, "The Cultural Apparatus" in *Power, Politics, and People,* edited and introduced by Irving Louis Horowitz (New York, 1962), pp. 415–16.
26. Hughes, *op. cit.,* p. 81.

Hegel, whom Marx had turned "rightside-up," what is this, in the end, but another skirmish in the never-ending battle of the human mind? Polarization leads to confrontation, which in turn, without effacing boundaries, leads to a better understanding of the dialectic which, in Lenin's shorthand, is the unity of opposites.[27]

27. A Marxist would, of course, insist that, even though subjectively rejecting bourgeois attitudes, Pareto still remained objectively a bourgeois incarnate.

When Karl Marx quoted Hegel's remark that "all facts and personages of great importance in world history occur, as it were, twice," adding, "the first time as tragedy, the second as farce," he had the two unlike Napoleons in mind. Are then all successors of a great man necessarily farcical? Is there not a touch of the tragic in the attempt of the inheritor to make the heritage his own and to obliterate the memory of the forbidding ancestor? There was a hint of farce in the relationship of the two prophets, Elisha and Elijah, as presented earlier, but there was also suffering, revolt against a cruel fate, the melancholy of the second-string performance. And when the successor of Vladimir Lenin turned out to be not his partner, Leon Trotsky, but a man whom he considered to be his inferior—that was tragedy, not farce. The "genial" Stalin buried Lenin, praising him; he also buried Lenin's team, still praising Lenin. It was a tragedy that Trotsky, who, after Marx—the greatest revolutionary intellectual of all time—was perhaps the greatest intellectual revolutionary of our time, had stepped down from the historic stage, having barely finished the first act.

No, it was not a farce. But there was irony in Trotsky's failure to identify the real nature of the Stalinist regime, refusing to name it by its true name exactly as Karl Marx before him had refused to see through the trappings of Bonapartism, a power based not on a class but rather on a parasitical form of domination over all classes. There was irony in Trotsky's defense of Stalin's rule as socialist. The Marxian heritage imposed its limitations. It was the cage out of which even the titanic will of the great exile could escape only when death came to him from the usurper's hand.

8 The Dialectics of Succession

A revolutionist may win or lose, but above all he must feel he is right about the revolution, even if the revolution has gone wrong. How else could he (in his own conscience) justify all the enormities committed in the name of revolution? Dismissal, prison, exile, all these he can endure, but one thing never: to be proved wrong.

Dismissed, in prison, exiled—he still seeks proof, if only for himself, that he is right. He can neither call on God to be his witness nor simply say to himself: "*I know* for I believe," because he has no faith in faith. Experience must stand the cold scrutiny of science, which, in turn, must be tested by experience.

Happy is he who in his youth finds the right science to instruct his indignation; his indignation will again instruct his science. The early influences become all-important, for they determine, once the choice of science has been made, what the young man will make of it. He may become a quiet scholar, content to prove to his own satisfaction that he sees things right. But if he is a revolutionist by nature, his science will provide him with two keys; the first, to leave the prison of inaction, and the second to lock permanently behind him the prison door of revolutionary science. When at last the revolution is spawned, the revolutionary faces the inevitable quandary: Shall he try to subdue the monster and keep it caged, or follow it wherever it might lead?

Again, the answer to this question may be found in the beginnings. Character and role of the young revolutionist, though still amorphous, are already dialectically locked in battle; in the end each may destroy the other.

SONS AND FATHERS

And Hegel begat Marx, and Marx Plekhanov, and Plekhanov (with a slight assist from Kautsky) Lenin. But of Lenin, do we know the son? The secretary-general who claimed that name, he had disowned in his last will and testament. There were some minor heirs: Bukharin, of whom he was fond in his remote, abstracted way; the old companions, Kamenev, Zinoviev, all destroyed by the new Sultan, the very man his last will had warned against.

He had no children of his own. There was Krupskaya, his wife, companion, and secretary. There were other women serving him. One won his love; he loved her shyly. She would play the piano for him; Beethoven's *Appassionata* was his favorite sonata, but, he said, it was too powerful for him; he was afraid of sentiment. And his work, to keep the friends in line, to split the enemies, left little time for Inessa. When she died, he for once lost control over himself. Krupskaya wrote the short obituary; she knew.[1]

He had no children of his own because he did not need them. Lenin had the Party. Thinking of himself not as a person but as thought, one single thought in action, his creation too could only be something impersonal, or superpersonal: the human phalanx of the new elect, the happy few, conspiring, agitating for the great day. The concept of the conspiratorial elite was nothing new: Blanqui in France, Nechaev in Dostoevskii's *The Possessed* had practiced the idea before Lenin. But he gave it a new turn:

1. See Bertram Wolfe, "Lenin and Inessa Armand," *Encounter*, Vol. 22, No. 2 (February, 1964), pp. 83–91.

his Party was not to achieve the revolution *for* the masses; it became the Party *of* the masses by a process of pure cerebration. Lenin decreed that its role would be to bring class consciousness to the still dormant proletariat "from without": by a band of classless intellectuals who would imbue the workers with a sense of their historic mission. Politics was, to be sure, mere "concentrated economics" in the orthodox tradition of Karl Marx, but Lenin, when he forged his organizational weapon, put the stress back on the other, half-forgotten Marx who called for *political* action.

It has been said that Lenin falsified Marx's testament by tearing off the teacher's democratic codicil. But Marxism was not a doctrine but a method, and the method must yield practical results, or else it remains abstract theory. It also must take stock of the historic circumstances. Lenin did just that. Plekhanov had convinced him of the capitalist character of the Russian economy; the only thing left was to do away with the retarding Czarist superstructure. So the coming revolution was to be bourgeois in character. But since the bourgeoisie would be too weak to "consummate its own revolution," Lenin was prepared to do it *for* the bourgeoisie and to administer capitalism until it would be ripe for his own, socialist revolution. Power would rest with a "dictatorship of workers and peasants." That was in 1905.

It was a daring substitution, still remaining faithful to Marx's *word* but stretching its meaning to the limit. It probably did not occur to Lenin at the time that the same substitution might one day be necessary to maintain himself in power: that his Party would have to administer the Soviet system *for* the proletariat.

The thought might have led Lenin to give up his enterprise, but then he would not have been Lenin. To ask whether or not Lenin lapsed into Marxian heresy at some point seems rather pointless, when one considers that Lenin had turned himself into a beautifully functioning machine, controlled by three sets of directives, each interrelated with the others, and each representing its own set of tensions:

Lenin was the Party, the Party was the Revolution, and the Revolution was still in the future.

The utopian leaps into the future, and the pragmatist copes with the present. By Lenin's definition, the Party, working on the present for the future, represents the *subjective* element (of proletarian consciousness), and its task is to absorb the harsh realities of Russia's economic backwardness ("an objective condition")[2] into a coherent "scientific" action program.

Any revolutionary party, that is, an organization whose whole *raison d'être* commits it to the twin tasks of destruction and reconstruction, must know how to recognize the boundary between the possible and the impossible. But that same party also must be ready to experiment, in order to find out whether what seems impossible is possible. It must be willing to treat a whole country as the laboratory of a revolution that may or may not succeed; it must subject the living organism of society to the bold probings of exploratory surgery. The social engineer cannot afford the tender sentiments induced by Beethoven's *Appassionata*.

The historic role assumed by Lenin's Party was well suited to the character he had given it. Being an extension of his own strong personality, the Bolshevik *persona* could be both utopian and pragmatic, flexible and stiff-necked, just as Lenin would hold out for realism in assessing the class character of the impending revolution (bourgeois) between 1905 and 1915, then convince himself that it had already entered the stage of monopoly imperialism and was therefore ripe for socialism. Two years later, a few months before assuming power, Lenin tried to visualize the new society, and for once the utopian vision took possession of his usually cautious mind: the state was to be managed by the many and there was to be no bureaucracy; the Party was hardly mentioned.[3] The awakening to the hard facts of social and political reality was cruel.

Even his own Party did not fail to disillusion him: Before October two of the old guard refused to follow him to the assault on Kerensky's bourgeois republic. Three years later he had to impose draconian discipline on the whole party, which threatened to fall apart over such matters as the role of labor unions in a proletarian state and the demand for more democracy within the party. What has been ascribed to Stalin was already Lenin's doing. Threatened on all sides, the narrow basis of control made it imperative that party unity take precedence over all other considerations, however important they might be.

2. Lenin, "Two Tactics of Social-Democracy in the Democratic Revolution," *Selected Works*, Vol. I (London, 1947), p. 352.
3. In *The State and Revolution*, 1917.

All revolutionary leaders have to work with doubtful, often shoddy, human material. Lenin's case was no exception. What was so unique about him was the perfect unity of character and role that made his party leadership appear less dictatorial than in fact it was. This bookish, unassuming man could at the same time be considerate and harsh, magnanimous (as toward his old friend and adversary, Julius Martov, leader of the disgraced Mensheviks) and unforgiving when the purity of Marxist doctrine was at stake. He would permit himself to be outvoted on occasion, confident that his view would be vindicated in the end. He had to drag the comrades into the October *coup;* he had to drag them into the abject surrender to victorious Germany at Brest-Litovsk, but he predicted also that the Germans would not last another year. He had to force the Party into the retreat of the New Economic Policy in 1921, which gave the capitalists, and the country, the short breathing spell that he himself was not to survive. He could afford to make and to acknowledge tactical mistakes because he was able to correct them; there was very little vanity in him. But one thing he could not give up: his power-grasp on the envisioned future. To the present he would often close his eyes. Human suffering had to be discounted if his work was to go on. And when "this honest functionary of disorder" [4] finally succumbed under the superhuman, inhuman burden, he was spared to see the outcome of his enterprise. The last years of the invalid were overshadowed by misgivings ("Ours is a workers' state with bureaucratic deformations" which he tried to cure by setting up another bureaucratic organ, the Workers' and Peasants' Inspection); he was worried by quarrels among his lieutenants. Like most self-made rulers, Lenin, who controlled so much, could not appoint his own successor. He had to look on while the two leading men contended for his mantle, one with cunning and political ability, and the other, greater man, who had created the new state in close companionship with Lenin, without him could not prevail against his enemy and soon was lost.

---

4. Curzio Malaparte, *Le bonhomme Lénine* (Paris, 1932), p. 385.

A FAILURE OF NERVE?

That a Trotsky was defeated by a Stalin is not in itself so difficult to comprehend, for history knows many examples of a genius bested by a lesser man: Napoleon was in the end outwitted by Fouché and Talleyrand, and the Germanic saga has its Siegfried felled by the invidious Hagen. Trotsky's fall from power is so puzzling not because he lost but because he lost without putting up a fight while he still had a chance of winning. Trotsky's own explanation, that he had to lose because the revolution had run out of steam, is hardly more than a face-saving rationalization for the benefit of his bewildered followers. Trotsky himself was too intelligent to believe it. It has been said that he did not attempt to contest the succession because, as the outsider, he was distrusted by the Party, by then already controlled by Stalin. Trotsky, according to this view, did not fight because he knew he had no chance of winning. But that explanation is as unconvincing as that offered by Trotsky himself. His whole life, before and after Lenin's death, is proof that he would carry on a fight, if so disposed, against all odds.

The answer to the riddle is most likely to be something so self-evident, that even Trotsky himself remained unaware of it. His lack of fighting spirit at the most decisive moment of his whole career may be to some extent explained by Trotsky's background. Son of that then rarest of all creatures, a Jewish farmer, the boy grew up without any of the stigmata inflicted by the ghetto. His spirit of revolt showed early, but it was a protest against not racial but social injustice. The luciferic pride of the young man was not the overcompensation of inherited resentment but the overweening confidence of a first-generation intellectual, who, however, never lost his contact with the soil and its antean consolations. To the last he loved to hike and hunt; he happened to be hunting in the south of Russia when in Moscow Lenin's funeral was stage-managed by Stalin.

It was this pride which seemed to make it so unnecessary for him to compete for power. The idea that anyone might question his claim to be, second only to Vladimir Lenin, the greatest revolutionary seemed absurd. And it is not impossible that a contributing factor was the atrophy of the competitive instinct so strong among the Jewry confined in the ghetto, under conditions impossible even to imagine by those growing up outside. Trotsky very likely despised bidding for support; his inability to play the game of politics, to compromise and flatter, is on record; so is his haughtiness. His genius for antagonizing the sensitivities of minor people was as great as his ability to generate abiding loyalties of people ready to be killed for his sake. But they were few in number, and the many who admired him never quite breached the enormous distance he put between them and himself. He was born to be a loner; he had needed Lenin's backing for all major undertakings, and he had received what he himself would never ask for because he took Lenin's help for granted. When it was no longer to be had, when Lenin was no longer there to hold his shield over the conqueror of Petrograd and the great organizer of the new, Red Army in the civil war, Trotsky was defenseless to his many enemies. They dealt him blows he could not parry. They remembered Trotsky's past as Lenin's enemy and all the acerbities that had long separated the two men before the revolution. Lenin never mentioned that past but they did. And Trotsky, autocrat in his own right, was faced with an impossibly hard choice. He could proclaim himself the authentic Marxist heir of Lenin's power and maintain that claim against the ruling Party as the prophet crying in the wilderness. Or he could humble himself, in order to retain his foothold in the Party, by acknowledging the superiority of Lenin as the only true *disciple* of Karl Marx. The latter choice would have been tantamount to denial of his own, proud record, which established him—or should have established him—as the man who had been ahead of Lenin in predicting the eventual course of the Russian revolution. But Trotsky tried hard, and almost managed to convince himself and others that he, who was Lenin's equal, was in fact his intellectual son. As long as Lenin lived, the thought did not occur to Trotsky; only the dead Lenin could become his freely chosen and adopted father.

All of Trotsky's later writings show him busily engaged in reinterpreting the past. He never stooped to hagiography: The fragment in which he attempted to recall the young Lenin is a study in studied "frankness": The warts are all painted in. It remains a picture of belated love mixed with regret: I should have loved him earlier, and I should have recognized his greatness from the start. For recognizing Lenin's stature was a way of also elevating to the same height the companion of his later years. The Trotsky pride was mirroring itself in Lenin's fame: The man in exile wanted to convey that he was great enough to recognize the other's superiority as a rich man might give freely because he need not be afraid of being thereby diminished. Sometimes a pleading note intrudes. "Remember what your Lenin said of me, 'Trotsky long ago said that unification [with other socialist parties] is impossible. Trotsky understood this and from that time on there has been no better Bolshevik.'"[5] He glossed over the fact that Lenin, though admiring Trotsky, never truly "took" to him. The sober teacher and the fiery tribune of the people remained worlds apart.[6]

A CONFINING HERITAGE

The ideological convergence between prodigal son and adopted father was a fact of history, but by exaggerating it, by trying to erase all vestiges of past as well as of potential future quarrels, Trotsky found himself entrapped in a condition all the more confining for being of his own making: The new Leninist became the captive rather than the master of a doctrine to be questioned only at the risk of falling into heresy. It was a trap from which he never managed to escape. He had to fight his enemies within the party with his hands tied. Even when his second exile should have enabled him to speak his mind freely, he persisted in defending a regime that he should have condemned, and in attacking those he should have joined in criticizing not merely the "bureaucratic deformations" of the new regime but its essential nature. Yet like his great predecessor, Marx, who shied away from drawing the conclusions from his own analysis of Bonaparte's regime, Trotsky stubbornly refused to recognize the truth of the new Soviet state. Worse still, he never could unmask the false Dimitri who had stolen his inheritance. Insisting to the bitter end that Stalinism was a mere distortion of what still remained authentic socialism, Trotsky failed to recognize the true proportions and the sociological significance of his opponent. When he wrote

5. Trotsky, *The Stalin School of Falsification* (New York, 1937), p. 105.
6. For a good confrontation of the two types, see Isaac Deutscher, *The Prophet Armed: Trotsky 1879-1921* (London and New York, 1954), pp. 341-43.

what was intended to become the literary execution of the man but remained only a fragment when Stalin's long-armed executioner reached him instead, he was forced to make of Stalin the mediocre front man of the new bureaucracy, a puppet mysteriously become puppet master.[7]

This was not mere invidiousness: It was the underestimation of a major historic personality. But this underestimation was itself the logical result of Trotsky's half-hearted analysis of the new system. Did it represent the "Thermidor" of Lenin's revolution? In 1930, he predicted that the further growth of Soviet bureaucracy "must inevitably lead to a crisis of the proletarian dictatorship which will be resolved either by a re-emergence of the revolution on a higher level, or by the restoration of bourgeois society." [8] He toyed with the idea that the new bureaucracy, though not a class in the Marxist sense, for it played no direct role in production, might transform itself into a genuine ruling class by finally restoring private property. By 1937, however, Trotsky had to recognize that public ownership of the means of production had come to stay, and he scaled down his earlier prediction to the mere statement that "the transformation of the bureaucratic class [*sic*] into one of property owners is an historic possibility, not an accomplished fact." [9]

The basis of the Soviet system remained socialist; nothing the two early theorists of the *New Class* (Machaisky, Bruno Rizzi; see above p. 112) could say would shake this conviction. In 1937, he proclaimed the economic basis of the Soviet Union to be sound; only the parasitic superstructure needed changing:

> The revolution which the bureaucracy is preparing against itself will not be social, like the October revolution of 1917. It is not a question this time of changing the economic foundations of society, of replacing certain forms of property with other forms. History has known elsewhere not only social revolutions which substituted the bourgeois for the feudal regime, but also political revolutions which, without destroying the economic foundations of society, swept out an old ruling upper crust (1830 and 1848 in France; February 1917 in Russia). The overthrow of the *Bonapartist caste* will, of course, have deep social consequences, but in itself it will be confined within the limits of political revolution.[10]

7. *Stalin*, 2nd ed. (New York, 1946).
8. *Toward Capitalism or Toward Socialism?*
9. *Once More: The USSR and its Defense.*
10. *The Revolution Betrayed*, p. 288.

It is the *Bonapartist caste* now: once more not a class. But just as Marx had found it difficult to discover the real ruling class behind the bureaucratic power, so now Trotsky had to keep up the pretense that Russia was still governed on behalf of, if not by, the proletariat. To restore true socialism, nothing more was needed than the introduction of political *democracy*.

The Phrygian cap of liberty sits oddly on the head of the great autocrat who had once mercilessly crushed the Kronstadt rebels when *they* called for democratic soviets. It was only after Trotsky fell from power that he rediscovered freedom to be indispensable to socialism. This is not to question the sincerity of his conversion, but if Trotsky had succeeded Lenin, he might have found that democratic rule was out of character: out of his character and, in addition, not well possible. But once he had embraced the notion of democracy, he carried it to the extreme of asking for the overthrow of the regime while the country was already at war with Hitler. He took recourse in the precedent of Clemenceau, who overthrow the French war government while Paris was being shelled by German guns.

A year before the Nazi armies moved into the Soviet Union, Trotsky had consolidated his own front. The Marxist critic recognized the "enormous progressive significance" of state-controlled production. But, he added, "the ruling caste has been transformed into the greatest brake upon the development of the productive forces," and continued:

> Socialist economy must by its very essence take as its guide the interests of the producers and the needs of the consumers. These interests and needs can find their expression only through the medium of a full-flowering democracy of producers and consumers.

The Stalinist bureaucracy must go precisely because it "cannot assure the necessary proportions between all branches of the economy, that is, the necessary correspondence between producers and consumers." One man's lust for power is an insufficient explanation of the Soviet state's malfunctioning. Here Trotsky seems already to reject, ahead of time, the Khrushchevite apology for all the errors of the past as a mere lapse into the "cult of personality." Not so, says Trotsky: "Stalin is not an individual, but a caste symbol. . . . The reactionary bureaucracy has to be overthrown and it will be overthrown. The political revolution in the USSR is inevitable." [11]

He greeted the war almost on a note of jubilation: "The Second World War has begun. It attests incontrovertibly to the fact that society can no longer live on the basis of capitalism." The Old Man reverted to the bold hopes of his beginnings: "If this war provokes, as we firmly believe, a proletarian [world] revolution, it must inevitably lead to the overthrow of the bureaucracy in the USSR and the regeneration of Soviet democracy on a far higher economic and cultural basis than in 1918." He added, addressing once more the heretic theorists of "bureaucratic collectivism," representing a third type of exploitation that is neither socialist nor capitalist: When my revolution comes, "the question as to whether the Stalinist bureaucracy was a 'class' or a parasitic growth on the workers' state will be automatically solved."

Then a doubt arises in Trotsky's mind and it will not be dispelled: What if the present war should not result in world-wide revolution but in "a decline of the proletariat"? And he answers his own question: The alternative would be "the further decay of monopoly capitalism, its further fusion with the state, and the replacement of democracy wherever it still remained by a totalitarian regime." Worse still, "then we would be compelled to acknowledge that the reason for the bureaucratic relapse is rooted not in the backwardness of [Russia] and not in the imperialist environment but in the congenital incapacity of the proletariat to become a ruling class."

A terrible alternative, and even to consider it must have been utterly repugnant to him. This was indeed thinking the unthinkable: If Stalin should eventually be proved right, then Trotsky must be wrong. But that was not all. If the war should not end with a world-wide revolution, what would be the inescapable conclusion? The mere glimpse of it must horrify the faithful Marxist, but Trotsky had never lacked courage. So he set the answer down:

"Then . . . nothing else would remain except only to recognize that the socialist program, based on the internal contradictions of

11. *Bulletin Oppositsii, issue 66–67.*

capitalist society, ended as Utopia. It is self-evident that a new 'minimum' program would be required—for the defense of the interests of the slaves of the totalitarian bureaucratic society." [12]

No mention of Lenin; Trotsky is alone with Marx. If even Marx's authority were shattered, if the mightiest of Lucifer's whole progeny should stand revealed as a utopian, then indeed all sufferings had been in vain, from the first Siberian exile to the final wanderings from Prinkipo to Norway to Coyoacan, Mexico. He had accepted the hard life, but now it seemed that even the decision that had cost him most, the surrender of his intellectual ego to Lenin, had been a mistake. Did Leon Trotsky now regret the years spent in the shadow of a grave? Did it occur to him that Lenin, whom he, after all, had brought to power, might himself have sown the evil seed—that Lenin's true heir was Stalin and not Trotsky? [13] Could it be that 1917, the Year of Wonder, had been a mere mirage, and that one could do no more than scrounge for a minimum, a pittance doled out to that disappointing class, the proletariat, by the "new exploiting regime" arising "on an international scale"? [14]

He probably forgot these nightmare thoughts a few days later and continued to harass the distant tyrant who still feared him. And with reason. The Old Man's new International was nothing, but his intellectual influence remained a menace. So the Kremlin sent someone to beat his brains out.

Leon Trotsky was that rare example of a revolutionary leader

12. "The USSR in War," written September 25, 1939, and first published in *The New International*, November 1939. The quotations in the text are taken from the reprint of the essay in the posthumous collection of Trotsky's last publications, *In Defense of Marxism* (New York, 1942), pp. 8–9.

13. This chapter was already written when the present author found, in a review of *The Bolsheviks* by Adam B. Ulam (New York, 1965), that "Stalin did not, Ulam thinks, pervert Leninism but in most respects fulfilled it. . . . Trotsky overstated the intimacy between himself and Lenin and—perhaps unknowingly—exaggerated Lenin's respect for him." *The New Yorker*, November 20, 1965, p. 244.

14. Trotsky, *op. cit.*, p. 9. Still in the future was another variant: Castro's charismatic communism which "establishes a direct, personal, almost mystical relationship with the masses that frees him from dependence on classes. It also frees him from what Lenin thought was indispensable for a communist revolution—a party." Theodore Draper, *Castroism: Theory and Practice* (New York, 1965), p. 133. See also Ernest Halperin's brilliant analysis of "Castro's Revolution" in *The New York Review of Books*, Vol. 5, No. 4 (September 30, 1965), pp. 11–12. The Leninist Trotsky would have found the Cuban version unacceptable; the charismatic leader, Trotsky, might have been attracted.

whose career reversed the usual sequence from rejected prophet to accepted leader. But his ruin, as spectacular as his success, did not lack greatness when he finally had to confess: We may be wrong. Few prophets equaled Trotsky's tortured honesty. He may have lived and died in vain.[15] *Sed victa Catoni:* The honors in this case go to the vanquished man.

15. "After his exile, Trotsky became a revolutionary without a revolutionary context, a bureaucrat without a bureaucracy, a politician without a party. He had the will, the motive, but neither the means nor the opportunity—the two are always relative—to make a revolution." C. Wright Mills, *The Marxists* (New York, 1962), p. 149. Trotsky's biographer, Isaac Deutscher, disagrees. He is convinced that Trotsky's vindication is bound to come before too long. See "Postscript: Victory in Defeat," *The Prophet Outcast: Trotsky* 1929-1940 (London, 1963), pp. 510ff.

This is the first of two chapters dealing with *intercession:* preventive counterrevolution. It succeeded in Italy where Mussolini exploited an exaggerated popular belief in an imminent communist take-over. Intercession likewise was a full success in Germany where Hitler appealed to the same fears. Usually a counterrevolution is the answer to a revolution already successful. Fascism seems to reverse the sequence, unless one accepts the fascist claim that their intervention arrested a revolution already in progress. The contrary view seems more convincing: that the fascists exploited all the discontent ripe for a revolution that had never taken place, although a revolutionary situation had existed in both Italy and Germany. The fascists drew their strength from an abortive revolution: Their own revolution was the stunted form in which the body politic at last expressed its revolutionary urge.

It is in this context that the less well-known attempt at intercepting Hitler's drive for power must be viewed. It was made by a group of intellectuals working with the German army, trying to anticipate a Hitler take-over by a coup d'état from above, to be sanctioned by the President, von Hindenburg. The intercession failed for reasons that will become clear in a report drawing on evidence of which this writer had personal knowledge.

9 The Fascist Syndrome[1]

Was fascism in Italy and Germany a revolution or a counter-revolution? Again, the answer to this largely academic question is that it was both. A brief look at the origins of the two similar but distinct movements will be helpful in discovering the reason.

MUSSOLINI

Mussolini started as a left-wing socialist, impatient with what he regarded as the treacherous, "revisionist" timidity of the old party leaders. Syndicalist influence, then prevalent among the Left, informed his direct-action tactics. He encouraged violence

1. "Fascism is . . . nationalism, expressed in emphasis on the primary importance and necessary unity of the cultural in-group, and in a tendency toward economic autarky; state intervention in socio-economic life, which can now be explained more plausibly as popular action to prevent the alleged dangers of free-market capitalism than as a tyranny designed to preserve monopoly-capitalism and to suppress the masses; the proposal of an alternative totalitarian ideology to Marxism-Leninism, allowing for imitation of communist organization and propaganda methods; focus on a

and strikes against the government's colonial war (in Africa, with Turkey over Tripoli). That was in 1912.

Three years later, Mussolini changed his line and came out for Italian intervention in the first World War. It was his final break with the old party, which overwhelmingly preferred neutrality. The internationalist had discovered the Italian nation; Mussolini himself went to war, fought bravely, was wounded, decorated, and discharged. He now converted the external war into a civil war fought on two fronts: against the liberal establishment and the old comrades of the Left. He spoke a language that the nation had not heard before: a syndicalist-patriotic blend.[2]

In the meantime, Italy had technically won her war but was in fact among the losers, in the company of Germany and Russia. Her economy was dislocated, unemployment high, the living standard of the lower middle class depressed. This had two consequences: on the one hand, a sharp radicalization of the proletarian movement, now much heartened by the success of the Russian revolution. On the other hand, the frightened little people, caught between the millstones of Big Capital and Big Labor, became ready for a counterrevolution in two directions: against a status quo that could no longer guarantee their status, and against what they saw as a threatening Red take-over. They found their man. They joined his combat squads, which grew from a core of displaced veterans led by ex-officers to a large movement. First based on the lower middle class of small-town lawyers and other minor notables and their despondent following, it finally became a cross-section of all classes, representative of all and of none. The last to join was the Italian proletariat. When the historic

---

single personality as leader." David Ashton, letter in The [London] Times Literary Supplement (February 24, 1966), p. 143.

"We propose to bypass all semantic traps by calling Fascist all of the not clearly communist or socialist regimes which have adopted anti-democratic, dictatorial systems, usually based on a single, privileged mass party, and informed by a mystique glorifying strength, violence, belief in a national or racial community, personified in an inspired leader figure. Negatively, that mystique will reject Reason, Individualism, and Equality. The system also cultivates an 'anti-capitalist' bias, although it is not averse to making use of the existing capitalist establishment, exploiting rather than abolishing it." James H. Meisel, The Fall of the Republic (Ann Arbor, 1962), p. 4. See also chapter 1, n. 7.

2. The mixture was not his invention: a few years before the war, some syndicalist friends of Georges Sorel had tried to combine with the extreme French Right against the Republic, but the merger did not succeed. The situation in France was not favorable to the intellectual construct. In Italy Mussolini made it work.

chance—signaled by the occupation of some factories—had been missed by the reluctant socialist elite, it was Benito Mussolini's turn to pursue the withdrawing Left, while still maintaining his old, revolutionary stance against the liberal regime and still vowing to abolish Crown and Church. The question whether Mussolini was sincere in uttering these revolutionary threats is immaterial. What matters is that the regime was not prepared to take him seriously. It regarded him as merely another ambitious party leader, biding his time to accept, eventually, some share of power in another typical combination in the game of politics so masterfully played by generations of Italian Machiavellis.

They were right, and also wrong. The Duce entered the establishment, but only to defeat and overthrow it from within. Unlike Lenin, Mussolini did not "smash" the state. He did not have to. All he needed was to master the old structure and to use it for his own designs. He had to pay a price, and in the end this proved his undoing. By tolerating Crown and Church within his own party state, he left Trojan horses for the day of his defeat by an external force, in still another war that saw his country finish on the losing side.

He had more than twenty years to make his face known to the world. His histrionic posturings could never, even at the height of his success, deceive that world about the basic ambiguity of the regime. It was a halfway house with an imperial grand façade behind which hid a semi-slum shored up by welfare-state props, its economy, under corporate trappings, ruled by the bureaucracy. Presiding over it, the Bonapartist ruler had deprived the bourgeoisie of its political control. To that extent the fascist movement had achieved a partial, revolutionary victory. But the bourgeoisie could well afford the loss, as long as it retained its economic privilege, as did the bourgeoisie that had submitted to the third Napoleon as the minor evil, in the face of the imagined proletarian threat.

The fascist movement had derived its great initial impetus from the, imagined, strength of the Red enemy, and its second wind precisely from his weakness. By inserting himself between the beginning surge and the ebb of the Italian revolution, Mussolini managed to enact two roles: first that of the counterrevolutionary, then of the revolutionary against the discredited bourgeois regime. He could pose as the savior of the bourgeoisie who had arrested bolshevism in Italy, inasmuch as bolshevism had already shot its bolt by the time he made his claim. He could occupy the empty battlefield, remaining the most revolutionary leader on the scene.

After his successfully completed intercession, the remaining revolutionary militants—now dressed in black shirts—kept reminding Mussolini of past promises. He did not hesitate to remove that threat to his control. Already in the early stages of the March on Rome he had disciplined his radicals. There was no need to call upon the army—he was his own Monk, and he based his rule on patronage to keep the satraps of the realm in line. There was some grumbling among those who had been dreaming of the perfect republic that D'Annunzio had, for one brief moment, conjured up in Fiume. Fascism, born out of war, had been domesticated, but its origins could never be denied: The instability of the regime compelled the Duce to return to war, first in Ethiopia, then in Spain, then in Albania, to collect cheap victories, until a bigger Mussolini forced his teacher into the ultimate adventure which ended in catastrophe for teacher and disciple alike.

HITLER

The dialectics of succession moves in subtle ways: The father is revered and emulated; the son tries to be a greater father. He may try to blot out the paternal memory, but not the heritage; that is, unless the son denies his very origin, insisting that the father has no real claim on him. Then he will spend a lifetime trying to erase the image and memory of the false father. Such a son was Adolf Hitler. He denied the father who gave him his name. The fact that Hitler also knew the other name—that of the Jew who was his spiritual progenitor—is attested by the very force of his denial and by his unceasing struggle against Karl Marx and his Russian legacy.

Mussolini was the Marxist apostate who, like all renegades, was harder on his former comrades than all anti-Marxists put together. When, defeated, he tried to revert to his republican and social-revolutionary origins, it proved to be too late: He was no longer creditable.[3]

3. His credibility can be discounted even in the quite unlikely eventuality that his Republic of Salò could have survived German tutelage and Hitler's downfall.

Hitler, on the other hand, was the authentic anti-Marxist lumpen-proletarian to whom Marxism meant everything that had gone wrong with a civilization in which he was bound to be a misfit. It is customary to attribute his ideas to the cumulative influence of thinkers such as Julius Langbehn, Houston Stewart Chamberlain, Paul de Lagarde, and Adolf Stoecker, not to forget Friedrich Nietzsche, about whom he probably heard through his mentor, Dietrich Eckhard.[4] But these men provided Hitler with no more than the mere frostings for a home-baked cake. The tawdriness of the official Nazi *Weltanschauung* is deceptive: It obscures the real source of strength that fed the movement to its dying days. In Italy, the fascist creed was never more than skin-deep, but in Germany the desperation over the lost war and the loss of identity had gone much deeper. It had rendered Germans far more vulnerable and more anxious to be cured of their disease at any price. The healer's popularity owed little to the promised cure; it was an indication of the patient's critical condition.

Hitler did not have to diagnose the illness. The slow accumulation of civilization's discontents, of all the helpless raging against forces unknown, had become personified in him and he in turn was able to personify the enemy. His double trauma, Marx and the Jews, merged into one. He led the counterattack of resentment. From re-acting he went on to re-enact the Marxist revolution with a twist: By substituting biological for economic materialism, race for class, he managed to turn "Marx" against the Jews: Anti-capitalism became narrowed down to antisemitism.

It was not the only point of difference between the Fuehrer and the Duce. Mussolini started as a political, civilian militant and ended as a self-appointed honorary corporal in charge of an Italian war society, while Hitler was a corporal turned politician. But the difference did not amount to much. Both men, in uniform or not, performed the role of Bonapartist tribunes of the people, and like Napoleon III they based their power on the masses whose "consent" was obtained, from time to time, by "democratic" plebiscites and kept in line by para-military party armies. Propaganda had been helpful, but it was intimidation rather than persuasion that kept the domestic peace. No revolutionary situation, even if it did objectively exist, could possibly come to a

4. See George L. Mosse, *The Crisis of German Ideology* (New York, 1964), especially chapters 2 and 17.

head as long as both the Gestapo and the OVRA did their work.

They could perform it so efficiently because both fascist movements had come to power not at the beginning but at the end of the authentic revolutionary situation. In Italy its high point had been passed in 1920, two years before Mussolini assumed the premiership. Germany too had her moment when she seemed ripe for a repetition of the Leninist October. German versions of Soldiers' and Workers' Soviets sprang up in all major German cities late in 1918, and soon thereafter the first native communist organization, taking its name from the proto-revolutionary, Spartacus, made a strong bid for power. The new, right-wing, socialist regime took fright and called for help. It was obliged by the former imperial army, or what was left of it. Berlin was made secure from the wild men of the Spartacus League. Their leaders, Rosa Luxemburg, the Polish Marxist, and Karl Liebknecht, the Reichstag deputy, were arrested by young army officers. One of them, later a friend of the present writer, stood by when the two captives were transported from their temporary place of detention, the Hotel Eden, to police headquarters. A private, standing guard outside, could not contain himself when the two were led out. Before anyone could prevent it, he brought the butt of his gun down on the two skulls. The witnessing lieutenant, Friedrich Wilhelm von Oertzen, never forgot the sound: It reminded him of walnuts cracking.[5] The unconscious prisoners were picked up by the officers and packed into a waiting car, which they drove through the Tiergarten, deliberating what to do. Finally, one of them shot and killed the already dying victims. There was a trial later, but the case was easily dismissed.

The unholy alliance between socialists and Reichswehr killed the German revolution in its infancy. The Spartacus revolt was premature. The socialist regime in turn was dilatory. So between too little and too much the proper revolutionary dose was never given to an awaiting body politic.

The arrested revolution begot Hitler.[6] His dictatorship was the delayed and warped version of the renaissance that did not come. National Socialism nationalized socialism's squandered energies.

5. Oral communication to the present writer. See also J. P. Nettl, *Rosa Luxemburg* (Oxford University Press, London, New York, 1966). Vol. II, pp. 774 f.

6. What follows is an enlarged variant of a study entitled "The First Conspiracy against Hitler," *Queen's Quarterly*, Vol. 56, No. 3, 1949, pp. 331–46. Reproduced by permission.

It did not socialize big business. Instead it let rearmament expro-
priate the same small enterprises the Party program had once
promised to protect. Grown strong by its conservative appeal to
independence and tradition, the Third Reich accelerated the
advent of mass society and technocratic rationalization. It was the
peculiar manner in which Germany resolved her hesitation between a capitalist past that was far from dead and a socialist
future that still had to prove its case in Soviet Russia. The result
of that historic German doubt was a mongrel system that was
neither a choice nor a compromise between capitalism and socialism but a protest against both. This fact explains, in part, the
extreme vigor of this double-faced rejection, which it took the
conjoined efforts of Western capitalism and Eastern socialism to
defeat.

THE CONSPIRACY OF
THE INTELLECTUALS

Hitler was responsible for many crimes against his country and
mankind, but of one crime he was quite innocent. Tradition has
it that Germany's short-lived republic was destroyed by him. But
when he came to power—in perfectly legal fashion—that republic had already been stripped of the essential requisites we associate with democracy. That scavenger job was performed by a
small Bonapartist clique who took advantage of the deadlock of
the social forces caused by the depression to establish the "authoritarian" regime of the Field Marshal-President, von Hindenburg.
They had his ear, and through him they controlled the Reichswehr. It represented not only the ultimate resort of the regime:
It was the only force that stood between legality and revolution.
But which revolution? Hitler's or that of the Communists (who
were growing stronger as unemployment increased)?

Well-informed people knew that the real danger came from
Hitler. Among the knowing were the journalists. A group of
them may serve here as a good example of the disarray in which
the German people found themselves. The famous publishing
house that mass-produced a fare diversified enough to suit all
tastes, from tabloidiocy to the last word in literary fashion cir-
cles, was a microcosm of all the contending ideologies, and the
Vossische Zeitung, a mildly progressive daily, which was as re-

spected as it was unprofitable, particularly reflected the confusion. Some of the younger editors were Marxists, even Communists, and after Hitler came to power they were joined by *alte Kaempfer*, Nazi veterans delighted that their time of unemployment was over. Their hiring contract, an insurance policy the employer took out against rainy days, did not prevent his ultimate expropriation.

Few of these men believed in the Republic. One group in particular excelled in this rejection, which included, with fine impartiality, the Marxist and the Nazi substitute. They were conservatives, but at the same time revolutionaries.[7] One of them had, under an assumed name, published a book signaling the end of nineteenth-century society, a kind of economic counterpart of Spengler's *Decline of the West*.

Their lack of faith in democratic government was matched only by their ironic disbelief in the reactionary holding operations of the day. Their dislike of the Fuehrer, although genuine, was an aesthetic rather than an ethical reaction. For they, like Hitler, were for strong, if necessary even extreme, means; they objected not so much to Hitler's program as to his vulgarity—not to the content but the style. In the opinion of the senior colleagues on their editorial board, these rebels were a badly confused, rather irritating lot needing to be watched but not to be taken seriously.

Their confusion did not paralyze their action, however, and they had a gifted leader. Hans Zehrer, who survived Hitler and became a leading German newspaperman, was tall, good-looking with a saturnine grin, secretive and soft-spoken, creating the impression of a Talleyrand's *finesse*. Like so many other diplomats, he was also known to write verse, and outside his close circle nobody would have suspected the intense ambition behind the appearance of a ladies' man. He liked to while away his nights pretending to be a gay blade, but he was mostly engaged in Socratic probings into the charades of power and how to unriddle them.

It was the heyday of astrologers and soothsayers in Germany; Hitler was their best-known devotee. One of these prophets found out that the name of the man who would vanquish Hitler,

7. See Klemens von Klemperer, *Germany's New Conservatism* (Princeton, 1957), and Armin Mohler, *Die konservative Revolution in Deutschland 1918–1932* (Stuttgart, 1950).

began with the initial Z. (Alas, it was Zhukov, the Soviet Marshal who was to "liberate" Berlin thirteen years later.) The prediction did not, even then in 1932, quite fit the case of Zehrer. Where was his army to combat the storm troopers? He did not even have a sounding board for his opinions. He was only a proficient editorial writer, wisely limiting himself to international relations, a safe subject.

His first chance came when a distinguished publisher invited him to resurrect *Die Tat*, a failing literary monthly. After protracted soul searching, Zehrer accepted, and before too long the ancient *Zeitschrift* had become a radical organ that created a stir among the young intelligentsia. Its murky terminology appealed to the idealism of people who had lost their humanistic moorings and had turned to the new Hitler cult.

Here they were offered by Zehrer and his staff a fascism in gloves, developed along anti-Marxist lines but in a pseudo-Marxist idiom that appeased suspicious radicals. As for the Hitler movement, it was neither praised nor criticized, but treated with a sociological detachment proper to its bulk and ominous ubiquity.

Soon afterwards (in 1932) Zehrer became editor-in-chief of *Die Tägliche Rundschau*, a small daily paper (not belonging to his old employers). He built up its circulation with a great expense of energy although he could not overcome a chronic deficit. People wondered about his financial backers, who preferred to remain in the background. Who could have an interest in subsidizing a small sheet, and at a time too when the great depression of those years had reached its very nadir?

Just then, the German President had named another Chancellor. It did not remain unnoticed that Hans Zehrer echoed in his editorial policy the line of the new government of Kurt von Schleicher. It transpired eventually that Schleicher, if not personally, then through the agency of interested parties, was the daily's backer. He also happened to be the one man in Germany who, at the time, was still a match for Hitler. The editorialist had found his general, and with the general an army—a professional army, to be sure—that was as superior, in military striking power, to the Nazi militia as it was inferior to it on the battlefield of politics. Both qualities, the military proficiency and the political deficiency of the German Reichswehr, circumscribed the assets and the limitations of the man who had become the latest Chancellor of the Republic.

The Field-Grey Eminence

Kurt von Schleicher belongs among the great might-have-beens of history, great not so much in character and talent as by virtue of the opportunity conferred upon them by a quirk of the historic situation. Schleicher's fluorescent charm blurred rather than illuminated the dimension of his undertaking, but his failure need not lessen recognition for a gallant effort.

Already as a Major in the then young army of professionals, von Schleicher had earned for himself the title of "Grey Eminence." It summed up the reluctant admiration for his special ability to get along well with the new regime of blundering civilians who found themselves, after the *débâcle* of the German empire, suddenly in charge of sulking generals. Von Schleicher's ability to convince politicians that he was no old-style Junker made him the natural liaison officer between the Reichswehr ministry and the Republic. Much of the credit that was given to the frosty and sardonic grandee, Hans von Seekt, belongs to Schleicher, the burgeois administrator of the new regime's praetorian guard. Overshadowed by the famous strategist of World War I, von Schleicher more than helped to forge the instrument that almost won, for Adolf Hitler, World War II.

The most engaging side of this superb quartermaster-general was that he could lift all those heavy loads without perspiring. Nothing was more alien to this gourmand of the table than the attitude of the fanatic. Between him and the hermit-teetotaler, Hitler, there was an almost physical barrier. Von Schleicher's gift for fun and relaxation was as great as that of Julius Caesar; or, if the comparison seems too pretentious, Schleicher may be likened to Spain's dictator-general of the 1920s, Primo de Rivera, whose *alter ego* he was even in physical appearance, at least as much as a Prussian can look like a Spaniard.

That he remained unknown for a whole decade must be credited, or charged, to the characteristic which his admirers called a virtue and his enemies a vice: Von Schleicher made it a rule never to reveal himself. Instead, he elevated men through whom he worked. For the greater glory of his Reichswehr, he employed and wore out countless puppets. When they had ceased to be useful, when they became a nuisance, like his friend, von Papen, or a laughing-stock, like his old patron, General Groener, he would, with a fine, regretful smile, undo them. His reluctance to wear the insignia of the power he wielded may have been due to a constitutional inability to act in the open, for his fiber was delicate, his nervous system not well geared to shocks. Yet he had proved himself, through many years, to be a man of firmness. As the zero hour of the Republic approached, not a few Germans set their hopes on him as a dictator of the "lesser evil," to use the euphemistic term by which the moderate and left-of-center parties meant to justify their "policy of toleration"—the policy of boys who suffer themselves to be bullied, hoping that the bully will protect them against still more dreaded toughs.

To these hopeful Germans Zehrer and his little group belonged. One of them was Herr von Oertzen, the same man who had helplessly stood by when Rosa Luxemburg and Liebknecht were struck down. He came from a military family and had good contacts with the Reichswehr ministry. Official liaison was now established, linking the circle of young intellectuals without power to the general in need of a political idea. For von Schleicher, eminent tactician, had no strategy. He might postpone the end by many little makeshifts, but as a soldier he knew that a mere holding action means defeat unless it is followed by a strong offensive. The governing by bayonets could not continue much longer: Schleicher's front man No. 1, the austere Dr. Heinrich Bruening, had exhausted his usefulness. He was replaced by Baron Franz von Papen. That dashing cavalier drove German socialism out of its last stronghold, the government of Prussia: He tried to wear down Hitler by alternately offering and withholding junior partnership in power. He also tried to overcome the economic slump by pump-priming. It did not work; the situation was not one to inspire the business community with confidence. Or perhaps it was a case of too little and too early.

Von Papen, as the world found out, was that surprising animal, a fox in fox's clothing. But he too, for the time being, had exhausted all his tricks. The dreaded moment had arrived when the great puppet-master had to step into the limelight, when General von Schleicher himself had to become Chancellor, if only to protect his precious instrument from further damage. For was not the entire Reichswehr, from the majors on down, infected by the Nazi virus? The young lieutenants, sons of the bankrupt Junkers, could they be relied upon to remain loyal to a system that failed to provide them with paternal subsidies?

Von Schleicher had to sacrifice his carefully nursed anonymity; he had to place himself between his Reichswehr and the Nazi pied piper. But if the General von Schleicher wanted to keep his fine army out of politics, the Chancellor von Schleicher would have to mobilize another army. He needed the assistance of the German people.

The Social General

The missing platform was provided by Hans Zehrer and his friends. The formula they had discussed in their political salons and propagated in the journal quietly subsidized by the Chancellor, now became a matter of state policy.

Hans Zehrer had no difficulty showing that the methods used by Dr. Bruening and Baron von Papen had not worked. They had not worked because they were anachronistic. Mass rebellions of the twentieth century, as formidably organized as that of Hitlerism, cannot be stopped with the police and fiscal techniques of Prince Metternich. In an era of total politics, there was no longer room for a view of the State confronting a passive citizenry. If the government intended to save Germany from Hitler, that could not be done for her, but only with and through the Germans.

Unfortunately, most political organizations of the German people were no longer serviceable for that purpose. As the year 1933 dawned, there was nothing left of their imposing structures but empty shells. Party and trade-union leaders no longer represented anyone but themselves. If the Chancellor intended to break through to the authentic people, to the masses, he would have to outflank the obsolescent party cadres and create a network of new cross-connections.

This network would need to enfold the Right, the Center, and the non-Communist Left, all the employers and all the trade unionists, regardless whether they belonged to Socialist or Catholic organizations. The resulting rally of all sober citizens, however, would still be of no avail unless it could attract the young, the teenage German who was unemployed and was radical not so much because he had not quite enough to eat, but because he was not allowed to *work*. To win him over, the defensive tactics of the past two years would have to be discarded. The thing to do was to carry the battle into the enemy's camp, to attack Hitler's "German Socialism" by creating German socialism without Hitler.

The General's cause, then, was no longer to be a thinly disguised economic royalism. Although the master of the Reichswehr could not and would not, call himself a Socialist, he let it be known that he intended to act henceforth as the "Social General." Captain Roehricht had been von Schleicher's intimate collaborator. He later reported that his chief was "very sympathetic towards, and popular with the trade unions, while suspected by the Conservatives on account of his tendency to social reforms." [8] There can be no doubt of the suspicions of the Right. But the confidence of the Left was at that moment something to be won rather than taken for granted. If labor listened to the General's proposals, it was because they had no other place to go. Von Schleicher in turn needed them, and they knew it. However, even if they were willing to taste his pudding, they could not furnish the cook with a recipe. It took more powerful ingredients than the labor unions in their much enfeebled state were able to provide.

Von Schleicher's brain trust therefore conceived the daring plan of raiding the Nazi rank and file by an act of wholesale bribery: to lure away the unemployed young storm troopers into the government camp. The moment was propitious, for the Nazi party, which had clad, fed, and partly housed hundreds of thousands in its barracks, had begun to run out of funds, for the financial angels, sorely tried by the Fuehrer's repeated refusal to enter a Rightist cabinet, were beginning to leave what they thought was a sinking ship.

But because the bulk of the Hitlerian private army would not betray the cause unless expressly ordered to do so by at least one outstanding leader, such a person had first to be found. It was exciting news when Gregor Strasser, one of the more serious-minded members of the inner ring of Nazi leadership and a skilled organizer, entered into negotiations with the soldier-chancellor. Strasser, who in an important Reichstag speech had coined the phrase "the anti-capitalist yearnings of the German

8. B. H. Liddell Hart, *The German Generals Talk* (New York: Morrow, 1948), p. 82. Roehricht was a General when he was interviewed in 1945.

people," was slated by von Schleicher for the post of Minister of Labor and Public Works, a bailiwick including the administration of all work camps. Comparable to the American CCC of the same period, they were to be vastly expanded and provided with funds sufficient to take care of the jobless in brown shirts.

Stealing Hitler's thunder: an ingenious stratagem. Those who conceived it had the right idea, without any clear awareness of its meaning in the context of the revolutionary situation. What they were aiming at was intercession: the attempt to insert countervailing forces into an historic process *before* it comes to a head.

Had Schleicher's grand design succeeded, the result would still have been some sort of fascism, but one administered by military gentlemen assisted by the bureaucrats of both the public and the private sector, and not by a gang of demagogues and terrorists. But the mere inkling of von Schleicher's "bolshevist plot" was enough to frighten the reactionary camarilla about President von Hindenburg. The formal presentation of Strasser to the Chief Executive, set for a certain date, was cancelled at the last moment.[9]

Hitler, faced with the prospect of a Reichswehr-Labor Axis, at long last consented to the twice-rejected deal with the industrialists and Junkers. Exploiting their fears of the "leftist" Schleicher, his ambitious and disgruntled friend, von Papen, now became the architect of the pact between conservative and revolutionary nationalism—the leonine pact from which was to issue the Third Reich.

The Verdict

General Roehricht, judging his old chief in retrospect, confided to Liddell Hart: "Kurt von Schleicher was a very skillful and astute political tactician, but without the personality of a statesman that was needed at this period." The opinion of von Oertzen

9. Hitler treated Strasser as a traitor and he had him killed a year later. This would seem to prove that Hitler had not sanctioned Strasser's negotiations with von Schleicher. Since Hitler's chances of succeeding the General were then still doubtful, Strasser possibly had his tacit permission at least to be the entering wedge in Schleicher's cabinet—that wedge to be widened afterwards, just as the Fuehrer later managed to transform a cabinet controlled by Papen's friends into a body dominated by his own men. For details of the affair, see Karl Dietrich Bracher, *Die Aufloesung der Weimarer Republik*, 2nd ed. (Stuttgart and Duesseldorf, 1957), pp. 673ff.

was even blunter: "We overrated the fellow. We pumped ideas into him and blew him up, like a balloon. But he was nothing but a drawing-room intriguer."

This repudiation of the "chosen instrument" conveys the bitterness of disappointed men. However, lack of statesmanship was not the cause of Schleicher's failure. There are situations in which even the most astute statecraft will accomplish nothing. Schleicher's failure had two causes, and in both situations he confronted forces beyond his control. There was his record as the general who had kept his Reichswehr aloof from the nation ever since the early days of the Republic. When at last the era of ill feeling was to end, could the people really forget that the armed force of the Republic had always refused to be a people's army? How could they now have faith in the "Social General?" Then, had not his front man, Dr. Bruening, sapped the strength of the trade unions with his stern deflationary policy? Who had administered the death-blow to the Social-Democratic Party but von Schleicher's Sassenach, von Papen?

Roles can be changed. What matters is whether the change be creditable. Suppose the leopard could have changed his spots: Suppose the General could have convinced the people that he was their man. His concept of an anti-Hitler rally of all moderates was sound. But to impress force, counterforce too must be creditable. There were no longer any groups left to be rallied, only social atoms, flotsam ready to be picked up by the great garbage collector from the Brown House. When Schleicher's scheme forced Hitler into the alliance with reaction, it proved to be the superior combination: It was solid, based on a coherent mass organization reinforced by the hard core of capital.

Schleicher's game was lost. What could he do? Use force, attempt a coup d'état, arrest von Hindenburg? He momentarily thought of it. But when the trustee of the German army called upon his fellow-generals, their faces betrayed nothing but a wooden loyalty to the old war lord, the senile incumbent of the highest office who had just changed chancellors again and who wished only one thing—to be left alone. So he bequeathed his country and, almost the world, to Adolf Hitler.

Should the General have shot it out with his successor? It was the one thing he would not do. It was unthinkable, although not for the reason he had given at a time when he could still count on the army: That his troops could not be asked to fire on patriotic Germans. The truth is that the Hitler revolution could have been defeated only by a real counterrevolution—by another attack on the *status quo*. But the General had never meant his popular front to be anything but a temporary combination, to be disbanded after serving his purpose, which was to bring the antagonist to reason and, if possible, into the fold.

The Aftermath

Zehrer and his friends continued to put out their paper during the first months of the Third Reich. Their attitude was one of watchful assent; they went so far as to endorse the boycott against Jews that went into effect on April 1, 1933. Among themselves (not publicly!) they argued, as new Machiavellis, that the Nazi attack against part of the economy could not be halted there and had to spread to the whole system, an end they heartily endorsed. Their awakening to the true, parasitical character of Nazi rule was hastened by the great purge of June 30th, 1934, when the revolution, which had benefitted from the premature repression of its predecessor, was in turn arrested by its Cromwell who smashed, with a twin-blow, both right-wing and left-wing opposition to his middle course.

It has been argued that the purge had been *imposed* on Hitler by the Reichswehr, unwilling to share control over the future national army with the leaders of the party army. If so, the old army paid a heavy price, because the purge did not spare its own representatives in public life, not even its old leader: Kurt von Schleicher, living in retirement, but still a man to watch, became, with his wife, the victim of Goering's thugs. Hans Zehrer and von Oertzen, forewarned by friends within the party, took to the woods, to reappear when things calmed down. In the mid-1930s, Zehrer became a member of one of the many cautious opposition groups that tried to operate within the lion's den, while Herr von Oertzen, despairing of all action, found some comfort in the Protestant resistance church. In 1939, he volunteered for active service and died at the Polish front a perhaps not unwelcomed death. But other members of the circle crawled deeper into the Hitlerian den, and at least one of them became a rather high official in a Nazi ministry.

Those of the group who managed to survive the war had time

to realize that intellectually conceived solutions to a problem cannot be hitched to the star of history like an outboard motor to a fishing boat. That does not mean that intercession cannot possibly succeed. It may work when conditions favor it. That was the case in France where intercession *did* succeed—with General de Gaulle as intercessor.[10]

10. See chapter 12. As this goes to press, the news came that Hans Zehrer, editor-in-chief of the influential Hamburg daily, *Die Welt*, since 1953, died on August 24, 1966, in Berlin, at the age of sixty-eight.

What C. Wright Mills said about Trotsky, that he was "a revolutionary without a revolutionary context," applies with even greater justice to the Englishman of many names, one of them being Thomas Edward Lawrence. The two careers show certain striking similarities: both men were writers of distinction. Both led armies, although the armies were not comparable in size. But if guerrilla combat is bound to be typical of future wars, then Lawrence was, in that respect, ahead of Trotsky who commanded mass formations. Both men reached the pinnacle of fame quite early and had to climb down again, and thereafter for each of them life was one endless anticlimax. Displaced prophets both, they tried new ways to solve their problems, but in vain.

The similarities end here. For Trotsky could, in exile, take some consolation in the thought that he had made his revolution. All he had to do was to keep fighting for it, saving it from the usurper. Lawrence, on the other hand, looks like a rebel without cause. His inability to reconcile the man of action with the man of intellect would seem to be a private rather than a public problem. Unlike Trotsky's exile, Lawrence's was self-imposed. Whereas alone, the Russian remained in full contact with national affairs, the Englishman felt alienated even when he was in touch. The following is an attempt to show that Lawrence was, in spite of all appearances, a public figure and his very isolation expressed needs, more felt than known, of people living in a period of transition and seeking a hero who would express revolutionary (counterrevolutionary) attitudes in a nonrevolutionary situation. To fill that role, the hero must become an anti-hero; his symbolic acts deliberate nonaction, and his life a myth.

10 The Mythmaker, T. E. Lawrence: An Existentialist Revolt

No single story can be told of him without at once provoking still another story to refute it. The subject of these stories, and of many drawings, paintings, and statues, for which many much more famous men might envy him, died more than thirty years ago, but there is still no end of him. They even made a movie about his Arabian war exploits, and were he still alive, he might have volunteered to write the script and serve as technical adviser, at the same time ridiculing the whole project, which would remind him of times and things of which he would no longer wish to be reminded.

A man who raised so many questions, most of which he asked himself, needs to be given a great deal of latitude and the benefit of every doubt. The proper thing, it would seem, is to start with a friendly testimonial, based for the most part on his own words. Next, it will be the turn of the critics, and lastly, only then, can an attempt be made to answer questions that the reader has a right to ask: Why Lawrence? In what sense was he a revolutionary? What is his importance in the context of this study?

These questions cannot be answered until we have seen the many faces of the man called Thomas Edward Lawrence, John Hume Ross, and T. E. Shaw, in all their contradictory variety.

A FRIEND OF FAMOUS MEN*

Somewhere in England, in an R.A.F. barracks, a lonely private "irk" was frantically typing letters. It was night, the other fellows were all gone on leave. Actually, it was *his* night off, but he had volunteered to stay on duty. He preferred to do his correspondence, which for a plain airman in his Majesty's service seemed rather copious. For hours he had been pounding the machine, but his fingers were still stiff. Because:

> It freezes: it snows: it blows. I'm cold as cold. The running rivers of my brain are all a-frozen. Don't expect coherence till a thaw sets in.
> The sweater: the Canadian sweater? I'm almost sure it's there. I can feel it, by hooking a finger between the third and fourth buttons (next above the belt) of my tunic. But this is sense evidence only. To make sure, I should have to unbutton my tunic, and look: and the wind is howling so terribly about this hangar that I don't dare.
> . . . They offer me huge prices here, for it: packets and packets of woodbine: spare pairs of boots, a "civie suit". . . . I refuse them all, frozenly waving one frozen hand, in icy refusal. Of course I should have written and told you: but . . . but . . . .
> It's cold.[1]

What is this? "Pretty" poetry, or mockery at pretty poetry? Both, very likely. Poetry ashamed of itself, sneering at itself. Airman Shaw (that was then his name) was fond of knitting together sentences, lines with the beat of music in them. Not fancy, far-fetched words—nothing but the plainest and most ordinary stuff, such as befitted a simple soldier. A soldier who, however, would arouse a friend whose invitation he could not

---

* A different and longer version of this section appeared under the title "The Mystery of Airman Shaw" in the *Michigan Alumnus Quarterly Review* (now the *Michigan Quarterly Review*), Vol. 54, No. 24 (July, 1948), p. 327-39. Reproduced by permission.
  1. Whenever Lawrence speaks, unless another source is given, the quotations are from *The Letters of T. E. Lawrence*, ed. by David Garnett (New York, 1939).

accept with the imperious lines: "Fly down to me, some day, instead!" Tyrtaeus in overalls.

Sometimes he wrote to his great namesake, known throughout the world as GBS. There was nothing special about the author of *Heartbreak House* and *St. Joan* receiving fan mail from an ardent admirer in uniform. But, strangely, the fan mail worked both ways. Indeed, airman Shaw, on one of his rare leaves in London, lost a whole pack of letters signed Bernard Shaw, letters urging the airman to publish a certain Arabian book of his.

There are more famous correspondents—in fact, the best names England could boast of between the two wars. There was Sir Edward Elgar donating the records of his symphonies to private Shaw's hut; there was Noel Coward addressing him in a line that has become famous: "Dear 338171 (may I call you 338?)"; while he, T. E. Shaw, signed a note to Lady Astor with "Yours proletariately." And what a host of authors anxious to send him their most recent books and get his critical reaction! Indeed, it seemed as if that lonely hut somewhere in England was sheltering the general staff of national literature. They were proud to be his friends: Robert Graves, and Liddell Hart (who were both to become his biographers, with Lawrence scrutinizing every line, rewriting entire passages), E. M. Forster, Siegfried Sassoon, the poet, Archibald Wavell, the general, Ronald Storrs, the imperial proconsul, John Buchan, Winston Churchill—all agreeing that *The Seven Pillars of Wisdom* was one of the truly great books of English literature, and bemoaning the fact that its author had elected to be a ghost writer for his commanding officer:

> I write the letters, type them, and do not sign them. The poor C.O. takes that responsibility. Often it is a responsibility.
> Just now I am wholly M.B.C. [Motor Boat Crew], for the R.A.F. is at last trying to get some marine craft of modern design, a need I have been urging on them (per C.O.'s signature) for 18 months. . . .

One notes—and the examples could be multiplied—the close conjunction of humility and pride, of great amibition, but not for himself, of will to power, and the wish for self-abasement. In all earnest, he applied for the position of a night watchman in the Bank of England for his old age. He wanted to stay at the bottom.

He liked it there.

"They treat my past as a joke, and forgive it me lightly. The officers fight shy of me, but I behave demurely, and give no trouble." Lawrence of Arabia was accepted by the common fellow, because he was not a pale-faced and bespectacled professor. Quite the contrary: The young, lean archeologist with the large, horsey head and the short legs had given proofs of physical endurance that won him the admiration of the toughest Bedouin. So he was no push-over as a recruit.

As for the officers, they had, indeed, good reason to "fight shy" of him. Nobody much enjoys being served his meal by a waiter he knows was once a grand duke to the Czar. Nor would the idea of having one's shoes shined by the author of a book on Plato be too pleasant. And there, standing at attention, was a chap who knows more about soldiering than they. The blank submission on his face was even more insufferable than the smile for which they scrutinized it closely, but in vain. He did not buck the system; he accepted it, like an old, incurable disease: "Poor reptiles. . . . A word in your ear—discipline itself is not necessary. We fight better without it. Yet being Englishmen we are born with it, and can no more lose it than our finger nails."

One might bite them off, though. Sometimes his sense of humor got the better of him, and the sorcerer playing apprentice resorted to puckish pranks and impish slips: "I . . . find it difficult to give the right salutes with a pop-gun at short notice. . . . Sheer wind, of course, for actually I know the movements well." The wind that indicated the opening of the safety valves.

One evening he wished to attend a performance of the *Oresteia* of Aeschylus by the Balliol Players in Thomas Hardy's garden. "The Staff Sergt. knew I wanted to get off promptly from work, & so he put me on to job after job . . . till I was too late. This was his revenge for my having been clever a day or two before." Lawrence ended his account with the laconic remark: "The Staff Sergt. has had a bad life since, & is sorry." We can only guess what Private Shaw and his gang did to the poor man to make his hair prematurely gray, but the result was that he "says I can get off early any day I like: I don't like . . . now." A slumbering lion, annoyed, showed his teeth; from now on he would be left alone.

Another time he had tea with the Hardys and came to sit— in his plain uniform—next to the Mayoress of Dorchester, who never in her life had had a private soldier next to her at table and confessed her great embarrassment in French. Either the hostess did not hear, or preferred not to hear; at any rate there would have been no answer had it not been for the private soldier who with a sweet expression and in perfect Parisian addressed himself to the lady from Dorchester: "May I serve as an interpreter, Madam? Mrs. Hardy does not know a word of French."

Edward Marsh, who tells this story in his autobiography, *A Number of People,* without remarking on the cruel tastelessness of Lawrence's joke, has another one about a snobbish officer to whom the former colonel has been assigned as a temporary batman:

> Unpacking his kit [Lawrence] looked around and said: "I beg your pardon, sir, but I can only find one of your razors." "I've only got one razor." "Indeed, sir? I thought most gentlemen had a razor for every day in the week." After a moment he looked round again. "Sir, I can't find your left-handed nail-scissors." The poor man rushed out of the tent and applied for a less exacting batman.

It was the "Yours proletariately" touch with a by-mixture of Jeeves that made them rush out of the tent to try to get rid of him. But inasmuch as his conduct sheet remained impeccable, all they could do was to transfer him to some other place.

In their war with Private Shaw his officers had a strong ally in Colonel Lawrence, for his fame followed into all his hiding places, threatening his hard-won small security. It was this fame that drove him from the fondly loved Air Force to the rugged Tank Corps. And again, when he was readmitted to the R.A.F., after some heavy string-pulling by influential friends—John Buchan, Churchill, Baldwin among them—two publications, by and on Lawrence, with all the flare-up of publicity, made his transfer to an East Indian airfield advisable.

He did not like it there: "England is the only place fit to live in!" he sighed behind the barbed wire of a frontier post. He was bored. His wish: "Put me back in England and you can keep your East!" was granted sooner than he expected: Newspaper rumor that had him organizing the Afghan revolt against their westernized King Amanullah caused the disturbed British authorities to place their prodigy under virtual arrest and to rush him home, to new oblivion.

We have a picture from his Indian sojourn with the legend written by himself: "T.E.S. against a Waziri desert, softly lit, nursing his excessive chin with one bent arm"—a grayish, graceful boy of forty. Yet a lady writing from Ohio had confessed to him: "You are my ideal of a real he-man." The notion made him wince. A cryptic chapter: Lawrence and women. Here his hide-and-seek technique had reached perfection:

"I like some women. I don't like their sex. . . ." Once he was genuinely impressed by a girl, but when she avoided him, he was relieved. The pattern of evasive action ran through his whole life. "The Viceroy came," he writes from India, "we worked for weeks beforehand collecting dust to throw in his eyes. . . . When the day came I dodged off on a side duty." He was always dodging off.

He wanted to write the warrants, to dictate the law, but not to sign it. As Private Meek in the "real" Shaw's play, *Too True to Be Good*, he is the orderly who runs the whole show for his colonel (whose preference is water colors). It is Meek who makes up the dispatches, translating into some uncouth native tongue nobody else ever took the pains to learn; he is the dispatch rider, too, delivering the ultimatum to the rebel chieftain, dictating his answer, translating it back into English; and having finally dealt with an operetta Revolt in the Desert in Julius Caesar fashion—with the Lawrentian variant: I came, I won, I vanished—he leaves his colonel but one choice: to concentrate on water colors from here on. He is terrific, and the model cloaked his pleasure with the modest statement that Meek is "unfortunately much nicer than the original."

When he is asked to furnish dates for the *Encyclopaedia Britannica*, he is amused but complies eagerly: "Yes, by all means. Let me try my hand. . . . Does that ring with the right loftiness . . . ?" It does not, and is significant less for what he divulged about himself than for the omissions. The war, and his own part in it are not mentioned; nor is his war book. He left this job to his correspondent, instructing him: "Don't overstress the war period. As it fades into distance, the war becomes a small affair."

But distance usually enhances, magnifies, and Lawrence knew it: "What's the cause that [we] can't get away from the War?" he wonders. "Me, in the ranks, finding squalor and maltreatment the only permitted existence: What's the matter with us all? It's like the malarial bugs in the blood, coming out months and years after in recurrent attacks." But it was the infection that kept him alive; recovery might have killed him.

The trouble with him was that his demonic driving power always overruled his will to stop:

> In the sports lately. . . . I was put down to jump, and refused because it was an activity of the flesh. Afterwards to myself I wondered if that was the reason, or was I afraid of failing ridiculously: So I went down alone and privily cleared over twenty feet, and was sick of mind at having tried because I was glad to find I still could jump.[2]

This expresses the whole man: his reticence in matters of the body, his wish to excel, and his disgust with himself because he enjoyed excelling. No wonder he was frightened: "This sort of thing must be madness, and sometimes I wonder how far mad I am, and if a mad-house would not be my next (and merciful) stage."

But Lawrence also knew: "There is no more rational being than myself alive. It's excess of reason which makes me seem mad to people." But he ever returns to his obsession, "the other fate I'm always fearing. You know, Robin, I'm hardly sane at times." And when his Father Confessor Socrates Mephisto Bernard Shaw wanted to find out at last "What is your game *really?*" his Alcibiades snapped back, "Please, don't think it is a game, just because I laugh at myself and everybody else. That's Irish, or an attempt to keep sane." [3]

His attitude in money matters was consistent with his whole philosophy of self-denial. Again and again he refused lucrative financial or job offers: "You see, I'm all smash inside: And I don't want to look prosperous or be prosperous, while I know

---

2. Another letter has the following variant: ". . . that craving for real risk. . . . I'm ashamed of doing it and of not doing it, unwilling to do it: And most of all ashamed (afraid) of doing it well."

3. "He had all the marks of the Irishman: the rhetoric of freedom, the rhetoric of chastity, the rhetoric of honor, the power to excite sudden deep affections, loyalty to the long-buried past, high aims qualified by too mocking a sense of humor, serenity clouded by petulance and broken by occasional black despair, playboy charm and theatricality, imagination that overruns itself and tires, extreme generosity, serpent cunning, lion courage, diabolic intuition, and the curse of self-doubt which becomes enmity to self and sometimes renunciation of all that is most loved and esteemed." Robert Graves, in Robert Graves and Liddell Hart, *T. E. Lawrence to His Biographers* (New York, 1963; copyright 1938), p. 186.

that." Was he a "red," then? Heavens, no. "The trouble with Communism is that it accepts too much of today's furniture. I hate furniture." Likewise, he is no reformer for reform's sake. "Democratize the Services?" he wrote a Labor Party friend, "O Lord, that doesn't matter. Make them decent for all classes, please, by delivering us of superstitions & callousnesses."

Among the superstitions he counted punishment for cowardice: "I have run too far and too fast under fire (though never fast enough to suit me at the time) to dare throw a stone at the fearfullest creature," he informed the same correspondent, responsible for the abolition of death penalty in the army. "You see, I might hit myself in the eye."

Meanwhile his outcry against the "foul-mouthed talk" of the barracks was muted, and he stated: "As I get older I feel safer and easier in contemplating the animal facts of existence. . . . I've lived in barracks now for nine years: preferring the plain man to the elaborate man. I find them forth-coming, honest, friendly and so comfortable. They do not pretend at all, and with them I have not to pretend." There had been a time when he was asking: "Do you think there have been many lay monks of my persuasion?" But he no longer considered himself to be a runaway from life, after having found it in his military monastery. For the first time he stopped looking backward: "Mark me down for a further spell of quite happy existence."

Nor did he continue to bewail his incapacity to write great books: "You have in me a contented being, and no literature rises out of contentment." He had long ago decided that *The Seven Pillars of Wisdom* was "a stodgy mess of mock-heroic egotism," and from the literary viewpoint, "one of the best dressed imitations of a book you'll ever see," and he declared indignantly: "Me to write again? God forbid . . . *C'est fini.*"

Not quite, though. Then he wrote *A Handbook to 37½ foot motor boats of the 200 class*, in which, he prides himself, "every sentence . . . is understandable, to a fitter." Like an incantation, exorcising evil spirits, he repeated: "The ancient self-seeking, and self-devouring T.E.L. is dead." How so? Hush. He shrinks from 'digging too deep into the happiness for fear of puncturing it.' "

Once he had groaned: "I have achieved [peace of mind] in the ranks at the price of stagnancy and beastliness"; later he would say that "Service life makes up for its roughness in many ways:—for instance one is never lonely—far from it . . ." and "one's bread and margarine is safe." Safe, he "feels safe," he has to be "in harness, for I am afraid of being loose and independent." He speaks for a whole generation craving for security.

Once he had been afraid of what he called his "power of molding men and things." Later he molded himself into a tool; he could not deny, with all his gift for understatement, that he was "a tolerable fitter, and handy on a motor-boat"; which in his language meant that he was running the whole show again. But this new power did not bother him, being impersonal and serving still greater powers—nature and its mastery: "Wherefore I get a sense of the sameness and smallness of everything, including us: and so I would not voluntarily put another in my place."

He may have changed but the brass hats never do. Because he had not quite given up the association with "elaborate men," the plain man, Shaw, got into trouble. He was seen chatting to some top people and was once more threatened with dismissal from the Air Force. He was ordered not to speak to certain "great men" who would cause publicity—for him. He was provided with a list of names in which, to Bernard Shaw's annoyance, Bernard Shaw was missing.

Then there was the ghost of Colonel Lawrence riding again: Sergeant Meek stepping from the stage down into life. Someone impersonating him, performing T. E. Lawrence at distinguished dinner parties. The airman came to town and looked him over. He was half-relieved, half-disappointed to find only "a worm." What if he would have met his very Self, reborn? A frightful, maddening idea. He meant to consult a lawyer, to protect, as it were, the copyright on his own personality. But did he, who had found the "sameness" of everything, still have a claim on being unique? A still more maddening idea.

The day was nearing when his service would come to its close. He looked forward to his house, for he was tired. "May I rest now? All the heat in me is gone out, and the endurance that was tougher than other men's," and "What a happy life it would be if one got up only when the sheets wanted changing! I grow so old and fat and white-haired. . . . Damn all letter-writing." And everything else besides: "Alas, how tired I am of bikes & books & music and food and drink & words and work." Tired as he was, the musical beat of a line still mattered to him. He heard that heath fires were raging near his cottage, and was "sad and afraid for the little place. I've grown to love it, I fear. What fools we become!" His greatest fear was *horror vacui:* "It will be queer to wake up . . . and to know that thence-forward there is not a single thing that I must do. . . . I wish there was any one thing in the world that I wanted to do."

His fear came true, and he wrote: "I just sit here in this cottage and wonder about nothing in general. . . . Am well, well-fed, full of company, laborious," but "there is something broken in the works . . . my will, I think. . . . In fact I find myself wishing all the time that my own curtain would fall. It seems as if I had finished, now." His wish was granted soon.

He had had many accidents in his career and on his motor bike rides had broken many ribs, his hands, thumbs, ankles. Now he crashed once more, while dodging a pedestrian. The police called it an accident. His giant will fought six days before it succumbed; he never regained consciousness.

LAWRENCE OBSERVED

There were those (their name is legion) who accepted him on his own terms and put him on a pedestal, which they then circled solemnly, reciting hagiographic poetry. He would have loved it, only to explode with laughter the next moment. In these edifying writings, whose sincerity cannot be questioned, Lawrence becomes "the destined prey of the sins of Lucifer . . . which spring from pride. The sins of the Angels." But "the bitterness of his failure saved him from falling to the level of a conqueror, or of a dictator. . . . It is as a monk that this man of action has kept his influence." [4]

We will be told by two of Lawrence's close friends that only his death saved him from the temptations of the dictator. But the monk's cowl fitted Lawrence very well indeed. André Malraux, a kindred soul, who might be called the Gallic Lawrence of the book and of the deed, also regards the Englishman as "one of the most religious minds of his time, if one means by religious to feel in the very depths of one's soul the anguish of being a man." In particular, "there was within him, beneath his pride, if not humility, at least a violent and intermittent inclination to

4. Victoria Ocampo, *338171 T. E. (Lawrence of Arabia)*, trans. by David Garnett from the original French edition of 1942 (New York, 1963), p. 68.

humiliate himself . . . the horror of respectability; the disgust for property, for money . . . a profound consciousness of guilt . . . and of the nothingness of nearly all that men cling to; the need of the Absolute, the instinctive taste for ascetism." But he was not religious in any conventional sense. "There was in him an anti-Christian of the first order; it was only from himself that he expected forgiveness." [5]

On a less exalted level we find two of his biographers. They look at Lawrence with the deep affection of a friendship that stood the test of many years precisely because love was tempered with detachment, admiration with judicious common sense. They were not blind to what Nietzsche called the human, all-too-human, in the make-up of their friend; his vanity, for instance, was perceived by one of them in all its disingenious playfulness: "Lawrence was always anxious to know of the effect he had on other people: He was like a child who hides behind a curtain and keeps showing little bits of himself to dramatize his sense of being in hiding." [6]

This and much more in the same vein in Graves and Hart's joint testimonial. But it is no demolition job, because that job had already been done by Lawrence himself. A careful reading of his letters and of what he said in conversation—eagerly recorded by his many visitors—leaves little doubt that almost anything that could be said against him, Lawrence had already said himself. His tendency to self-dramatization cannot be denied, but his histrionics never kept him from eventually confronting and acknowledging the truth, so often muddled and not in the least "heroic." The same Robert Graves is the recipient of a letter in which Lawrence tried to tell what motivated him to join the forces as a private after World War I:

Honestly I couldn't tell you exactly . . . though the night before I did. . . . I sat up and wrote out all the reasons. . . . But they came to little more than that it was a necessary step, forced on me by an inclination towards ground-level: by a despairing hope that I'd find myself on common ground with men: by a little wish to make myself a little more human . . . also I'm broke. . . . All these are reasons; but unless they are cumulative they are miserably inadequate. I wanted to join up,

5. André Malraux, "The Demon of the Absolute, a Study of T. E. Lawrence (2)," *World Review, London* (October, 1949), p. 37. For the first part of this essay, see the same journal. (September, 1949), pp. 9–12.
6. Robert Graves, in *op. cit.,* p. 172.

that's all: and I am still glad, sometimes, that I did. It's going to be a brain-sleep, and I'll come out of it less odd than I went in: or at least less odd in other men's eyes.

He knew how little we do know about the cardinal decisions of our life; no marble for the monument is being furnished here.

When Liddell Hart showed Lawrence the flamboyant peroration he contributed to the joint biography: "He is the Spirit of Freedom come incarnate to a world in fetters," Lawrence "contended that he did not respect others' freedom, so much as insisting on his own. He was the essential 'anarch'—the very opposite of Socialist." [7]

This is important. Lawrence knew that something was expected of him that did violence to his own nature, as he saw it: needing independence to be free—free to work out its own destiny. Others, in turn, sensed more than they understood what he expected of *them* and took fright. Impasse. But the mutual attraction and repulsion also generated a still fragile but intense awareness, on both sides, of a community of interests: Others could respect his struggle for autonomy, while he in turn confessed his fear "of being loose and independent." Lawrence knew and recognized his debt to others, without minimizing his own contribution: "When I see pictures of myself in Arab kit I get a little impatient—silly of me, for it was long ago, and did really happen." But he sneers at "Lurans Bey," well knowing that great enterprises are the sum of *many* individual efforts: teamwork. He will minimize his actual role but realistically accept the conversion of many merits into one—his own; the condensation of glories into glory, of collective history into a very personal mythology. The irony of it he knew, but also that it was immune to irony.

People have asked what Lawrence would have done in his retirement, had he lived. His two biographers tried to find out:

Did Lawrence really mean that his life was over? He was made (in a phrase that he had once applied to me) without a reversed gear. He had finished with digging up the past [as a young archeologist] making new military history, trying to be an "artist," being a plain man. Now came . . . the temptation to dramatize himself politically . . . to become a more legendary Hitler a shrewder and more powerful Mussolini. . . . He played

7. Liddell Hart, in *op. cit.*, p. 201.

with the temptation as an exciting alternative to the do-nothing
Sunday . . . that he had promised himself.[8]

Lawrence admitted that "the Fascists had been after him."
Apparently some followers, or even direct emissaries, of Sir
Oswald Mosley, "He had replied that he wouldn't help them to
power, but if they gained it, he would agree to become 'dictator
of the press'—for a fortnight." Lawrence then elaborated how
he would "stop all mentioning of anybody's name except public
servants" and "suppress the cheaper press, save the decent three."

This sounds like just another instance of Lawrentian leg-pulling,
with Liddell Hart the victim in the case, but Hart was uneasy
and pressed on. "T.E. said there was no doubt there was a big
call for a new lead. Would cease to be Fascist when gained
power. But said Mosley was . . . not likely to tolerate any really
good chief of staff. But his chance might come if somebody big
took him under their wing."

These are notes made from memory, but it is possible to re-
construct what went on in Lawrence's mind. There was indeed
a "call" for a new lead during the English 1930's. It is easy now
to cast aspersions on Sir Oswald, or "the Cliveden set," appease-
ment, Munich and the rest. But it must be remembered that there
also was in progress something like an intellectual counterrevolution against liberal and socialist incompetence in solving the great
economic crisis. It required strong means and new ideas. Not a
few distinguished writers flirted with the new philosophers of
power: Wyndham Lewis wrote *The Art of Being Ruled;* H. G.
Wells, in novel after novel, called on the new technocrats and
managers to engage in "open conspiracy" to organize and rule
the world. Not even the great Yeats remained immune from
the infection. As for Lawrence, Fascism was to his restless mind
no more than just another means to new activity, itself a passing
fashion, which would not outlast the revolution. Still, it would be
in need of a good chief of staff, and private Shaw (ret.) might
be it.

So Hart puts Lawrence to the question: "Would he contem-
plate leading any movement? He said 'No'—still determined to
try and settle down in his cottage. But if he got tired of it, many

8. Robert Graves, in *op. cit.,* p. 185. Lawrence did not think much of the
Duce: "Lot of practical sense, but no capacity for abstract thought. Lenin
was the greatest man—only man who had evolved a theory, carried it out,
and consolidated." Liddell Hart, in *op. cit.,* p. 211.

things he could do. (His attitude is certainly changing—more than he is conscious of.)" [9]

But not the man who, tempted, instantly pulled the reverse gear Robert Graves could not detect, and backed into the safe position that the fascist revolution would have no use for him. Inasmuch as Sir Oswald would not give him *plein pouvoir*, perhaps some greater Lord Protector would turn up to let him play his customary role behind the scene: Drafting the new ordinances but not signing them.

The critic standing at the other end of the continuum in the scoffer's corner finds this whole last episode amusing, although otherwise no man could be called less amused by what he had discovered about T. E. Lawrence than his biographical inquirer, Richard Aldington. He comes to the conclusion that "the career of Lawrence the man of action . . . was of much less significance than is generally supposed," while "the establishment and growth of . . . the Lawrence legend . . . was largely Lawrence's own doing." Aldington does not deny "that Lawrence was a man of peculiar abilities." [10] But these abilities, he comments, which Lawrence used to practice "from a very early date" are "the systematic falsification and overvaluing of himself." And he sums it up, "the national hero turned out at least half a fraud." [11]

What is startling about this summation is the vehemence of the accuser, rather than that of the evidence, collected by him with an ardor worthy of a better cause. For all or most of the damaging facts can be gleaned from the Lawrentian correspondence, whose editor, David Garnett, already spoke of his great vanity, his masochism, his growing persecution mania. What can be more severe than Garnett's comment on Lawrence's habitual neglect of bodily injuries: "The courage of the boy too proud to make a fuss is something we admire; in an educated man it is ridiculous and a sign of abnormality." [12] Aldington's objective is not ridicule but the destruction of a myth that is a fraud, conceived and executed with painstaking exactness by the subject of the myth himself. He is, in Aldington's book, a superb public relations expert of the softest sell, relying on subliminal persuasion—unless something less effete is indicated: then, he will pull

9. Hart, *op. cit.*, p. 222.
10. Richard Aldington, *Lawrence of Arabia. A Biographical Enquiry* (London, 1955), p. 14.
11. *Ibid.*, p. 12.
12. *The Letters of T. E. Lawrence*, p. 350.

strings without any compunction; his collaborators in the war will slowly vanish from the scene, while the great Monologist, T.E.L., remains its sole, undisputed hero. But that hero is pursued by furies: His vainglory is nothing but a masquerade of guilt. The victor of Damascus is not able to live down the fact of his illegitimate origin. (His brothers could.) From the name Lawrence, assumed by the father, the son goes on to become, first Ross, then Shaw, forever searching for his true identity. His congenital deficiency explains, if it does not excuse, the congenital compulsion to invent a legendary figure as an armor in which the hollow man can disappear.

Aldington's attempt to psychoanalyze Lawrence is a matter for the psychoanalyst to analyze. He may decide that the reduction of a man's complexity to monocausal nudity may, in this case, have led to a *reductio ad absurdum*. As for Lawrence the mythmaker, the massively documented story makes a devastating impact on the reader. But the argument is also strangely self-defeating. One expects of Aldington not charity but an awareness on a par with his unquestionably great intelligence. It should have led him to the following consideration: Granted Lawrence wanted to be famous, why did he persist in hiding and continue to play ostrich even *after* his self-manufactured legend had become a public fact? How prove that Lawrence's flight *from* publicity was less authentic than his love of it?

This study, not concerned with personal pathology as such, but only as it impinges on the public role enacted by the subject, can and must ignore the private person, Lawrence, and the question of his authenticity or lack of it. The significant Lawrence is the one in whom people hoped—and for some still to be discovered reason—failed to find their superpersonal, collective working-contact and representation. More precisely: Lawrence is a case of a reluctant leader facing a reluctant if admiring public. The compounding of two hesitations on the one hand, and of two attractions on the other, has two contradictory effects: a widening communications gap, precariously bridged by imagination.

THE PROPHET DISPLACED

This is the story of a one-man revolution that remained a one-man revolution. If the radical rejection of received ideas, and the acceptance of and total dedication to new values are the preconditions of a real revolution, then the man called Thomas Edward Lawrence was a real revolutionary.

Revolutions do not happen in a void. They are the transformation of emotional or intellectual exchanges into combined practice. The complaints and blueprints for remedial action may originate in one man's mind, but if they remain his secret property, the revolution is not likely to succeed. He must communicate his grievances and his demands.

Or, if the message comes to him from other minds, the revolutionary must acknowledge it and signal either his consent or his refusal. Silence will not be accepted as an answer; come the revolution, he is likely to get hurt as badly if not worse than the avowed opponent.

But it may happen that the revolutionary is unable to communicate and share his problem with those of a like predisposition. In that case, his predicament would seem to be devoid of interpersonal significance: It has become his private business altogether. Only God can help him now, and if he has no God, his life will be a story of self-torture and despair, unless he has the strength to work out his own salvation as a solitary.

Even then he may, in some rare cases, still become a public figure, serving as a magnet for atomic particles of discontent, a catalyst for fear and hope. What is he: a false prophet? Or could the falseness be in his people? In the time of his arrival? Has he come too soon, or much too late, so that the "shock of recognition," although felt by the collective consciousness, is unable to generate collective action? The electric circuit is still uncompleted or already broken. For what reason? They will never know.

But they will keep on scanning the horizon for a sign, a signal from the desert. Unlike the great prophets of the past who stepped from it full of the spirit in the fullness of time, Lawrence came out of Arabia shattered by the magnitude of his "betrayal of the Arab cause," by the revealed duplicity of his own role as both a liberator and an agent of imperial interest. But that was merely the convenient rationalization of a greater guilt: the failure of an entire generation that had, singing, marched into the war to end all wars, and that was now faced with the collapse of its entire civilization.

It was the time of revolution, first in Russia, then in Italy; in Germany the revolution fizzled, and it never came to England, which was, after all, one of the winners of the war. But England was in crisis too: One of its spokesmen, D. H. Lawrence, had already left his country and was busily collecting deserts; finally he settled down in Taos.

In the meantime, the war veteran who would not live except in England tried to fit the shattered pieces of his life together. But they would no longer match. That made him what we now call a displaced or maladjusted person. Because it was not in his nature to express himself in any fashion short of the spectacular, he joined at once the company of England's great eccentrics.

They had always been a fixture of that country, so the odd behavior of the man at once established him as a figure in which England could take an indulgent pride. His shock tactics not only failed to shock his public, but endeared him to it. His deliberate "downward mobility" filled many whose existence was conventional with something like a sneaking admiration; those condemned to live a humdrum life find vicarious satisfaction in the daring of those living dangerously. England slept, but her sleep was uneasy, haunted by bad dreams, and Lawrence acted out those dreams for all to see, projecting them onto the public screen. Exaggeration, self-dramatization thus fulfilled a necessary function. In that symbolic Punch-and-Judy show, ex-Colonel Lawrence, now called Airman Shaw, became the rebel against old routine and obsolete authority; his pranks delighted his vast audience even if their deeper meaning remained unintelligible to most. His myth, self-engineered or not, for *them* it had reality. He was the bold deserter from *their* arid desert, the insurgent against a whole, unintelligible system they knew they would not dare to change. It was the kind of personal revolt they could still endorse, for it took place within and not without the system. It may strike us as a half-hearted sort of rebellion, as a classic case of what the upright Marxist would call "petty bourgeois radicalism": loud but ineffective and recoiling from the logical conclusion. But in fact, what Lawrence did was much more damaging than any overt action. It was possibly the most original way of combatting the establishment. By serving instead of attempting to destroy authority, he undermined it as effectively as conditions would permit. It was the very fact that he belonged to the Establishment as a voluntary menial that so endeared him to a country that refused to have its Lenin or its Hitler. Lawrence was a substitute, the only man who in his lifetime became myth, the only myth-man coming out of the great war. Churchill's hour would not arrive until the next great war, and Lawrence was the only one to fill the void, the common need.

But because his revolution did not face the question of a new authority, it militated against all authority. The hour of the "original anarch" had arrived.

It arrived; it passed; because the anarch balked at the idea of translating his personal rebellion into any "movement." It is more than likely that, if given the chance of becoming England's "leader," he would not have taken it but once more "dodged off" to a sideline.

What, then, *was* his revolutionary message? Inasmuch as Lawrence never clearly verbalized but "merely" lived it, we will have to guess. The atmosphere of mystery surrounding Lawrence served him well as a protective screen; it also magnified the ambiguity of his position. He was called a prophet and a saint; so possibly his very failure to communicate was deliberate refusal, and the silence was the message?

His hankering for anonymity cannot be questioned. But it brought him only pseudo-anonymity. He always remained in the world and knew it. His self-degradation was his form of service, and his place of service was within the only institution left for him—the only monastery not closed to the unbeliever which still stood intact and outside the disorder of the market place. Not that he had the slightest faith in soldiering; but while there was no longer anything worth fighting for, he stood guard waiting for the old flag to be lowered and a new one to be hoisted. He flinched from the notion of becoming a leader, except in the sense intended by George Fox, in Bernard Shaw's play, *In Good King Charles's Golden Days,* when saying: "I desire Friends, not followers."

The vision of a leader against "leaders," fighting in the Permanent Resistance, neither proletariately nor otherwise confined by anything less that the notion of humanity—there was the hint, the hope, the message of the man. There it still is.

In Italy and Germany the counterrevolution met with no overt and violent resistance; in Spain it prevailed only after a protracted civil war. In Italy and Germany the challenge to the state came from political mass movements tolerated by bureaucracies and armies. The Spanish insurrection came from the army, and although enlisting popular support, remained an army' matter. Against the generals, the ruling politicians mobilized the masses but could not unite them behind the Republic. Behind the civil-war front, soon another civil war broke out: The Spanish anarchists, distrustful of the state, of any state, defied the organizers of defense, the communists who tried to suppress the Bakuninites just as Karl Marx had tried it in his time. Marx won another battle, but the Spanish republic lost the civil war.

11 The Sputtering Fuse: Spain

ARMY AND ANARCHY

Spain ought to be the paradise of revolutionologists: In the past century alone, that country has had four major civil wars (1820, 1833-1840, 1854, 1868-1873) or, according to Sir Henry Maine's count, "forty military uprisings." [1]

Spain is, however, nothing of the sort. Its revolutionary record merely baffles and dejects the reader. Oversaturated with upheavals that seem merely repetitious and not in the least indicative of any real changes in the social system, he can see no reason why those Spanish revolutions and *pronunciamentos* had to happen.[2]

---

1. *Popular Government*, Preface, 1885, p. 16; cited by K. C. Chorley in *Armies and The Art of Revolution* (London, 1943), p. 100.

2. "The throne of Isabel II was in a precarious state. The Liberal Union was the only party that could withstand the tide of revolution. The old Progressive Party, now called the Liberal Party . . . advocated a constitutional regime of the European type . . . its members devoted most of their time to opposing the ultraconservatives, who were complete reactionaries. The Moderates became the Conservative Party. . . . The radicals of this party were constitutionalists. The center was larger but its principal objective was despotism. . . . A more conservative group . . . while sus-

Why, then, was the Spanish turmoil so endemic and so violent without producing any tangible result? One is reminded of the Sherlock Holmesian dog who did not bark: The significant point about Spain in the nineteenth century was that the revolution did *not* happen, for the simple reason that the revolution of the age, a bourgeois revolution, was still meaningless for Spain. Accordingly, the Spanish answer to it was at first a sullen silence. The rejection became violent when the intrusion from the French side of the Pyrenees became invasion by a foreign *army*. The reaction of the Spanish people could be all the more unanimous as the French revolution came to them, not in its prime, but in its late, imperial and imperious version, which, if Spengler is to be believed, was, in the last analysis, a British thing: "The tragic in Napoleon's life . . . was that he, who rose into effective being by fighting British policy and British spirit . . . completed by that very fighting the continental victory of this [commercial and industrial] spirit." [8] By the same irony, the Spanish allies of the Iron Duke became the first to sap the power of the Emperor but without benefit to their own country: Their revolt against the French was at the same time a rejection of the now triumphant "British Century"; it was the Spanish counterrevolution against Europe. The guerrilla war against Napoleon deflected Spanish history as much as the attack by the old monarchies had changed the course of the young French republic. With this difference: The French regime became more *radical*, whereas the Spanish masses battled the invader in defense of Church and Crown. Their war for independence was not favorable to the evolution of political and social freedom for a century.

---

taining civil authority, tolerated infractions of the constitution and appeared to support absolutism. The third party was the Liberal Union. Organized by O'Donnell, it consisted of the temperate liberals. . . . They were joined by the liberal conservatives of the Moderate Party, who opposed both reaction and absolutism. . . ." Rhea Marsh Smith, *Spain: A Modern History* (Ann Arbor, 1965), p. 334. No wonder the throne of Isabel II was in a precarious state. So is the mental health of the confounded reader.

3. *Decline of the West* (New York, 1939), Vol. I, p. 149. See also *ibid.*, pp. 150–51.

THE LUNAR DESERT

Each country has its poor, but Spain is a poor country. Heirs of a defunct imperial past, the Spaniards always have been, and still are, conditioned by their early role as conquering and re-conquering frontiersmen, pushing Africa back to the Straits but never quite expunging it from their own nature. Which leads to all sorts of imaginings about the Spanish character, proud, quixotic, and in love with death. One might in fact consider a foundation even more basic than history and blame the miseries of Spain on its geology:

> To know what we are up against we ought to go to Spain by aeroplane and fly to the centre of it. . . . For the most part we are looking down at steppe which is iced in the long winter and cindery like a furnace floor in the short summer. . . . Nine months of winter, three of hell . . . [Castile's] landscape is the pocked and cratered surface of the moon.[4]

But Andalusia is lush country, a country of large estates and of the largest concentration of exploited rural proletarians. The industrial revolution lagged behind; again the Spaniards seemed to demonstrate that strange unwillingness—or inability—to seize an economic opportunity. Their conquistadors had brought back the gold of the New World. But the hidalgo had no flair for commerce and finance; he left that new field to the Dutch and English interlopers. Similarly, in the nineteenth century, the Spanish urban middle classes seemed unable or unwilling to "understand the connection between capital and production and failed to make the bourgeois revolution which created the powerful industrialists of England, France and Germany. Power remained in the hands of the landlords, and their class enemy was the peasantry. It was a situation which favored the anarchism preached by Bakunin." [5]

But that was later. In the meantime, in the absence of *articulate* industrial and rural anarchism, there was anarchy. It found expression in perennial struggles between upper-class traditionalists and progressivists, with neither side prevailing. Hence that "equi-

4. V. S. Pritchett, *The Spanish Temper* (New York, 1954), pp. 4, 5, 38.
5. Robert Melville, "Picasso Dismissed," *New Statesman*, November 12, 1965, p. 758.

librium of instability" characteristic of the period between 1820 and 1874. The bourgeois revolution did not happen, and reaction did not fully triumph. To explain the reason for that deadlock two hypotheses suggest themselves: (1) The difficulty was that Spain had revolutionary forces but no genuine revolutionary situation to resolve, the class struggle still being in the early stages of bourgeois ascendancy. (2) The dilemma of Spain was precisely that the country was in a persistent revolutionary situation but without sufficient revolutionary forces to resolve it.

The historic record indicates that the second is closer to the truth than the first. In theory the situation was impossible and should have led to a complete paralysis if not to the breakdown of the body politic. But even anarchy will seldom lack the *mediating* organisms or institutions to maintain it in a state of being. Spain was fortunately not without them, although "two organizations only showed coherence and a capacity for disciplined action. These were the Church and the Army." [6] While the landowners looked to the Church to sanction the old social order, progress found its agents among Spanish army officers who, as a rule, were not recruited from the aristocracy but from the middle or even the lower middle class. It was the well-known situation in which backward countries find themselves: The army has to take the place of the still absent or still undeveloped social forces and becomes a social force in its own right. The Spanish officers corps had been prepared to play that role, although not always able to perform it, ever since "the collapse of Spain's colonial empire [had] thrust an inflated army back into metropolitan Spain. Hence the persistence of the *Ancien Regime*, the over-officered, underpaid, bureaucratic army, a branch of the civil service rather than a fighting machine." [7]

FOUR MILITARY TYPES

It may be useful to sketch a typology of army leadership on the basis of the functions it performs within the social structure. There is:

a. The army as one of the pressure groups; specifically as a public pressure group, akin to other groups of civil servants, such

6. Chorley, *op. cit.*, p. 99.
7. A. R. M. [Raymond] Carr, "Spain," in Michael Howard, *Soldiers and Government* (London, 1957), p. 137.

as government employees, postal clerks, and others, but, of course, incomparably more powerful.

b. A praetorian force, prepared to intervene in the political process, threatening, or actually resorting to, force, on behalf and in the service of a political faction.

c. A praetorian army intervening in the political process *in lieu* of other (sometimes nonexistent) political forces, making itself master of the state, but in the long run helpless without civilian guidance.

d. A political army properly speaking, acting on its own and trying to impose on the community an ideology that has assimilated, or originated, a full-fledged political and social program. This type is very rare; for two examples, see chapter 4, above, and chapter 12, below.

The Spanish army ran through all these stages; sometimes it straddled more than one, and even more than two of the four here identified positions. That is why historians sometimes seem to contradict each other and why even the same writer seems to contradict himself. For instance, Salvador de Madariaga gives a classical description of the soldier politician:

> He does not come to politics through the intellectual roads of the university and in his tender years. He arrives late, when he has already made his mark in the army. . . . His first attitude, therefore, is apt to be that of a natural observer who finds fault with "that whole lot of talkers" and feels sure that he can put everything right if he is only left to apply decent military methods. . . . He knows what is good. He sees what is good. He wants to go there direct. An argument is an obstacle.[8]

This characterization corresponds to both types B and C above: The Spanish officer is obviously a "military politician" among civil politicians who "can hope, not merely to be obeyed, but to be heard." His means are direct, military, but his ends do not transcend the limits of conventional, civilian politics. "We find [him] now on the liberal side (Riego), now on the reactionary side (Narvaez), now in a dubious zone hesitating between liberal leanings and friendships and a reactionary temperament (O'Donnell)." But "whether liberal or reactionary in his ideas, the Spanish military politician is a reactionary by temperament. He wants to have his way, not to pool his ideas or wishes."[9]

8. *Spain* (New York, 1930), pp. 96, 97.
9. *Ibid.*, p. 99, 96, 97.

The same author argues, quite convincingly, that "militarism is hardly a correct word in the case of Spain." Its army was unlike that of imperial Germany where "a military caste controlled the national policy. In Spain there is no such thing, and the evil would be better described as praetorianism." [10]

This is confusing, since Spain's policy *was* frequently controlled by her "praetorians." What Señor de Madariaga means, and says, is that, unlike the German army officer, his Spanish counterpart formed "by no means a caste." He "controls the political life of the nation" though "giving but little thought to foreign affairs." What matters to him is "the preservation of power" and "the administration and enjoyment of a disproportionate amount of the Budget." [11]

Almost imperceptibly, the author is here shifting to type A: the army as a pressure group, "branch of the civil service rather than a fighting machine," in the already cited words of Raymond Carr.[12]

Madariaga seems to have involved himself in contradictions. But not really. There is no reason why military politicians should not also constitute an economic pressure group; the two types are in fact quite complementary. The author's shift from political to pressure-group praetorianism is historically justified. The early army liberals hoped to reform and stabilize the state, with scant results. The sequence of *pronunciamentos* is a record of increasing disenchantment with progressivist ideas. The politically minded soldiers become more and more praetorian looking for an able king or statesman to bail them out of economic trouble, be he conservative or liberal; the public-minded military corporation is transformed into another vested interest.

It would be superficial to blame the calamities of nineteenth-century Spain on the army, for the army could usurp the functions of the state only because there was no state. The true opponent of the military was not this or that civilian coterie but the inherent anarchism of the Spanish people. And drawn from the Spanish people, the military men shared that propensity for anarchism, so violently antithetic to the view of military discipline: "Since every Spaniard is a unique political party in his own right and the military men are not immune to this individualism,

10. *Ibid.*, p. 237.
11. *Ibid.*
12. See above, p. 174, note 7.

they intervened in civil affairs not as soldiers but as Spaniards for what they considered the general welfare. They have led the nation out of many difficult situations, just as their subservience to tradition has produced others." [13]

This explains the failure of the Spanish military politicians to create a stable social system, also why the Spanish army did not, like its Prussian counterpart, become a homogeneous caste, or ruling class: The Spanish civil war in permanence was fought by army factions facing other army factions, one or both of them aligned with some civilian party, not one of them strong enough to crush the opposition. Only general exhaustion brought some temporary simulacrum of stability.

THE SPANISH ANSWER

"The basic assumptions of anarchism are all contrary to the development of large-scale industry and of mass production and consumption." [14] Anarchism is the Spanish "No!" to modern Europe. Its philosophy was first articulated in another backward country: Russia. (Although William Godwin in England had expressed this earlier, he had remained an isolated figure there.) One wonders why! Was it because a primitive society, when *suddenly* attacked by an advanced technology, imported from abroad, will be more sensitive to the experience, suffering a deeper trauma than did European society in which the process was indigenous and gradual?

But anarchism did not wait for a Bakunin to emerge; it was a natural, spontaneous attitude toward existence in society as old as the emergence of the *state.* In Nietzsche's view:

> the fitting of a hitherto unchecked and amorphous population into a fixed form . . . could only be accomplished by acts of violence and nothing else. . . . The oldest "State" appeared consequently as a ghastly tyranny, a grinding ruthless piece of machinery which went on working, till this raw material of a

13. Smith, *op. cit.,* p. 479.
14. James Joll, *The Anarchists* (Boston, 1964), p. 277. "When workers and peasants saw the Church allying itself with the industrial order, they lost their faith, and anarchism became a religion. It was preferred to Communism and Socialism because it was not materialistic, because it rejected industrial capitalism altogether and regarded the whole system as morally corrupting." V. S. Pritchett, *op. cit.,* p. 264.

semi-animal populace was not only thoroughly kneaded and elastic, but also moulded.[15]

Anticipating Freud's *Civilization and Its Discontents*, the Nietzschean genealogy of man's domestication is concerned not merely with the fact of his subjection, but—and even mainly— with the necessary internalization of that fact by the very "instinct of freedom forced back, trodden back, imprisoned within itself, and finally only able to find vent and relief in itself: this, only this, is the beginning of the 'bad conscience.' " [16]

This leads to the dichotomy of master-slave moralities (already recognized by Hegel in his *Phenomenology of Mind*) and to the Marxian alienation of the worker emptying himself into the product of his labor. It is, perhaps, the reason for the enduring vitality of such a preindustrial philosophy as anarchism that Marx remained concerned with *economic* alienation proper, whereas anarchism anticipated technological frustration.

It remained for Jacques Ellul to reinterpret the dichotomy of man and machine as dialectical and to proclaim "the great law . . . that all things are necessary to make a society and that even revolt is necessary to make a technical society." [17]

Anarchism, in that author's view, is an essential part of modern, technological society. What he calls "ecstasy," that is, all the "anarchic and antisocial tendencies as well as the more pleasant transports we usually associate with it," is the ground of war as well as of religion." [18]

Without these creative—and destructive—instincts technological society would die. So it must try to make them serviceable. In that struggle, the anarchist elites fail to attain their ends, but their attempt is not a total loss, because the happy few of anarchism mediate for all the millions of potential but not actual rebels their need for revolt and simultaneously appease it. "Their essential function is to act as vicarious intermediaries, to integrate into the technical society the same impulses and feelings which . . .

15. *The Genealogy of Morals,* section 17.
16. *Ibid.,* section 17, end.
17. Jacques Ellul, *The Technological Society* (Paris, 1954, and New York, 1965), p. 424.
18. *Ibid.,* p. 420, translator's note. But after 1936, the Spaniard Gaston Laval wrote that "war and anarchism are two conditions of humanity that are mutually repugnant; one is destruction and extermination, the other is creation and harmony; one implies the triumph of violence, the other the triumph of love." Cited by Burnett Bolloten in *The Grand Camouflage* (New York, 1961), p. 218.

would otherwise escape the jurisdiction of the technical society and become a threat to it." [19]

Ellul ends on a note of resignation. He expects that "with the final integration of the instinctive and the spiritual . . . the edifice of the technical society will be completed." Then, he continues:

> We shall have nothing more to lose, and nothing to win. . . .
> And the supreme luxury of the society . . . will be to grant the bonus of useless revolt and of an acquiescent smile.[20]

It is an Orwellian note, but Ellul's pessimism is French in its wry irony. He may still be too optimistic, for the strain that technological society imposes on its members may become too heavy and with a resurfacing of the anarchic instincts, the completed edifice may come crashing down in a colossal act of self-destruction.

WAY STATIONS TO SUICIDE

It was the tragedy of Spain that, when she had to face the supreme test, her government did not succeed in integrating the anarchic forces. They demanded All or Nothing. Only when the fall of the Republic was already imminent did the elites of anarchism, as Ellul would call them, recall their mediating role and join the ruling coalition, too late to stop Franco.

The story of the Civil War of 1936, not as a Spanish tragedy but as a world experience, remains to be written. The tragedy can easily be traced in the works, autobiographical or fictional, of French, English or American left-wing intellectuals, some of whom fought and died at the front. But less easy to isolate is the residue left in the minds of those who were young in the 1930s and who are now the old liberals. Their present numbness may well be the lasting effect of those years: the numbness of defeat. Their faith in the unerring good sense of The People, in the strength of the Great Proletarian, soured and became cynicism and political immobilism.

The Spanish people lost. But nothing can deprive them of the glory that they were the only ones in Europe who did not sub-

19. Ellul, *op. cit.*, pp. 423, 425, 426.
20. *Ibid.*, pp. 426-27.

mit to fascist rule without a fight. The fact that they were also the illiterates of Europe is disturbing. Could it be that education saps, instead of strengthening, the vigor of the body politic? [21]

The counterrevolution, which became a war in 1936 and lasted until 1939, began in 1923, when Primo de Rivera began playing Strafford to his Spanish Charles I, Alfonso XIII. Like his successor, Franco, Primo was a general, and his regime was strictly military. He lacked a political philosophy and the political mass basis that his son, José Antonio, worked out later. This lack explains the father's inability to intercept the revolution. His regime was never more than a benevolent dictatorship, and his withdrawal, after six years of maneuvering, was inevitable when the army, which had made him great, deserted him.

His master's abdication followed one year later, and Spain became a republic, the third European republic to come into being by default within a span of fourteen years. Now, after Russia (1917) and Germany (1918), democracy inherited the problems of a bankrupt monarchy in Spain (1931). It was a bloodless triumph, and few Spaniards guessed that it was not the end but only the beginning of a long and savage struggle.

The new rulers, a loose grouping of the Center-Left, combining bourgeois radicals and right-wing socialists, worked against time to do something about Church disestablishment and land reform. The dislocations of the past called for astringent social remedies, which in turn were bound to create new social dislocations and severe resentments. Wavering between impatience and timidity, the governors of the Republic disappointed their own followers and frightened the conservatives and moderates. The conflict could not be contained within the government; it soon involved the masses and so reached the streets. The provocation came first from the Right, not so much from the Monarchists as from intransigent high churchmen. Now the pent-up rage of centuries against the institution, which for the poor peasants had become identified with their own servitude, exploded in defilement and destruction of church property. The mass killings of priests came later. They are, of course, inexcusable, as are the acts of retaliation that were, after 1936, committed by the other

21. This question was raised by a German, Bernhard Guttmann, in "Die Aussichten der Freiheit" [The Prospects of Freedom] in *Die Gegenwart* (Stuttgart, August 31, 1947).

side. The terrible statistics of this war [22] only indicate that revolutions are not choosy in their human materiel. Its list includes both saints and criminals, fanatics and idealists, religious cranks and social crackpots, homosexuals, sadists, masochists, executives and executioners, drunks, millenarians, millionaires, sensation seekers, power addicts, addicts, intellectuals, morons.[23]

The first *pronunciamentos* of the Army were not slow in coming (late in 1932): One centered in Madrid and "frankly Monarchist—the first sign of a violent resurgence of Monarchism that had yet occurred. . . . Its rapid suppression, with its failure to evoke any marked popular response, must have been a sore blow to Alfonsist aspirations." [24]

General Sanjurjo's rising in Seville, likewise a failure, was non-Royalist in character and gives, in retrospect, a foretaste of things to come: an army insurrection not tied to the past and trying to exploit the growing discontent of both Republicans and Rightists.[25]

In addition, the Republic of the Left had to contend with the old trouble of all central Spanish governments: the polycentric tendencies most marked in Catalonia and the Basque frontier country along the Pyrenees. A Statute granting Catalan autonomy did not resolve the issue between Barcelona and Madrid; Spain's "Irish question" would remain perplexing.

In November 1933, the general elections disavowed the leftist government. A right-of-center coalition tried to steer the revolution into calmer waters. To the Left this was no mere recoil: It was the counterrevolution. The response came one year later: Catalonia, stronghold of the anarchist organizations, went on strike in 1934 (October); the Asturian miners followed suit and rose in arms against the government of the industrialist, Gil

22. According to Hugh Thomas, *The Spanish Civil War* (New York, 1961), Appendix II, "The Casualties of the War," p. 631, "the number of deaths . . . is customarily held to be one million," whereas the victors "estimated the numbers of assassinated on the Republican side at three to four hundred thousand. . . . Now, however, the calculation for those killed in that way has sunk to about 86,000. . . . The total number of Nationalist 'atrocities' . . . is unlikely to have been greater than 40,000."

23. This is a poor paraphrase of that great catalogue of counterrevolutionary elements provided by Marx in *the 18th Brumaire of Louis Bonaparte*, cited above, p. 101.

24. E. Allison Peers, *The Spanish Tragedy* 1930-1936 (New York, 1936), p. 117.

25. "*No era eso*—It wasn't this that we expected—said to have been first used by the eminent philosopher Don José Ortega y Gasset." *Ibid.*

Robles. The administration, which called itself republican, repressed the rising in a short but costly civil war.[26]

In the next election, in the early months of 1936, the revolutionary pendulum swung back to its position left of center, and the coalition of the *Frente Popular* took power. The attempt to stabilize the revolution short of civil war had failed. There was rioting in the streets, burning of churches, and an ever growing number of assassinations. Time, so the army leaders thought, to intervene and restore order.

Once more, General Sanjurjo was to be in charge of operations, but he perished in a plane crash. General Mola looked like his successor, but he proved no match for Franco, who was in control of all the Spanish units in Morocco. With the help of these tough troopers it should have been easy.

But the generals miscalculated. Spain was no longer the country that meekly accepted the *pronunciamento* like an act of God. The civil war became a struggle between armies in the field, around Madrid, along the Ebro, around Teruel, fighting for control of territory, of communication centers, for supremacy in natural resources. And from the start, resources, in manpower and material, were in short supply on either side. They had to look for foreign help. It came, in strength, to the insurgents, both from Italy and Germany; while the Republic was helped, to a lesser degree, by the Soviet Union. The internal struggle had become the dress rehearsal for the next world war.

A THREE-CORNERED CONTEST

The Spanish civil war not only split the nation into two camps; the dividing line ran also through those classes not initially opposed to the Republic. The whole situation was not unlike that of revolutionary England around 1640, when the forces previously united behind Parliament against an autocratic king split ranks as Parliament became intransigent and drove the moderates into the royal camp. In Spain, the process of republican disintegration was more gradual. The initial, fast success of the insurgents forced the government to mobilize the masses, since the army

26. Official figures "showed a total of 1,335 killed, of whom 1,051 were civilians. . . . The wounded numbered 2,951, rather more than two-thirds of whom were civilians. The buildings destroyed or damaged by fire totaled 730." *Ibid.*, p. 171.

cadres, with few exceptions, had deserted to the other side. A new republican defense force had to be created, so to speak, from scratch. This meant that it would be an army of the working class, and proletarian sacrifices had to be rewarded by a larger share in the political direction of the struggle. The Republic slowly gravitated to the extreme Left. Already "by the summer of 1936, the number of those who supported 'humanist socialism' and democratic processes as conceived in 1931 was diminishing rapidly. The militants were taking over from the moderates, the forces of political life had become polarized at the extremes." [27]

It proved to be the unchanged Spanish tragedy: The masses fought for the Republic, but they would not willingly submit to the authority of a strong Spanish *state*—which would have been the correct answer to the threat confronting democratic freedom. The late and reluctant entry of the syndicalist leaders into the official government did not reflect the true conviction of their followers. It spoke with an authentic voice in this confession of a fighting anarchist:

On some nights . . . I would rise from behind my parapet as if in a dream . . . gripping my rifle with a frenzied desire to fire, not merely at the enemy sheltered barely a hundred yards away, but at the other concealed at my side, the one who called me comrade. . . . In the barracks, I was on the verge of losing my personality, so severe was the treatment and the stupid discipline they tried to impose on me. . . . The militarists have surrounded us. Yesterday we were masters; today they are. . . . The popular army, which has nothing popular about it except that the people form it . . . does not belong to the people but to the government, and it is the government that commands, it is the government that gives orders . . .[28]

This must have been a typical reaction of the anarchist militias to the government decree incorporating them into the Army. The old feud between the Hebrew prophets and their kings was re-enacted by the followers of Mikhail Bakunin and Karl Marx on Spanish soil. Marx won the battle, but he lost the war, although the Communist Third International used every means, including "liquidation" of their anarchist opponents, to bring order into the confusion. It is a moot question whether the Republic could have

27. Raymond Carr, "The Spanish Tragedy," *The New York Review of Books* (November 25, 1965), pp. 23–24.
28. From the anarchist newspaper, *Nosotros*, March 12–13, 15–17, 1937, cited by Burnett Bolloten, in *op. cit.*, p. 218.

won the war without the massive intervention benefitting mostly Franco's side. But there can be no question that the civil war behind the front lines hastened the Republican collapse: "By May 1937 political infighting and communist tactics had destroyed the revolutionary coalition," while "on the other side built-in loyalties and the army imposed unity on Nationalist dissidents. A feuding government was fighting a political monolith." [29]

Comparatively speaking, this is true. The contrast between the two Spains at war made Franco's nationalist half indeed look like a monolith. On the Republican side, a weak multi-party government tried desperately to consolidate resistance, even if that meant accepting communist control. The anarchists fought bravely their own war, not that of the Republic. All they cared about was their own stronghold, Catalonia, while Castile, with the besieged Madrid, remained a distant, alien country.

It is the old Spanish story. The surprising thing is that the followers of Franco, being also Spaniards, acted differently. Their own factional and regional disputes, which were as passionate as those of their opponents, remained muted:

> There were almost as many possible fissures in the Nationalist side as there were among the Republicans. The delay in obtaining victory, and the incessant disappointments, gave many chances for the solidarity of the Nationalists to collapse. . . . Agreement . . . was made easier by a certain class desperation. . . . But it was Franco who turned this desperation, this fear of defeat . . . into engines of war.[30]

LA CONQUISTA DEL ESTADO

The decisive fact about the Spanish counterrevolution was that it began, and in the end remained, an army insurrection. This explains why the Nationalist camp was better disciplined, or why existing dissidence was never seriously disruptive. Franco's generals considered the whole territory occupied by their troops simply as a military zone subject to martial law, and their civilian sympathizers realized that they had better go along.

29. Carr, *op. cit.*, p. 24 For contemporary testimonials of "the other civil war," see Franz Borkenau, *The Spanish Cockpit* (London, 1937), and George Orwell, *Homage to Catalonia* (London, 1938); for a strongly anticommunist account, see Bolloten, *op. cit.*
30. Thomas, *op. cit.*, p. 610.

So much for discipline. But discipline was not enough. The population ruled from Burgos and Seville had also to be given a belief transforming a campaign of military mutineers into an ideological crusade. That much, however, was not in the power of praetorian generals to give. It was their old predicament: They had the will and they had the guns, but no idea what to do beyond the negative aim of destroying the Republic.

Their trouble was not that no ideology existed, for it did, but that it had developed independently and now made bold to discipline the population along lines distasteful to the military mind. The Spanish variant of Italian fascism, emphatically Catholic but at the same time social-revolutionary, had some interesting founding fathers, many of whom became martyrs in and after 1936. Ramon Ledesma Ramos had in 1931 proclaimed the program in the very title of his magazine, called *La Conquista del Estado*. But no state existed. It had to be *built*. Ledesma's articles of faith asked for a "politique of military feeling, of responsibility and struggle." The convergence of the military and civilian counter-revolution was in fact remarkable. "The centers of the movement were to be 'military-type teams without hypocrisy before the rifle's barrel.' " [31]

It was this very closeness of ideas that made the *Falange* [32] so distasteful to the generals. They rejected the civilian competition just as passionately as the German *Reichswehr* had refused the wholesale fusion with the brown shirt cadres. Hitler ruled in favor of the Army; the result was the great purge of 1934, which was a pyrrhic victory for the conservative professionals.

In Spain, the outcome of the confrontation was quite different. There Franco, the professional, won out over the para-military fascists. With the help of his Soustelle, who happened to be his brother-in-law, Ramon Serrano Suñer, Franco did what Charles de Gaulle would do in 1958 [33]: He confiscated the extremist movement of his insurrection by a real *coup d'état* in April 1937 and incorporated the *Falange* into his own forces. In a way, it was a counterrevolutionary "intercept" within the larger context of the Nationalist counterrevolution. Franco, with his genius

31. Cited by Thomas, *op. cit.*, p 69.
32. See Stanley G. Payne, *Falange: A History of Spanish Fascism* (Stanford, 1961).
33. See below, p. 197 f.

for mediocrity, not only had eliminated his own "anarchist" collaborators as an independent force; he had also, and by the same token, integrated and absorbed its ideological momentum into his own war machine. Thereafter, the *Falange* never were more than one of the various props buttressing Franco's power, but they gave him what he lacked: a semblance of totalitarian *Weltanschauung*. The result, if it did not exactly profit Spain, at least confirms Ellul's thesis that the fuel of disorder is essential to the life of the Establishment. It was, in Franco's case, essentially a military order, but:

> Franco's greatest military success was in fact political. He was politically successful because he treated politics as a department of military science. Political leaders were to General Franco merely divisional commanders. . . . He established himself as the political leader of the most passionately concerned country in the world by a contempt for political feelings. As a result, he was never in any real political danger at any time during the Civil War.[34]

The master politician who can do this does not have to be a general.

The defeat of the Republic cannot be explained by any single cause, but one will note a singular divergence of developments: The legal government was driven to the left by the sharp impact of the counterrevolution but failed in achieving order and coherence *à la Russe*. The counterrevolution, on the other hand, owed whatever popularity it had to its own radical totalitarians but did not, in victory, become totalitarian. Franco's Spain is not a monolith. It sports a feeble fascist ideology, but it is not a fascist system. The regime remains authoritarian,[35] and, true to its origins, a *tetrarchy*. Its structure rests on the four pillars of the Army, Church, Big Business, and *Falange*, in that order of importance, although the *Falange* try hard to assert their role as the

---

34. Thomas, *op. cit.*, 610.

35. "Authoritarian regimes are political systems with limited, not responsible, political pluralism: without elaborate and guiding ideology (but with distinctive mentalities); without intensive or extensive political mobilization . . . and in which a leader (or occasionally a small group) exercises power within formally ill-defined limits but actually quite predictable ones." Juan Linz, "An Authoritarian Regime: Spain," in *Cleavages, Ideologies and Party Systems*, ed. by Erik Allardt and Yrjö Littunen (Turku, 1964), p. 297.

187 The Sputtering Fuse: Spain

main guardian of the corporate organization of society.[36] Francisco Franco himself plays his role of Bonapartist linchpin with compelling artistry, relying more on his astuteness than on charisma. Spain's weakness and the cold war constitute the man's enduring strength.

Through Franco, Spain became at long last a contemporary *state*, still backward but, through her still unofficial but effective Nato affiliation, opened up to the industrial revolution.[37] Technological society was fated to come to the Spaniards, not with democratic institutions but forced on them from outside, first by armed intervention, next by American financial and industrial penetration. For better or worse, Spain has joined the century.

Or has the century joined Franco's Spain?

36. "In the Western world, some sort of corporatism has become a logical response whenever the revolutionary demands of workers cannot be resolved by ordinary economic means. Something very similar to national syndicalism was the only device that could be used to harness the Spanish working class after the outbreak of the war in 1936. This was the indispensable contribution of *falangismo* to the Franco regime. To be sure, the syndical system was organized entirely as the government saw fit, but it was vital nevertheless." Stanley G. Payne, *op. cit.*, p. 267.

37. "The Spanish Cortes (Parliament) meeting in one of its rare plenary sessions, approved today [December 20th] a law that at least in theory legalizes economically inspired labor strikes. . . . This means, in effect, that the unions should be dissociated from the regime's political party, the Falange movement." *The New York Times*, December 21, 1965, p. 18.

In France, the army insurrection (on behalf of French Algeria) was defeated by a general without an army but with popular support. De Gaulle's success is an example of a counterrevolution that prevented a potential revolution. Interposing himself between a rebellious army and a government he despised, the providential man got rid of both and took advantage of the Bonapartist opportunity to organize a state power essentially based on his personal authority. But in another sense, the grand old man merely presides over a technological and managerial revolution of which he is the unconscious agent rather than the representative and leader. Charles de Gaulle is here viewed as another Cromwell, as a figure of transition trying in vain to consolidate the flux.

12 Augustus Before Caesar: De Gaulle

STRENGTH AND WEAKNESS OF A COMMONWEALTH

Two years before he made his revolution,[1] Lenin asked himself the question: "What, generally speaking, are the symptoms of a revolutionary situation?" and his answer was that there were three of them: (1) there must be a split within the ruling class, which weakens its control; (2) "the want and suffering of the oppressed classes have become more acute than usual"; and as a consequence of (1) and (2), there will be (3) "a considerable increase in the activity of the masses."[2]

[1]. "The role the professional revolutionists played in all modern revolution is great and significant enough, but it did not consist in the preparation of revolutions. . . . Not even Lenin's party of professional revolutionists would ever have been able to 'make' a revolution; the best they could do was to be around, or to hurry home, at the right moment, that is, at the moment of collapse." Hannah Arendt, *On Revolution* (New York, 1963), p. 263. This was true of the March revolution of 1917, but the November revolution Lenin did prepare and "make."

[2]. Lenin, "The Collapse of the Second International" (Summer, 1915), *Selected Works* (New York, 1943), Vol. V, p. 174. As summed up by *Historicus* (George Kennan), "Stalin's necessary 'objective' conditions for revolution" were "bourgeoisie isolated and disorganized, proletariat aroused to revolt and supported by the masses, and a favorable balance of proletarian against bourgeois aid from outside the country." "Stalin on Revolution," *Foreign Affairs*, Vol. 27, No. 2 (January, 1949), p. 189.

In short, the weakening of the political elite (which need not be a consequence of the increasing power of the ruled) and greater mass activity (which may be caused by an extrinsic factor, such as war or a depression causing unemployment and mass suffering) have to occur together to create a revolutionary situation. Lenin does not claim that the elite loses strength *because* the opposition gains in strength; there is no necessary causal link between the two phenomena: They merely complement and reinforce each other.

At first, this would not strike us as an earth-shaking discovery. But it is one which, if considered as a starting point, may yield further insights of considerable interest. For one thing, Lenin understood the relativity of power. The disintegration of the ruling class is not enough to make a revolution possible, unless the masses also increase their activity; that is, unless they become stronger. But *this* increase cannot be assumed to follow automatically from *that* decrease.[3]

"Want and suffering of the oppressed" may equally well bring about a weakening of their organizations (labor unions lose notoriously in membership, hence in financial power, during a depression). In that case, the loss in power of the ruling class would have to be considerably greater than the loss in strength of the opposing forces to enable them to rise successfully. In Lenin's case, the power of the bourgeois government had reached its nadir in the fall of 1917, whereas the Bolsheviks, although still a minor party, were in the ascendancy and, failing any strong resistance, could afford to make their bid for power without too much risk. But their success does not bear out the "breakdown theory of power."

One may pursue this trend of thought and think of situations where "power" is not the result of conflicting drives but where the ruling power is, for the time being, uncontested. In that case, a show of governmental strength will not be necessary. This does *not* mean that strength would be lacking in emergencies, only that it need not be in evidence and fully organized. There is no need for that as long as the consensus of the social forces lasts, or if potentially disruptive elements are negligible. The govern-

3. Lenin would not have agreed with Hannah Arendt's claim that "Tocqueville's observation in 1848, that the monarchy fell 'before rather than beneath the blows of the victors, who were as astonished at their triumph as were the vanquished at their defeat,' *has been verified over and over again.*" Arendt, *op. cit.* Our italics.

ment of such a system may be, technically, "weak" to an extreme degree; politically it is likely to be stronger than the most elaborate police state. Power, in this case, is a communal force, invisible and not "in being," but unquestioned. Under such conditions, nothing would seem more unlikely than a civil war. Not even major technological and economic changes need result in social dislocation and political malaise: The "revolution of things" may proceed apace without provoking any revolutionary struggle between men.

But just as a community rent by internal conflict may try to externalize and exorcise its troubles by exporting them, say, by a war, in the vain hope of recreating unity at home by fighting the external, real or imagined, threat,[4] so a community free from or unaware of its domestic problems may be forced to face them in its international relations; for instance, if the nation is unwilling to release dependencies abroad from their colonial bondage in an age of decolonization. In that case, the conflict will recoil upon the mother country, and the problem, germane to the system but cloaked by an outlandish disguise, will be converted into an internal conflict, the more virulent the longer it remains unrecognized.

THE TWO FRANCES

Habitually, that phrase refers to the perennial cleavage between the official French tradition of a democratic lay-republic and the other, Catholic, aristocratic, and monarchic France, which never recognized the revolution and its principles.

But here the term will be employed to point up two divergent tendencies *within* the framework of the French Republic, although both also reflect, at least in part, the other, more traditional distinction.

While the Third Republic lasted—and it lasted longer than all governments preceding it since 1789: for sixty-five years, and its end was not due to internal causes—there was never any lack of critics, foreign and domestic, to bewail the instability of the regime, with its cabinets succeeding one another within months

---

4. The relation of internal and external conflict has been systematically studied by Nicholas S. Timasheff, *War and Revolution* (New York, 1965). About the conjunction of war and revolution, see also Elie Halévy, *The Era of Tyrannies*, transl. by R. K. Webb (Garden City, 1965), pp. 211ff.

or even weeks. At the same time, other critics could be overheard to say that *"plus ça change, plus c'est la même chose,"* meaning that the system was not *really* unstable, for the French executive branch went right on administering the country, thus safeguarding the essential continuity of the regime. That administration has been inherited from the *ancien régime;* its principle of centralized control had become ever more astringent with the times, no matter whether sovereignty had been imperial, royal, or republican.

This bureaucratization of the state conflicted sharply with the fragmentation of the democratic will, the people legislating through their representatives in Parliament. French parties were notoriously unable, and perhaps unwilling, to assure political stability. If not a revolutionary, then a Bonapartist syndrome may be called the typically French affliction. "Bonapartism has a permanent and solid basis in our country. It sums up the call to national grandeur, the monarchic tradition, and the Jacobin fervor for national unity." [5] That fervor becomes fearful if the price of union is the loss of liberty. It is a cloud, most of the time not larger than the hand of such a Bonaparte *manqué* as Boulanger, but it is something built into the very system of a country that, in an emergency, would find it difficult if not impossible to force its will upon a more or less unsympathetic or inert bureaucracy: "The administrative technocracy detests and envies politics, that foolish virgin gadding about in the streets, while she, the wise one, keeps the home." [6]

One instrument of government had never, under the French Third Republic, given any serious cause for apprehension and that was the French army.[7] It had served without much love for the Republic, but served loyally, not ever questioning the constitutional prerogative of the civilian power.

But the Fourth Republic had to send the army overseas to put down two colonial insurrections, first in Indochina, next in Algeria. The Asian territory was lost, and the French army took it hard. When it appeared that the Algerian operation would end with a similar surrender (and Algeria, technically, was a part of France), the army leaders became restive. The colonial war became a problem pitting Frenchmen against Frenchmen; was it

5. François Mitterand, *Le Coup d'état permanent* (Paris, 1964), p. 79.
6. *Ibid.,* p. 168.
7. Well, hardly ever, *l'affaire Dreyfus* being the exception.

threatening to turn into a civil war? Not yet. French intellectuals raised the moral issue of repressing natives fighting for the principles of the French revolution; they made much of the use of torture by the army of a nation just liberated from Gestapo rule.

It was treason. But the army remained hesitant to cross the Rubicon. So the white settlers, not debilitated by the military habit of obedience, formed their own, not in the least clandestine, para-military units in Algeria, to protect Algeria.

THE LINE-UP

The conspirators thought they could depend on the reluctance of the military to use force against their fellow countrymen. If the old generals were loath to gamble, most of the young colonels were converted to the cause.

We meet here with a new phenomenon: French military history knows of praetorian intervention in political affairs, although the number of such interventions tends to be exaggerated. The first Bonaparte, although a soldier, cannot be considered a praetorian in the sense of signifying apolitical, brute force. Napoleon III was a civilian who *made use* of some praetorian generals.[8]

Now, in Algeria, the French officer became an intellectual formulating his own ideology. It was his answer to the ideology that had confronted him in Indochina: Mao Tse-tung's theory of the guerrilla war as a *political* campaign. This answer was at the same time, its inversion, to be serviceable *against* Mao and the assumed global communist conspiracy now threatening Algeria. Transformed by the colonels, and enriched by some civilian thinkers of the extreme Right, the Chinese doctrine had become a theory of counterrevolution. It was, if not an argument for civil war, at least a grand design for the prevention, by all means in the totalitarian arsenal, of civil war.

It has been said of one of the French colonels that "he thinks badly, but he thinks." [9] The new school had its prophets and its pragmatists.

Marcel Bigeard is in the French tradition fathered by such men as Charles Péguy:

8. For a fuller presentation of this argument, see *The Fall of the Republic* (Ann Arbor, 1962) by the present writer, p. 152f.
9. A. P. Lentin, *L'Algérie des colonels* (Paris, 1958), p. 24.

Undisciplined, headstrong, a solitary . . . an innocent who, after struggling dumbly with an obscure private crisis, finally became a holy innocent. . . . Political action was anathema to this man who could rarely, however, keep quiet about political issues. . . . Instead of action on the plane of *la politique* he advocated action on the plane of *la mystique*. . . .[10]

This school had a small class of desert saints: Charles de Foucault, the priest; Ernest Psichari, the religious writer; St. Exupéry, the airman; and Malraux, the writer, joined these men to meet the myth-wish of their generations. The French counterpart of T. E. Lawrence, Bigeard, is the prototype of the new *uomo religioso* whose sect is his paratrooper unit, and whose creed is to give battle to a worthy foe. Bigeard's crusade for French Algeria seems to be no more than an excuse for fighting, enjoyed for its own sake. He is the aging scoutmaster singing of youth, and the lover of death:

Drunk with fatigue, we struggled on. The sharp stones knifed into our boots, our camouflage was torn by thorns. We struggled on by habit: fatigue had become a drug to give oblivion. . . . We were no caravan in search of water. . . . No, our rendezvous behind each corner of the trail, behind each crag, was with our death. To earn the right to die, we had to suffer first. . . .[11]

Bigeard's politics were ludicrous; the true tacticians of French counterrevolutionary warfare were three other colonels: Yves Godard, Antoine Argoud, Roger Trinquier. These men in turn were the disciples of Charles Lacheroy and Lionel-Max Chassin, a General who had "discovered" Mao's revolutionary theories for France.

It was Trinquier who managed to come unscathed through the vicissitudes of the Algerian tragedy, to write the book to end all books on counterrevolutionary theory.

---

10. F. W. J. Hemmings, "Holy Innocents," *New Statesman* (August 20, 1965), p. 258. The sequence of some of the sentences has been reversed.

11. Marcel Bigeard, *Aucune bête au monde*, quoted by Gilles Perrault in his *Les Parachutistes* (Paris, 1961), pp. 158–59; transl. and cited by the present writer in *op. cit.*, p. 138. Another expression of this attitude: "Woe unto those who have not known the silence [of the desert]. It is a bit of heaven descended to man." Ernest Psichari, *Le Voyage du centurion*, *Oeuvres complètes* (Paris, 1948), p. 69. Jean-François Six, *Witness in the Desert, The Life of Charles de Foucault*, transl. by Lucie Noel (New York, 1965).

There is in it no hint of politics, but then the author's entire purpose is to make an end to politics in the traditional sense of the word. Actually, his scheme demands the full politization of the mother country, to defend it against communism. For modern war is "an ensemble of actions of all kinds (political, social, economic, psychological, and military) which envisages *the overthrow of power in one country* and the substitution of a different regime." Against this threat, the nation must react accordingly: by full mobilization, already in peace time—because modern war "is not officially declared as used to be the custom"—and stand faithfully behind its own armed forces. Because this new-type, world-wide civil war, knows no frontiers, it must be fought at home as well as on the ramparts. The external enemy has his internal allies: They must be controlled. Accordingly, the entire country must be structured, overlaid with a whole gridwork of both vertical and horizontal checkpoints.

It is clear by now that politization logically has to end in militarization; the state of emergency becomes routine.[12] If this was madness, it was also perfect logic: If the colonels wished to keep Algeria French, against an apathetic mother country, they had to make France Algerian first.

"LIKE FISH IN THE WATER"

The theory was first tried in Algeria and it failed. It had to fail because the main assumption, that you had to win the people, presupposed that you were among your *own* people. But the natives of Algeria had already "gone over the hill," symbolically speaking. They were siding with their own guerrilla fighters who, indeed, could practice Mao's precept that the revolutionary army should move "like fish in the water,"[13] in the city blending innocently with the crowds after an act of terrorism and in the countryside fed, sheltered, informed by the villagers. It was too late to win these natives back for France with half-hearted concessions. The best efforts of the social workers in French uniform came to grief each time a village they had cared for was strafed by paratroopers trying to destroy a sniper's hide-out. The French

12. Roger Trinquier (Paris, 1961), pp. 15, 45–48, *passim*, 49, 51, 57.
13. Mao, *On Guerrilla Warfare* (New York, 1961), p. 93.

fish could not swim in the native waters; they were too con-
spicuous; they were white.

However, the same theory, when later practiced among *French*
Algerians, was a full success, and the French government was as
helpless in combatting the French terrorists as it had been before,
when trying to flush out their native counterpart. The European
population of the key Algerian cities could be mobilized and
used as a protective screen, once the French counterrevolutionaries, after two conventional uprisings, finally had reached the
point of no return and become killers. Something had gone
wrong with the design to keep the French flag flying in Algeria.
The traditional French cry: *"Nous sommes trahis!"* we've been
betrayed, was heard again in Algiers, the true capital of France
throughout those years. And this time, it was possible to pin the
blame on *one* man, the same man the Army had brought back to
power because he could be expected to defend Algeria against
the Parisian traitors, Charles de Gaulle.

THE DAY OF DUPES

The General, then in retirement, was not popular with the
French Army of Algeria, but his name was still one with which
to conjure. None of the French generals then in command at
Algiers, some of them quite willing to play Franco to the Fourth
Republic, had the charisma of the old man. But would he take
the lead in overthrowing the Republic and would he risk his
reputation?

It has been asserted that no less than thirteen plots were under
way that were to merge into the superplot exploding on May 13,
1958.[14] With the help of a computer, this claim may some day be
verified. Until that day, the number of conspiracies can be
conveniently reduced to three.

There were first the so-called activists including extremists of
all kinds, Pétainists, Poujadists, small but extremely vocal groups
of Monarchists, and of religious *exaltés,* hell-bent on bringing
down the lay-republic, and some army cells of officers who had
ideas about a French national and socialist revival.

Then there was the Army, or, to be exact, the high command,

14. Merry and Serge Bromberger, *Les 13 complots du 13 Mai* (Paris,
1959).

pushed into insurrection by its Young Turks: the new military intellectuals preaching the true gospel after Mao and minus Marx. At the apex of this hierarchy stood General Raoul Salan, an old Indochina hand, a cautious politician, unwilling to burn the bridges of legality.

And third, newly arrived on the scene, the Gaullists, trying to sell their man to Salan.

The outcome is well known: The Algiers activists, not hindered by the Army, stormed the seat of the administration and formed at once revolutionary *comités de salut public*, thereby reverting to the very Jacobin tradition they wanted to expunge from the French record.

It was the counterrevolution against the great revolution, a hundred sixty-nine years old.

The Army managed with some difficulty to restore a modicum of order, but with, not against, the activists who controlled Algiers and the main French centers of Algeria. It was clear that unless the movement could retain its first momentum, it was bound to peter out, for the French mainland showed no sympathy for the extremists. Poujade's tax rebellion had calmed down. With the exception of some rural districts, France was prospering; she did not wish to be disturbed. The Government reacted timidly to the Algerian insurrection, but it did not panic. Not yet.

There was, in short, no revolutionary situation. But it could, perhaps, be engineered. The conflagration must be spread beyond its local limits, into trans-Mediterranean France, by the fully mobilized French Army. But on what authority?

The question was resolved by General Salan on the third day of the rebellion, when he showed himself to the assembled masses and was booed. After some hesitation, and some prompting by a Gaullist standing behind him, he intoned the name of Charles de Gaulle, and the crowd cheered. What seemed to be a leonine pact between an all-powerful French Army and a venerated figurehead had been concluded. It was formalized a few days later by De Gaulle's proconsul, Jacques Soustelle, a former governor of French Algeria, very popular with the white element. Soustelle played Bonaparte to Charles de Gaulle's Sieyès by making him acceptable to the Algerian Vichyites who still detested the old liberator. Some years later, Jacques Soustelle would find the roles exchanged, when his chief, no longer a diffident Sieyès but a serene Augustus, dismissed his lieutenant as a Bonapartist hot-head. Poor Soustelle! He deserved a better fate. But then, all revolutions eat their children, and the counterrevolutions do not like their parents, who might well be revolutionaries in disguise.

The question is: What did De Gaulle know about the con-spiracy of May 13th? We know the answer: He was kept in-formed and he did not discourage the rebellion. When it hesi-tated at the waterfront, De Gaulle encouraged the insurgents to proceed and leapfrog into Corsica, as the last stepping stone to the French mainland. In the meantime, he continued negotiations with the caretakers of the Republic, offering to mediate the quar-rel if they would invest him with supreme authority. Thus, with one hand restraining and the other beckoning to the insurgents, he became acceptable to the French parties as the Prince of Peace and Savior of the Constitution. At the same time, De Gaulle "pocketed the *coup d'état*" [15] and turned it to his own advantage.

But it took him four more years to liquidate the French posi-tion in Algeria.[16] For this, he has been attacked both by the Right—outraged by what they thought to be a breach of prom-ise—and by the French Left, annoyed with what they thought was his procrastination. But no matter what De Gaulle's inten-tions were, he was not a free agent during those four years—not until he had subdued the Army, the one force on which his own authority rested. Until he had weathered two more armed re-bellions and the terror of the "Secret Army," the Algerian settle-ment had to be shelved. De Gaulle throughout that time ruled by a paradox: Returned to power as the Lord Protector of the Right, he ruled, or was believed to rule, as the defender of democracy against the Right. On one occasion, when insurgent troops were rumored about to prepare an airdrop upon Paris, Gaullist ministers officially encouraged something like a latter-day *levée-en-masse*, and ragtag volunteers presented themselves at the armories to fight for the Republic. So De Gaulle's strength may be said to have *depended* on the presence of the hostile army as a "countervailing force," enabling him to rule by a "consensus of anxiety" in a comparatively democratic fashion. As soon as the army and its radical affiliates ceased to be a threat, the weak-

15. Mitterand, *op. cit.*, p. 61.

16. The settlement of 1962 was most unfavorable for the colonists, one million of whom (more than 90 per cent of the total) had to leave Algeria.

ness of De Gaulle's plebiscitarian power base became apparent, and it is no accident—nor the result of one old man's megalomania—that the Fifth Republic, from then on, became increasingly authoritarian.

This development is well attested to by witnesses as far apart as François Mitterand, a Liberal, and Jacques Soustelle, the former Gaullist leader, now a fugitive from Gaullist justice. Mitterand gives chapter and verse, documenting what has happened to the French judicial system, how it has been made subservient to the depolitization of all public life, the prevention of all criticism, particularly criticism of the head of state. Republican legality is being made a mockery; the democratic process has been superseded by the arbitrary rule of the police. The state monopoly of news subverts the pluralism of opinion.[17]

The distinguished archeologist, Soustelle, one of the first to join De Gaulle in London after the *débâcle* of 1940, organizer of his secret service, more than any other man responsible for rallying the army high command behind his patron in 1958, master builder of the UNR,[18] now has to issue his *"J'accuse!"* from unknown places "somewhere in Europe." He accuses the French President of "neo-Caesarism" and speaks of his regime as being "a one-man, one-party autocracy thinly disguised under the veil of a rubber-stamp parliament." He does not stop at calling his old chief a "tyrant." [19]

Should one dismiss this as the fury of a lover scorned, as the resentment of a son whose father image has been shattered?

The case of Jacques Soustelle is not that easily resolved. Here is a man, not unlike Trotsky, who has taken a deep fall and now abjures the gods he once had worshipped. In the early days, he and Michel Debré had been among the Gaullist Jacobins. But it so happened that De Gaulle in power turned to the Gironde and replaced Debré with Georges Pompidou, the banker. Revolutionary history was thus reversed, and Jacques Soustelle found himself relegated to the background. But it was his firm attachment to the cause of French Algeria that led to his break with the regime.

17. See Mitterand, *op. cit.*, pp. 127–247, *passim*.
18. *Union pour la nouvelle République*, the Gaullist party holding a majority in the National Assembly.
19. Jacques Soustelle, *A New Road for France* (New York, 1965), pp. 13, ix, 11. The book is the enlarged English version of *Sur une route nouvelle* (Paris, 1964).

There is no doubt about the deep sincerity of his belief in freedom and Republican legality. True, as a hunted exile he may now feel differently about certain civil rights which, in his fight against the Fourth Republic, he may not have cherished quite as ardently. About Algeria, though, he has not changed his mind; this speaks for his tenacity if not his political acumen. He refused to disavow the Secret Army when it was accused of murderous activities. In 1961 he declared in an interview:

The Algerian *resistance* honors itself by opposing [the abandonment] with all its might. It's struggle is that of all men in love with liberty. . . . The domination of the FLN over Algeria —that would be the greatest of all evils. Against this mortal peril all means ('I repeat: all means') must be employed.[20]

Three years later, his analysis of the Algerian tragedy is more elaborate, more guarded. But he still thinks that the terroristic acts "imputed to the [Secret Army] organization were an understandable reaction to the terrorism of the other side." [21]

It is a pity to see a man of Soustelle's achievement prematurely trapped by an historic avalanche. One of the iron laws of politics says that a leader who commits himself too early in a fluid situation commits suicide.

Confined now to the role of angry prophet in the desert, Jacques Soustelle has time to reflect on his return to a France *sans* De Gaulle. It would be unfair to expect him to be fair to Charles de Gaulle, although he tries and, grudgingly, observes that "the Gaullist regime is the expression of a declining society whose decadence it reflects and at the same time precipitates." [22] A penetrating observation, for De Gaulle himself, a Catholic and, at the same time, pragmatist, only presides over the change now taking place in France; he does not represent or lead it. He is

20. Reprinted in Soustelle's *L'espérance trahie* (Paris, 1962), p. 261. FLN is the Front de libération nationale, the Algerian revolutionary movement. The parenthetical quotation is an ironic reference to words used by de Gaulle when, during the "Four Generals" Putsch of 1961, he enjoined the French army to use all means to restore order, if necessary by committing acts of military disobedience.

21. *A New Road for France* (New York, 1964), p. 71.

22. *Ibid.*, p. 11. "A political system can be said to degenerate . . . when there is a decline in the capacity of the ruling elite to define the purposes of the political system in relationship to society and to express them *in effective institutional terms.* . . ." Zbigniew Brzezinski, "The Soviet Political System: Transformation or Degeneration," *Problems of Communism*, Vol. 15, No. 1 (January–February 1966), p. 14. Our italics.

the mere agent of a "revolution of things" about which he knows next to nothing; as for its meaning he could not care less. But he makes use of all its incidentals: Planning and technological advance serve him to concentrate all the apparent power in his hands, while the new managers hold the effective power, using him as much as he is using them. "The administrative technocracy endorsed the Gaullist victory, but only after the event. The managers obey and aid, they execute and profit but they feel no love. Their real love belongs to the French *State* which they have made their own." [23] The General presides but hardly ever interferes. His thoughts are elsewhere; his designs transcend the limits of the country and the age. He towers over the French land like an erratic block left from the past. He is no member of the present French establishment, although it profits by his presence. Gladly did it pay the price he exacted for his intervention.

THIRD MAN

De Gaulle's achievement was unique in that he triumphed where a Schleicher failed; using tactics that would have aroused the envy of a Machiavelli, he succeeded in arresting an extremist movement, at the same time using it to gain control, to play one side against the other, and emerge as the supreme arbiter. His intercession was superbly timed and executed: Under the pretense of shielding the Republic, he first neutralized and then disarmed all parts in the incipient civil war. He stole the thunder of rebellion from the activists and then proceeded by applying his "disarming" tactics to the politicians of the Fourth Republic.

Double-dealing and self-seeking as he may have been, De Gaulle must nonetheless be credited with having broken the political immobilism of the country, and with hastening the peaceful revolution of the managers and technocrats.[24]

But De Gaulle's success was only a beginning, and the question is: What did he make of his stupendous victory? The rule of the politicos was over, Parliament no longer sovereign. What

23. Mitterand, *op. cit.*, p. 167. Our italics.

24. A counterrevolution really, if one goes all the way back to the first French Revolution; revolution inasmuch as both rebellions, activist and Gaullist-managerial, were directed against the inertia of the Fourth Republic. Many of the military politicians were decidedly unsympathetic to the social *status quo*.

fills the void? What Gaullist institutions spell out the new Gaullist order?

To begin with: It is by no means clear whether there is, or will ever be, a Gaullist order. The new system is, for the time being, an elective monarchy, with Charles de Gaulle as temporary monarch.[25] Some observers have compared his rule to Louis Philippe's July monarchy, while others are reminded of the third Napoleon. But the Bonapartist system lacked the underpinnings of a mass-based, monolithic party structure. There are intimations of that party type in the French Fifth Republic. But the UNR is hardly monolithic. It is a mere congeries of floaters and disintegrated groups that have sought shelter under the umbrella with the famous label. "Gaullist France," Soustelle reminds us, "is not a one-party State, but a State with one official party," which, to be sure, "has the vigorous support of the administration . . . in exchange for a complete, totalitarian submission to the Master's will." [26] That submission is perhaps not quite as total as it looks: "We serve the General," declared the secretary general of the UNR in July 1959, "without receiving direct orders." He continued hastily: "We are his tool, he is not ours." It seems the Lady does protest too much.[27]

The Gaullist party performs best in national elections, but below that level, in municipal and other contests, it still has to show true grass-roots strength. The party managers are vividly aware of how much remains to be done to build the kind of machine strong enough to carry on without De Gaulle. A hard-nosed, very able lot, such party satraps as Fouchet, Frey—and perhaps, again, Debré [28]—cannot count on much help from the patron when it matters most: *between* elections. It is difficult to gauge their progress in creating the conditions under which a Gaullist order could survive without the De Gaulle charisma. The real strength of the regime is elsewhere.

---

25. It is well known that the General would like the Count of Paris to succeed him.

26. *A New Road for France*, p. 235.

27. *Le Monde*, Paris, July 21, 1959, cited in Henri Claude, *Gaullisme et grand capital* (Paris, 1960), p. 19. A Marxist analysis to which we shall return.

28. A few weeks after this was written, Debré returned to power as an economic "Czar" in charge of social legislation. *The New York Times*, January 8, 1966, p. 2. *Cf.* below, pp. 191–92 and note 36 on the deficiencies of Gaullist social policy.

THE FUSION OF BUREAUCRACIES

Intercession of necessity means also reinsertion into the existing socio-economic fabric. No contemporary "tyrant," not even De Gaulle, can govern by mere fiat; the regime depends on substructures, both public and private, if it refuses to rule through elected representatives. However, because the General would not or could not be a revolutionary Caesar, but made bold to start as a serene Augustus, he was forced to make accommodations.

It has already been noted that, whenever the *pays légal* was out of touch with the *pays réal*, or *vice versa*, the estrangement between the French people and their legislators did not lead to much more serious dislocations because the executive branch would step in and carry on. The centralized administration with its network penetrating into all the nooks and crannies of society was in such intervals omnipotent. Its functionaries could feel that they *were* the State, that they "in lieu of all the quarreling and deadlocked parties, and in place of a submissive parliament . . . now were the only ones to represent the absent sovereign." [29]

But that could only be an interim solution, not a full equivalent for the direct assertion of the democratic will. In France, the state bureaucracy before De Gaulle confronted and, at best, directed but did not itself directly operate the vast bulk of the national economy. (The nationalized sector, though important, was still the exception from the capitalist norm.)

The *rapprochement* between the public and the privately controlled administrations was already begun under the Fourth Republic, but the Fifth brought an acceleration of the process that amounted to a "change from quantity to quality." State managerial freedom from the apron strings of Parliament, instead of being the exception, now became the rule. What had been confrontation became interpenetration, almost fusion. Private businessmen and government officials, under "voluntary planning," became interchangeable.

29. Mitterand, *op. cit.,* p. 167. See also Ralf Dahrendorf, *Class and Class Conflict in an Industrial Society* (London, 1959), p. 309: "In its most limiting aspect, the process of political democracy allows for a rapid succession of governments which can prevent any one ruling group from remaining in power long enough to make its influence felt. For all practical purposes, the top of the political hierarchy of authority is unoccupied. In this case, the bureaucracy of the state becomes its own master."

The business affiliations of the Gaullist ministers and party leaders are no secret; Marxist propaganda had a field day demonstrating "the true nature" of the new regime. One might have guessed it. The example *par excellence* is the Prime Minister, Georges Pompidou, a Rothschild man; Couve de Murville, the Foreign Minister, was "sent into the government" by *l'Union Parisienne-Mirabeaud;* a third bank, *Lazard Frères,* has their man, Louis Jacquinot, in still another ministry (his wife owns 20 per cent of Lazard stock). Giscard d'Estaing, the ex-Minister of Finance "represents" (again by marriage) the Schneider-Creuzot armament combine. Debré, De Gaulle's first Premier, is another monetary oligarch. And so one could go on for pages, citing from the Marxist black book.[30] De Gaulle himself turns out to be affiliated, through his mother, with most powerful industrial interests in Northern France, while brother Pierre had served as a director with the Paris bank firm mentioned in connection with the Foreign Minister. So one is not surprised to learn that "De Gaulle has been the instrument enabling the grand bourgeoisie to smash the obstacles which blocked its way to total domination over France." [31]

Thus, in the Marxist view, De Gaulle is not another Bonaparte,[32] for he is clearly taking orders from a class. But it is one which had not been the undisputed ruling class before. "The Gaullist regime is an original version of the dictatorship of Big Capital which has broken with traditional bourgeois democracy; *but it is not fascism.*" The rule of finance capital and the reduction of parliament are two decisive landmarks in "the general evolution of French capitalism after the second world war." However, this has to be qualified, because "the economic base of Gaullism does not extend over the whole of French capitalism but is confined *to its most modern and most cosmopolitan part—* the part which forms *the spearhead of a capitalism invigorated by* [state-directed] *economic planning.*" Under De Gaulle, the French economy has reached "the most advanced capitalistic stage: that of monopoly state capitalism." [33]

There is more here than meets the eye.

The admission that De Gaulle's rule is not fascist may seem

---

30. Henri Claude, *op. cit.,* pp. 33ff.
31. *Ibid.,* p. 71.
32. In the non-Marxist sense, defended in this study. See above, chapter 6.
33. *Ibid.,* pp. 208–9. Our italics.

startling, for in the official Marxist canon fascism is the political form of monopoly capitalism in crisis: Fascism is bourgeois decadence.

But the economy of Gaullist France, we just have been informed, is anything but decadent, and therefore Gaullism cannot be fascist. *Q.E.D.*

The non-Marxist agrees: Resistance to De Gaulle, right after his return to office, did in fact come from the outright fascist groups reflecting the malaise of the more hidebound, rural and industrial elements, who in the past could always count on the protectionist help of the state.

The Marxist author quotes Maurice Duverger at great length, in order to refute this argument:

Those who try to analyze the present situation in terms of class will easily make the chief of state an instrument of big capital. But that is to simplify the problem grossly, to the point of total deformation. Even if the statement were correct, we must not overlook the basic fact of the French situation: the rivalry between one type of capitalism which is modern, dynamic, competitive, and unafraid of international cooperation and global competition on the one hand, and an archaic, sclerotic capitalism on the other, incapable of facing foreign markets and, consequently, forced back on positions of political and economic nationalism. . . . In spite of all the social forces which control the public power now, it represents a liberal and hence progressive element.[34]

Clearly, the two writers agree on the facts: One sector of the French economy fares well under the new regime: the one that is "most modern and most cosmopolitan" (Claude); "modern, dynamic," internationally competitive (Duverger). But when the latter proceeds to call economic Gaullism a "liberal, and hence progressive" force, the Marxist balks. Does he remember Eugene Varga's punishment for daring to assert that, under war conditions, the imperialists were able to transcend the narrow limits of monopolistic interests and benefit the entire bourgeoisie? That was no longer Lenin; that was Djilas.[35]

---

34. Maurice Duverger, "La gauche et le Parlement," *Le Monde*, January 16, 1959, cited in Claude, *op. cit.*, pp. 212–13.

35. About Varga's heresy, see Leonard Schapiro, *The Communist Party of the Soviet Union* (New York, 1960), pp. 532–34. Djilas, *The New Class* (New York, 1957), pp. 211ff. See also above, chapter 7, p. 112, and note 15.

THE OUTLOOK

If it is true, then, that the issue is between a France intent on growing into Common Market Europe, and the other France, parochial and protectionist, then the developments of the most recent past may cause alarm. De Gaulle's insistence on an independent French deterrent may place too much of a strain on the economy; his isolationist imperialism, with its bias against Britain and full continental integration, and his agricultural protectionism in defiance of the Common Market—all this augurs ill for the perhaps not distant future when the strange great man with the distant look of the myopic will no longer be the "guide" of his beloved France. His presidential rule has style, but style is not enough. "There has been no corresponding transformation of the quality of life in France. There have been no radical departures in dealing with the social problems of a large and growing country." Living costs continued to climb (5 per cent in 1962 and 1963); so did taxes. A stabilization program introduced in 1963 "has succeeded in slowing but not stopping" that process, but it had two adverse consequences: economic stagnation and a cutback in economic planning, once the pride of France. "Now the studious planners are in eclipse." [36]

If it is true that the essential strength of the regime is not political but economic-managerial, then the General must be a worried man. His re-election line of 1965 that Frenchmen had the choice between De Gaulle or chaos, indicates some doubt in his own mind, a fear that Gaullism may, after all, be a transitional phenomenon. But like Marx, who said that he was not a Marxist, Charles de Gaulle has often indicated that he is no Gaullist. Fond of history and its comparisons, he might find comfort in another figure of transition: Cromwell. Both the Frenchman and the Englishman were generals, the latter by historic accident, the former by profession. Both arrested and contained the revolution that had swept them into power. Like Francisco Franco, neither of the two men were "first choices." Both men became agents of a movement that they did not truly represent. Both had to purge their armies. Come to power, they had to maintain themselves

---

36. *The New York Times*, December 3, p. 10, and December 4, 1965, p. 7, *passim*.

against conservatives and activists. The Lord Protector tried but was unable to consolidate his rule. De Gaulle received a foretaste of defeat when he presented himself for a second presidential term in 1965. He failed to gain an absolute majority at the first try (December 2), and he barely attained 54 per cent a fortnight later. Indications are that, as in Louis Philippe's time, *La France s'ennuie*. Bored with grandeur, the country eyes new party combinations with impressive, younger leaders.

Augustus before Caesar: Will the sequence be reversed, must a French Caesar *follow* the Augustus? Has the revolution only been delayed? Those who believe in iron laws of history and see catastrophe ahead for France may wait in vain. There have been governments so strong that, theoretically, they should have gone on forever, only to collapse all of a sudden, vanishing without a trace. The Gaullist system, with some minor readjustments, may survive precisely because of its built-in weakness. The French managers and technocrats may, in the long run, find the price of *gloire* excessive. In that case, they may decide to cut their losses and, without abolishing the presidential system, restore some of Parliament's historic powers. As a last resort, the rulers could still count on army help, but that would lead them to the point where they came in. If they prevail, however, it will be the end of revolution, and the glamorous regime of Charles de Gaulle will be replaced by competent mediocrity, the great Augustus by the little Caesars.

▣ Conclusions:
A Surfeit of Answers

Of course a few conclusions are desirable, one for each problem: a good formula defining "revolution" [1]; one good methodology for studying the causes (origins); one comprehensive characterization of the types of people who make revolutions, and a testing of their motivations and beliefs—their revolutionary ideology.

The profusion of contemporary studies of the field is intimidating, and like other disciplines of recent origin, the science of revolution seems to be in need of a new, esoteric language that avoids the vagueness of untested common nonsense. This first phase of Withdrawal and Return [2] is also one of sharp dissensions: The historians, some of them at least, look with suspicion at the work of the more radical sociologists who are the vanguard of revolutionology: "Some of the writings of contemporary social scientists," writes a distinguished expert on the Great Rebellion, "are ingenious feats of verbal juggling in an esoteric

1. See also chapter 1, above.
2. Toynbee's terms.

language, performed around the totem pole of an abstract model, surrounded as far as the eye can see by the arid wastes of terminological definitions and mathematical formulae. Small wonder the historian finds it hard to digest the gritty diet of this neoscholasticism, as it has been aptly called." But the curse is softened by a semi-blessing: "The more historically-minded of the social scientists, however, have a great deal to offer . . . [They] can supply a corrective to the antiquarian fact-grubbing to which historians are so prone; they can direct attention to problems of general relevance, and away from the sterile triviality of so much historical research." [3]

Many have attempted to define what constitutes a revolution. The answers show a great deal of divergence but not much dissension; a common pattern does emerge. Here are a few examples:

A revolution is:

> A sweeping, fundamental change in political organization, social structure, economic property control and the predominant myth of a social order, thus indicating a major break in the continuity of development.[4]

> It is a breakdown, momentary or prolonged, of the state's monopoly of power, usually accompanied by a lessening of the habit of obedience. . . . Revolution prevails when the state's monopoly of power is effectively challenged and persists until a monopoly of power is re-established. Such a definition avoids a number of traditional problems: the fine distinction between a *coup d'état* and a revolution; the degree of social change necessary before a movement may be called revolutionary . . . the uncertain differentiation between wars of independence, civil wars and revolutions.[5]

> It is a kind of social force that is exerted in the process of political competition, deviating from previously shared social norms, "warlike" in character (that is, conducted practically

---

3. Lawrence Stone, "Theories of Revolution" *World Politics*, Vol. 18, No. 2 (January, 1966), pp. 175–76.

4. Sigmund Neumann, "The International Civil War," *World Politics*, Vol. 1, No. 3 (April 1949), pp. 333–34, n. 1.

5. Peter Amman, "Revolution: A Redefinition," *Political Science Quarterly*, Vol. 77, No. 1 (March, 1962), pp. 38, 39. But *cf.* Eugene Kamenka's critique of Amman's non-distinction between *coup d'état* and revolution in *Revolution, Nomos VIII*, ed. by Carl J. Friedrich (New York, 1966), pp. 131–32.

without mutually observed normative rules), and involving the serious disruption of settled institutional patterns.[6]

It is the resultant of special limiting conditions surrounding conflict situations.[7]

Still another formulation, this one by a well-known sovietologist, combines lucidity with brevity, while making an additional important point:

I would define a revolution as two or three distinct processes which often are lumped together. One is the destruction of the old order or the old political system; another is the creation of a new one; and a third is the inevitable period of chaos that comes in between the two. The fallacy of seeing these three distinct processes as one lies in regarding all destruction as the creation of something new. Yet the false starts and abortive undertakings of the interregnum dramatize the break between the destructive and the constructive phases. So does the leadership turnover: The creators are usually people other than the destroyers. Indeed before the new system is built, the destroyers themselves are usually destroyed.[8]

Another approach stresses various *types* of revolution. Chalmers Johnson, in his useful survey of the field, distinguishes (1) The Jacquerie "to characterize a mass rebellion of peasants with strictly limited aims," The Millenarian Rebellion, such as studies by Eric Hobsbawm in his *Primitive Rebels* and by Norman Cohn in his *Pursuit of the Millennium,* crypto-political movements of sectarian character whose language is that of religion (our own second chapter fits into this pattern); (2) The Anarchist Rebellion, a reaction, counterrevolutionary in intent, to major changes in the social system which are viewed as dysfunctional by displaced minorities; (3) The Jacobin Communist Revolution of the classic type; (4) The Conspiratorial *coup d'état;* and finally (5) The Militarized Mass Insurrection, the political guerrilla warfare as developed by Mao and practiced by the revolutionary

6. Harry Eckstein, "Introduction" to *Internal War,* ed. by Harry Eckstein (New York, 1964), p. 12.

7. David Willer and George K. Zollschan, "Prolegomena to a Theory of Revolutions" in *Explorations in Social Change,* ed. by Zollschan and Hirsch (Boston, 1964), p. 133.

8. Alfred G. Meyer, "The Functions of Ideology in the Soviet Political System," *Soviet Studies,* Vol. 17, No. 3 (January, 1966), pp. 275–76.

leaders of colonial countries.[9] A sixth category, not mentioned by Johnson, would be the revolution staged by professional army leaders, acting in lieu of absent or still insufficiently developed social forces and civilian parties (see chapters 11 and 12 above).

The Johnsonian typology has been questioned by Lawrence Stone, author of what is perhaps the best brief critical analysis of the whole problem. He points out the frequent overlap of revolutionary categories as well as the great variety of subtypes we can find under each heading.[10] It is for this reason that other writers prefer definitions bypassing, for instance, the sharp distinction between *coup d'état* and revolution (see Peter Amman on p. 210, above, and note 5).

As for explanations of the origins of revolution, they are in open controversy. It is here that methodological revisionism amounts to a revolutionary reinterpretation of long-accepted stereotypes. Some revolutions are now held to be caused by the rising expectations of an ascending class rather than by universal misery,[11] whereas other revolutions are explained as actions of a

9. Chalmers Johnson, *Revolution and the Social System* (Stanford, 1964), pp. 26ff. The classical (French, Russian) type of revolution presupposes "a ruling class, separated from a formerly passive people by the privileges of power and property and culture, [which] has remained isolated, has decayed in function, in leadership capacity, and in motivation toward measures needed for growth and advancement of the society or community. Here we have a mass phenomenon, a people rejecting its government and the ruling class. It moves by plan, but the events constantly contradict the plans, and the results can be measured only long after the event. . . . The process is in some respects like the business cycle, a mass action by a great number of individuals, with the course and outcome on a basis that is statistically and historically logical, *but not understood by the participants*." George Pettee, "Revolution—Typology and Process," *Revolution, Nomos VIII* (New York, 1966), pp. 16–17.

10. Lawrence Stone, *op. cit.*, pp. 163–166.

11. "It is the dissatisfied state of mind rather than the tangible provision of 'adequate' or 'inadequate' supplies of food, equality, or liberty which produces the revolution. . . . Revolutions ordinarily do not occur when a society is generally impoverished—when, as de Tocqueville put it, evils that seem inevitable are patiently endured. They are endured in the extreme case because the physical and mental energies of people are totally employed in the process of merely staying alive. . . . It is when the chains have been loosened somewhat, so that they can be cast off without a high probability of losing life, that people are put in a condition of proto-rebelliousness." James C. Davies, "Toward a Theory of Revolution," *American Sociological Review*, Vol. 27, No. 1 (February, 1962), pp. 6 and 7. The East-Berlin uprising after Stalin's death, as well as the Polish and Hungarian upheavals of 1956 would seem to be examples for Professor Davies' thesis.

class descending the social scale and anxious to maintain its status. Sometimes the historians are not certain which way the rebellious class is moving, up or down.[12] The first French revolution has been subjected to a very radical restudy; the dramatic canvas of that great event has been replaced by a *collage* of minute fragments: "It is becoming increasingly apparent," Professor Hampson says, "that conditions in France, both before and during the Revolution, varied very widely indeed from one area to another. A detailed survey of one Department—which itself may be a collection of contrasts—offers no safe basis for generalization about others." [13] Another British scholar goes so far as to question the bourgeois origins of the French revolution: "The grievances of the lower and therefore more dissatisfied elements in town and country were not so much against the survival of an old feudal order of society as against the coming of a newer capitalist one." [14] The bourgeois revolution here becomes almost a counterrevolution of conservative protest against the bourgeoisie.

But the human mind, faced with the evidence of scientific truth, recoils and tries to protect the old image, even at the peril of indulging in pure fantasy. Man, we are told, is bound to be an architect of universals. So, no matter whether we engage in theory or practice, if presented with a choice between the utter fragmentation of existence and totalitarian integration, we will choose the latter, even if it should mean intellectual or actual slavery.

But in reality the choice will rarely be between extremes, and concept-building man, just like political man, will be happy with

---

The rising-expectations theory of revolution found its eloquent contemporary advocate in Crane Brinton; see his *Anatomy of Revolution* (New York, 1952), p. 32; "The men who made the French Revolution were getting higher and higher real income—so much that they wanted a great deal more." Temporary setbacks suffered by ascending groups may have a catalytical effect: see Brinton, *op. cit.*, pp. 34–36.

12. A case in question is the socioeconomic situation of the British gentry prior to the Great Rebellion; see p. 102 and note 16, above.

13. Norman Hampson, *A Social History of the French Revolution* (London, 1963), p. vii.

14. Alfred Cobban, *The Social Interpretation of the French Revolution* (Cambridge, 1964), p. 167. See also p. 103 and note 19, above.

a generalization large enough to create order out of chaos while still close enough to the established facts. Such a "half-way universalism" [15] might lead to an understanding in particular of the two questions raised about the type of people who are revolutionaries and about their ideology.

A crude distinction, made before if only casually, might help us. It is the distinction between changes not induced or even consciously demanded by all or some members of society, and changes that are so demanded and induced; between what has been called a revolution of things (technological, impersonal) and a revolution of men. The two are complementary in that all drastic change in the modalities of our existence will produce equally drastic responses of rejection or approval. Change acknowledged becomes change desirable or undesirable; change implemented by one group may be objected to by other groups, but even the obstruction will result in change extending to all or most aspects of communal life.

But how does this conversion of specific grievances by individuals and/or subgroups into collective form take place? The Marxist answer is simplicity itself: The matured consciousness of rising classes will adapt the lagging institution of the superstructure to the changes in the economic base. Yet our curiosity remains unsatisfied. We still would like to know precisely how the signals of change are transmitted to our consciousness, and if they reach it, how reliable these signals are. Non-Marxists will prefer to start at the beginning and consider individual grievances within the range of individual activity. Man's drive for economic betterment, for the protection or improvement of his social status will depend on the extent to which his interests are being fostered by the socio-economic subgroup to which he belongs by habit or training; on the role he plays within that group; and most of all on the importance of his group in the society as a whole.

15. Discovered after this had already been written: "A few years ago it seemed that history was becoming an atomized pile of trivia of no interest to anyone but the narrowest of specialists. . . . But we are now at the stage of being stunned by a barrage of *organizing hypotheses of middle magnitude*, which are supported by a good deal of plausible-seeming data, but which cannot yet be firmly embedded in the historical evidence. To document, to quantify, and to qualify these generalizations is the primary task of the current generation. . . ." Lawrence Stone, "The Century of Crisis," *The New York Review of Books*, Vol. 6, No. 3 (March 3, 1966), p. 16. Our italics. Professor Stone is the author of *The Crisis of the Aristocracy, 1558–1641* (Oxford, 1965).

The individual will habitually expect his wishes to be met by the, loosely organized or fully structured, sub-collectives of his trade. He will accept conditions as they are, however unsatisfactory, as long as he can discover *reasonable* causes for his failure to advance or hold his own within the system. But he will not do this indefinitely: "The truth is that interest as a collective force can be felt only where stable social bodies provide the necessary transmission belts between the individual and the group." [16]

Once the belief in the intrinsic rationality of interpersonal relations and the reasonable expectation of rewards for rational behavior have been shattered, as for instance in a prolonged economic crisis, the collapse of all the class and party shelters follows logically:

> The fall of protective class walls transformed the slumbering majorities behind all parties into one great unorganized, structureless mass of furious individuals who had nothing in common except their vague apprehension that . . . the most respected, articulate and representative members of the community were fools and that all the powers that be were not so much evil as they were equally stupid and fraudulent. [17]

Deprived of his now useless shelter, thrust into an alien, terrifying vacuum, the individual experiences a dreadful freedom from which he is anxious to escape, we have been told. [18] But his new cage is no longer of one-man size; he shares it with all others. He is being offered membership in the community of all, for nothing but the whole community, of class or race, would now seem strong enough to contain and to muster the collective strength of the new masses; no order could be as absurd as that of the discredited old masters. [19]

It is then, and only then, that the *new* masters look like liberators to the individual, happy to give up his separate identity. Fate has unplugged him from his narrow circuit and connected him with the big network. He can pull some bigger levers now, if only in his own imagination. His old drudgery remains the same or even worsens, but with compensations: After work he

16. Hannah Arendt, *The Origins of Totalitarianism* (New York, 1951), p. 338.

17. *Ibid.*, pp. 308–9.

18. By Erich Fromm in his *Escape from Freedom* (New York, 1941).

19. "Totalitarian propaganda can outrageously insult common sense only where common sense has lost its validity." Arendt, *op. cit.*, p. 342.

can march, demonstrate, become a minor leader. However temporary, the liberation from routine is in itself a revolutionary act.
A war, an air attack, an electronic blackout are occasions of that
liberation. This writer still remembers how in August 1914 Germans from all walks of life welcomed the declaration of war with
a feeling that was more than mere relief from the suspense of
the preceding days and weeks. Their singing and parading were
not only expressions of their patriotism: They were the joy of
the escaping galley slave. All over Europe, young men went to
war just as they would go on an unexpected holiday, delighted
to escape the daily boredom of their clerking. It was the upheaval of the masses against the bastilles of technological society.[20] Ironically, that revolt was masterminded by the very lords
of the bastilles.

Where the great unplugging of the mini-circuits is not the
result of a catastrophe disrupting the whole system (such as a
severe depression), or centrally directed (as it is in an external
war), the new consensus is not likely to materialize spontaneously. It must be generated by an act of will compounded of the
wills of individuals acting as a group. It takes at least two major
grievance groups to force the necessary breakthrough to the
masses. The beginning of the English Great Rebellion came with
the convergence of religious and political dissent; both Jacobins
and Bolsheviks had to enlist the peasants.

The consensus does not last, of course, and in the leading
group it is, from the beginning, never more than an appearance.
Classless by definition, the regime is really a throwback to the
mass-based rule of the Greek tyrant, under a new name. Only
the tyrant may now be a group of leaders fighting their own
private civil wars within the larger one. The source of their
precarious power is the deadlock of class interests; the state
looks strong because the groups engaged in conflict remain weak.
Once the situation has been normalized, the strongest class will
reassert itself. For a short while, the situation remains "revolutionary," with the same old actors still playing the youthful
leads. Their heavily rouged cheeks deceive nobody. Order has
returned, although it will to some extent be a new order, which

20. See p. 178f., above.

will stand until the next historic flood rolls in. As Robert Michels said in the concluding sentence of his well-known work: "It is probable that this cruel game will continue without end." [21]

In that mood of Ecclesiastes, it will be considered the last word of wisdom to regard a revolution as a question loudly raised; the answer raises a new question; and so on and so forth to eternity. Bored with all theorizing, the survivors of the revolution will be satisfied with morsels of pragmatic advice. The fate of a Sieyès or of a Soustelle is likely to suggest to them the rule that "he who commits himself too early in the revolution commits revolutionary suicide." But even in this modest claim the enemy of theory at once discovers the pretensions of an iron law which can be falsified. For instance, Lenin could be quite inflexible; his premature commitments to a fixed line cost him a few battles, without losing him the war.

It is perhaps no accident that some ex-Marxists, disappointed by the turn their revolution took, reverted to the older theory of the historic cycle that expresses Machiavelli's somber creed: *il mondo e sempre eguale* (the world will always be the same). It is the denial of progress; the historicism of Karl Marx is superseded by Pareto's ahistoricism.[22] Franz Borkenau proclaims the "law of the twofold development of revolutions. They begin as anarchist movements against the bureaucratic state organization, which they inevitably destroy; they continue by setting in its place another, in most cases stronger, bureaucratic organization, which supresses all free mass movements." [23] Arthur Koestler believes that "we seem to be faced with a pendulum movement in history, swinging from absolutism to democracy, from democracy back to absolute dictatorship"; he continues:

> Every jump of technical progress leaves the relative intellectual development of the masses a step behind, and thus causes a fall in the political-maturity thermometer. . . . When the level of mass-consciousness catches up with the objective state of affairs, there follows inevitably the conquest of democracy, either peaceably or by force. Until the next jump of technical civil-

21. *Political Parties* (Glencoe, 1949), p. 408.
22. See chapter 7, above.
23. Franz Borkenau, "State and Revolution in the Paris Commune, the Russian Revolution, and the Spanish Civil War," *Sociological Review*, 29 (1937), p. 41. Quoted by Eugene Kamenka in "The Concept of a Political Revolution," *Revolution, Nomos VIII* (New York, 1966), p. 131.

ization . . . again sets back the masses in a state of relative immaturity, and renders possible or even necessary the establishment of some form of absolute leadership.[24]

Seen from such stellar distance, the objective of the revolutionary struggle has become irrelevant, although the struggle may still thrill us and enlist our sympathies.

Is there something like a revolutionary *type* of human being, psychologically predisposed toward dysfunctional behavior? The suspicion, widely held at times, that revolutions are the work of psychopaths and criminals, is alien to the scholarly mind: "The aspect of psychological studies of revolution that we do not find useful is the misinformed generalization of micro data without reference to a macro model—namely, the derivation of revolution from psychological studies of individual revolutionaries and the resultant value judgment that because some revolutionaries are lunatics, revolution is a form of social lunacy." These elements may flock together and "exploit any fissure in the . . . system in order to attempt the seizure of political power. If such a fissure appears, they may even succeed." [25] But the fissure is not the result of their activities; it pre-exists and merely gives them scope to act politically within larger groups of socially displaced and disturbed elements. "The 'order' characteristic of any social system consists both of regularized patterns of action *and of institutions that control, ameliorate, and canalize the conflicts produced by persistent social strains. . . .* Revolutions result from unsuccessful tension-management." [26] At the pre-revolutionary stage, "the early articulations of such groups, being too limited, die with the failure of the groups. It is the widespread acceptance of a single set of ideas among such frustrated tributary groups that forms the impulse needed for the growth of a fully fledged movement. This is the work of ideology—ideology being viewed as a system of articulations." [27]

Hitler did successfully appeal to such conflicting interests as those which pitted rural against urban Germans, labor against capital. "A major source of the complexity of historical ideolo-

24. Arthur Koestler, *Darkness at Noon* [1940] (New York, 1946), pp. 168–9.
25. Chalmers Johnson, *op. cit.*, p. 25.
26. Arnold S. Feldman, "Violence and Volatility: The Likelihood of Revolution," in Harry Eckstein, *op. cit.*, p. 117.
27. Willer and Zollschan, *op. cit.*, p. 139,

gies springs from the necessity of appealing to diverse types of people faced by different exigencies. . . . [The] ideology must minimize differences between them." It must "emphasize some shared characteristics (real *or fictional*) which all the groupings concerned have in common." [28] Hitler's racial myth served just that purpose. Lenin never tired of pointing out that the aim of his proletarian party was to carry with it all the classes opposed to the Czarist system. The terror regime of the Jacobins derived its rationale from the appeal of their patriotic and equalitarian ideology. It lingered on long after Robespierre had reached his end. The ideology of revolution, without the *terribles simplificateurs*, becomes a phantom, a nostalgic memory.

Because the break-out of the individual from his subgroup did not in the past result in the complete alienation of his special interests but only in their brief suspension, the historic revolutions studied here effect change but not the destruction of the social system. There remains the possibility, however distant, of a final revolution, to destroy not just a special order but order itself: the inherited civilization. Once it is conceded that the economic factor need not be the only cause of alienation, somber vistas open up of an advanced society refusing to advance, of well-fed, well-housed people suffering from multiple neuroses.

Joseph Schumpeter, himself no socialist, wrote:

> the bourgeois finds to his amazement that the rationalist attitude does not stop at the credentials of kings and popes but goes on to attack private property and the whole scheme of bourgeois values. . . . There is inherent in the capitalist system a tendency toward self-destruction which, in its earlier stages, may well assert itself in the form of a tendency toward retardation of progress.[29]

Why not even more so in its later stages? The self-destructive tendency may not be gratified by a mere change in property arrangements: It may turn against machine culture itself. The kind of alienation caused by an increasingly complex technology and science will continue to exist long after economic alienation has become extinct. The first industrial revolution had its Luddites; the new electronic revolution may be threatened by more expert wreckers.

28. *Ibid*. Our italics.
29. Schumpeter, *Capitalism, Socialism, and Democracy*, 2nd ed. (New York, 1947), pp. 143 and 162.

We know of great societies of the past that have perished from an excess of organization. Both the Western and the Eastern Roman Empires literally overtaxed the strength of their own citizens: Rome her municipal elites; the Byzantines their Anatolian peasant-soldiers.[30] One risks ridicule by mentioning that some societies were great as long as they were struggling against poverty and that they died of apoplexy in a state of affluence.[31] A preview of the self-destructive culture that may be our destiny is already provided by the vandalized new schools of our suburbias and by all those automobile tops and tires slashed every night by juveniles by no means poor and lacking nothing except reverence for a community that gives them little scope for their abundant energies.

The coming revolution—if it ever comes—is likely to be one of total abnegation. Those of us who are no longer young can only hope that the new Luddites will not turn into what one of them called anarchist totalitarians.

30. M. Cary, *A History of Rome* (London, 1949), pp. 635–36; Arnold J. Toynbee, *A Study of History*, Vol. IV (London, 1939), pp. 72–73.
31. "Is there a substitute for the creativity of misery?" Michael Harrington, *The Accidental History* (New York, 1965), p. 132.

▣ Selective Bibliography *

GENERAL

Adams, Brooks, *The Theory of Social Revolutions* (New York: Macmillan, 1913).

Amman, Peter, "Revolution: A Redefinition," *Political Science Quarterly*, 77 (1), March 1962, 36-53.

Andrzejewski, Stanislaw, *Military Organization and Society* (New York: Humanities, 1954).

Arendt, Hannah, *On Revolution* (New York: Viking, 1965).

Brinkman, Carl, *Soziologische Theorie der Revolution* (Göttingen: Vandenhoeck & Ruprecht, 1948).

Brinton, Crane, *The Anatomy of Revolution* (New York: Random House, 1957).

Brogan, D. W., *The Price of Revolution* (New York: Harper, 1951).

Burns, C. D., *The Principles of Revolution* (London: Allen & Unwin, 1920).

Canetti, Elia, *Crowds and Power* (New York: Viking, 1962).

Chorley, Katharine, *Armies and the Art of Revolution* (London: Faber, 1943).

---

* This list does not include all the sources used in the text and mentioned in the footnotes.

Cohn, Norman, *The Pursuit of the Millennium* (New York: Oxford University Press, 1957).

Davies, James C., "Toward a Theory of Revolution," *American Sociological Review* 27 (1), February 1962, 5-19.

Dumont, Jean (ed.), *Les coups d'état* (Paris: Hachette, 1963).

Eckstein, Harry (ed.) *Internal War* (New York: The Free Press, 1964).

Edwards, Lyford P., *The Natural History of Revolution* (New York: Russell, 1965).

Ellul, Jacques, *The Technological Society*, transl. by John Wilkinson (New York: Knopf, 1964).

Finer, S. E., *The Man on Horseback* (New York: Praeger, 1962).

Friedrich, Carl J. (ed.), *Revolution: Nomos VIII* (New York: Atherton, 1966).

Goodspeed, D. J., *The Conspirators: A Study of the Coup d'État* (New York: Viking, 1962).

Gottschalk, L., "Causes of Revolution," *American Journal of Sociology*, 50 (1), July 1944, 1-8.

Griewank, Karl, *Der neuzeitliche Revolutionsbegriff* (Weimar: Hermann Boehlhaus Nachfolger, 1955).

Hatto, Arthur, "Revolution: An Enquiry into the Usefulness of an Historical Term," *Mind*, 58, October 1949, 495-517.

Hobsbawm, Eric J., *Primitive Rebels* (New York: Praeger, 1963).

Hoffer, Eric, *The True Believer* (New York: Harper, 1951).

Hopper, Rex D., "The Revolutionary Process," *Social Forces*, 28 (3), March 1950, 270-79.

Howard, Michael (ed.), *Soldiers and Governments* (London: Eyre & Spottiswood, 1957).

Johnson, Chalmers, *Revolution and the Social System* (Stanford: Stanford University Press, 1964).

———, *Revolutionary Change* (Boston: Little, Brown, 1966).

Joly, Pierre, *Contre-revolution* (Liège, 1943).

Kirchheimer, Otto, "Confining Conditions and Revolutionary Breakthroughs," *American Political Science Review*, 59 (4), December 1965, 964-74.

Meusel, Alfred, "Revolution and Counter-Revolution," *Encyclopedia of the Social Sciences*, Vol. 13, 1934, pp. 367-76.

Nomad, Max, *Rebels and Renegades* (New York: Macmillan, 1932).

———, *Aspects of Revolt* (New York: Twayne, 1959).

Pettee, George S., *The Process of Revolution* (New York: Harper, 1938).

Postgate, Raymond, *Revolution from 1789 to 1906* (New York: Harper, 1962).

Preston, Richard A., et al., *Men in Arms* (New York: Praeger, 1962).

Reeve, S. A., *The Natural Laws of Social Convulsion* (New York: Dutton, 1933).

Riezler, Kurt, "On the Psychology of the Modern Revolution," *Social Research*, 10 (3), September 1943, 320-36.

Rosenstock-Huessy, Eugen, *Die europäischen Revolutionen und der Charakter der Nationen* (Stuttgart: W. Stollhammer, 1951).

Sorokin, Pitirim, *Social and Cultural Dynamics*, Vol. 3 (Totowa, N. J.: Bedminster, 1962).

Stone, Lawrence, "Theories of Revolution," *World Politics*, 18 (2), January 1966, 159-76.

Timasheff, Nicholas S., *War and Revolution* (New York: Sheed & Ward, 1965).

Willer, David, and George K. Zollschan, "Prolegomena to a Theory of Revolutions," in *Explorations in Social Change*, George K. Zollschan and Walter Hirsch, eds. (Boston: Houghton Mifflin, 1964), pp. 125-51.

ROME

Adcock, Frank, *Roman Political Ideas and Practice* (Ann Arbor: University of Michigan, 1959).

Cary, Max, *A History of Rome* (New York: St. Martin's, 1954).

Cowell, F. R., *Cicero and the Roman Republic* (Massachusetts: Peter Smith, 1956).

Dickinson, John, *Death of a Republic* (New York: Macmillan, 1963).

Ferrero, Guglielmo, *The Greatness and Decline of Rome* (New York: Putnam, 1907-9).

——, The Life of Caesar (New York: Norton, 1962).

Haskell, H. J., *This Was Cicero* (New York: Fawcett, 1964).

Oman, Charles, *Seven Roman Statesmen of the Later Republic* (London: St. Martin's, 1902).

Rolfe, John C., *Cicero and His Influence* (New York: Cooper Square Publishers, 1963).

Scullard, Howard H., *From the Gracchi to Nero*, 2nd ed. (New York: Barnes & Noble, 1965).

Smith, Richard Edwin, *The Failure of the Roman Republic* (Cambridge: Harvard University Press, 1955).

Syme, Ronald, *A Roman Post-Mortem: An Inquest on the Fall of the Roman Republic* (Sydney: 1950).

—— *The Roman Revolution* (New York: Oxford University Press, 1939).

ENGLAND

Aston, Trevor (ed.), *Crisis in Europe 1560-1660* (New York: Basic Books, 1965).

Davies, Godfrey, *The Restoration of Charles II* (San Marino, Calif.: Huntington Library, 1955).

——, The Early Stuarts 1603-1660 (New York: Oxford University Press, 1959).

Firth, Charles Harding, *The Last Years of the Protectorate 1656-1658*, 2 vols. (New York: Russell, 1964).

Gumble, Thomas, *The Life of General Monck* (London: 1671).

Hexter, J. H., *Reappraisals in History* (Evanston, Ill.: Northwestern University Press, 1962), Chaps. 5-7.

Hill, Christopher, *Puritanism and Revolution* (New York: Schocken, 1964).

———, *Intellectual Origins of the English Revolution* (New York: Oxford University Press, 1965).

James, Margaret, *Social Problems and Policy during the Puritan Revolution* (London: Routledge, 1930).

Jones, I. Deane, *The English Revolution 1603-1714* (Chester Springs, Pa.: Dufour, 1960).

Laslett, Peter, *The World We Have Lost* (London: Methuen, 1965).

Lenz, Georg, *Demokratie und Diktatur in der englischen Revolution* (München-Berlin: 1933).

Mathew, David, *The Social Structure in Caroline England* (New York: Oxford University Press, 1948).

Pease, T. C., *The Leveller Movement* (Massachusetts: Peter Smith, 1916).

Stone, Lawrence, "The Century of Crisis," *The New York Review of Books*, 6 (3) March 1966, 13-16.

———, *The Crisis of the Aristocracy 1558-1640* (New York: Oxford University Press, 1965).

———, *Social Change and Revolution in England 1540-1640* (New York: Oxford University Press, 1966).

Trevor-Roper, Hugh, *Historical Essays* (London: Macmillan, 1957), Chaps. 27-36.

Walzer, Michael, *The Revolution of the Saints* (Cambridge, Mass.: Harvard University Press, 1965).

Yule, George, *The Independents in the English Civil War* (New York: Cambridge University Press, 1958).

FRANCE

Carr, Edward Hallett, *Studies in Revolution* (New York: Barnes & Noble, 1962).

Cobban, Alfred, *The Social Interpretation of the French Revolution* (New York: Cambridge University Press, 1964).

Fisher, H. A. L., *Bonapartism* (New York: Oxford University Press, 1957).

Gaxotte, Pierre, *The French Revolution* (New York: French & European Publications, 1932).

Godechot, Jacques, *Les institutions de la France sous la Révolution et l'Empire* (Paris: Presses Universitaires de France, 1951).

———, *La contre-révolution, doctrine et action 1789-1804* (Paris: Presses Universitaires de France, 1961).

Guérin, Daniel, *La lutte de classes sous la première République*, 2 vols. (Paris: 1946).

Guillemin, Henri, *Le coup du 2 Décembre* (Paris: Gallimard, 1951).

Hampson, Norman, *A Social History of the French Revolution* (Toronto: University of Toronto Press, 1963).

Hobsbawm, Eric J., *The Age of Revolution* (Cleveland: World Publishers, 1962).

Lefebvre, Georges, *The French Revolution*, 2 vols. (New York: Columbia University Press, 1964).

Madelin, Louis, *La contrerévolution sous la révolution 1789-1815* (Paris: Plon, 1935).

Marx, Karl, *The Class Struggles in France* (New York: International Publishers, 1964).

———, *The 18th Brumaire of Louis Bonaparte* (New York: International Publishers, 1964).

Mathiez, Albert, *The French Revolution*, 2 vols. (New York: Grosset, 1964).

Palmer, R. R., *Twelve Who Ruled* (Princeton: Princeton University Press, 1941).

———, *The Age of Democratic Revolution 1760-1800*, 2 vols. (Princeton: Princeton University Press, 1959, 1964).

Robertson, Priscilla, *Revolutions of 1848* (New York: Harper, 1960).

Rudé, George, *The Crowd in the French Revolution* (New York: Oxford University Press, 1959).

Sieyès, Emmanuel Joseph, *What is the Third Estate?* Transl. by M. Blondel and ed. by S. E. Finer, intro. by Peter Campbell (London: Pall Mall Press, 1963).

Soboul, Albert, *The Parisian Sansculottes and the French Revolution* (New York: Oxford University Press, 1964).

Sydenham, M. J., *The French Revolution* (New York: Putnam, 1965).

Thompson, J. M., *The French Revolution* (New York: Oxford University Press, 1955).

Tilly, Charles, *The Vendée* (Cambridge, Mass.: Harvard University Press, 1964).

Tocqueville, Alexis de, *The Old Regime and the French Revolution* (New York: Doubleday, 1955).

RUSSIA

Basseches, Nikolaus, *Stalin* (New York: Dutton, 1952).

Berdyaev, Nicolas, *The Origins of Russian Communism* (Ann Arbor: University of Michigan Press, 1960).

———, *The Russian Revolution* (Ann Arbor: University of Michigan Press, 1960).

Black, Cyril E., and Thomas P. Thornton (eds.), *Communism and Revolution* (Princeton: Princeton University Press, 1964).

Deutscher, Isaac, *Stalin* (New York: Oxford University Press, 1949).
———, *The Prophet Armed: Trotsky, 1879-1921* (New York: Oxford University Press, 1954).
———, *The Prophet Unarmed: Trotsky, 1921-1929* (New York: Oxford University Press, 1959).
———, *The Prophet Outcast: Trotsky, 1929-1940* (New York: Oxford University Press, 1963).
Djilas, Milovan, *The New Class* (New York: Praeger, 1957).
———, *Conversations with Stalin* (New York: Harcourt, 1962).
Fischer, Louis, *The Life of Lenin* (New York: Harper, 1964).
Howe, Irving (ed), *The Basic Writings of Trotsky* (New York: Random, 1963).
Malaparte, Curzio [Suckert], *Coup d'état, The Technique of Revolution* (New York: Dutton, 1932).
———, *Le bonhomme Lénine* (Paris: Grasset, 1932).
Nettl, J. P., *Rosa Luxemburg*, 2 vols. (New York: Oxford University Press, 1966).
Shub, David, *Lenin* (New York: New American Library, 1948).
Sorokin, Pitirim, *The Sociology of Revolution* (Philadelphia: Lippincott, 1925).
Souvarine, Boris, *Stalin* (New York: Alliance Book Corporation, Longmans, Green & Co., 1939).
Trotsky, Leon, *The History of the Russian Revolution* (Ann Arbor: University of Michigan, 1957).
———, *The Revolution Betrayed* (London: Doubleday, 1937).
———, *In Defense of Marxism* (Kearney, Nebraska: Pioneer Pub. Co., 1942).
———, *Stalin* (New York: Harper, 1941).
Ulam, Adam, *The Bolsheviks* (New York: Macmillan, 1965).
Wolfe, Bertram, *Three Who Made a Revolution* (New York: Dial, 1964).

ITALY AND GERMANY

Bracher, Karl D., *Die Auflösung der Weimarer Republik*, 2nd ed. (Stuttgart: Ring-Verlag, 1955).
———, et al., *Die nationalsozialistische Machtergreifung* (Cologne: Westdeutscher Verlag, 1960).
Bullock, Alan L., *Hitler. A Study in Tyranny*, Rev. ed. (New York: Harper, 1964).
Carsten, Francis L., *The Reichswehr and Politics 1918 to 1933* (London, New York: Oxford University Press, 1966).
Chakotin, Serge, *The Rape of the Masses* (London: The Labour Book Service, 1940).
Eyck, Erich, *History of the Weimar Republic*, 2 vols. (Cambridge, Mass.: Harvard University Press, 1962-63).

Foertsch, Hermann, *Schuld und Verhängnis* [about Schleicher] (Stuttgart: Deutsche Verlagsanstalt, 1951).

Friedrich, Julius, *Wer spielte falsch?* [About Schleicher] (Hamburg: Hermann Laatzen, n.d.).

Gordon, Harold J., *The Reichswehr and the German Republic* (Princeton: Princeton University Press, 1957).

Klemperer, Klemens von, *Germany's New Conservatism* (Princeton: Princeton University Press, 1957).

Mohler, Armin, *Die konservative Revolution in Deutschland 1918-1932* (Stuttgart: Friedrich Vorwerk, 1950).

Mosse, George L., *The Crisis of German Ideology* (New York: Grosset, 1964).

Niekisch, Ernst, *Das Reich der niederen Dämonen* (Hamburg: Rowohlt, 1953).

Nolte, Ernst, *Three Faces of Fascism*, transl. by Leila Vermewitz (New York: Holt, Rinehart and Winston, 1966).

O'Neill, Robert, *The German Army and the Nazi Party 1933-39* (London: Cassell, 1966).

Organski, A. F. K., *The Stages of Political Development* (New York: Knopf, 1965), Chap. V.

Stern, Fritz, *The Politics of Cultural Despair* (New York: Doubleday, 1965).

Wheeler-Bennett, *The Nemesis of Power. The German Army in Politics 1918-45* (New York: St. Martin's, 1953).

SPAIN

Bolloten, Burnett, *The Grand Camouflage* (New York: Praeger, 1961).

Brenan, Gerald, *The Spanish Labyrinth* (New York: Cambridge University Press, 1943, 1950).

Carr, Raymond, *Spain 1808-1939* (London, New York: Oxford University Press, 1966).

Cattell, David T., *Communism and the Spanish Civil War* (New York: Russell, 1965).

Jackson, Gabriel, *The Spanish Republic and the Civil War 1931-39* (Princeton: Princeton University Press, 1965).

Linz, Juan, "An Authoritarian Regime: Spain" in *Cleavages, Ideologies and Party Systems*, ed. by. Erik Allardt and Irjö Littunen (Turku, 1964).

Livermore, Harold V., *A History of Spain* (New York: Farrar, Straus, 1959).

Madariaga, Salvador de, *Spain, a Modern History*, Rev. ed. (New York: Praeger, 1958).

Payne, Stanley G., *Falange* (Stanford: Stanford University Press, 1961).

Sandoval, José, and Manuel Azcarate, *Spain 1936-1939*, tr. by Nan Green (London: Lawrence, 1963).

Smith, Rhea Marsh, *Spain: A Modern History* (Ann Arbor, The University of Michigan Press, 1965).

Thomas, Hugh, *The Spanish Civil War* (New York: Harper, 1961).

Welles, Benjamin, *Spain, the Gentle Anarchy* (New York: Praeger, 1965).

DE GAULLE

Aron, Robert, *An Explanation of De Gaulle* (New York: Harper, 1965).

Bloch-Morhange, Jacques, *Le Gaullisme* (Paris: Plon, 1963).

Claude, Henri, *La concentration capitaliste-Pouvoir économique et pouvoir gaulliste* (Paris: Editions Sociales, 1966).

Fauvet, Jacques, and Jean Planchais, *La fronde des généraux* (Paris: Arthaud, 1961).

Gillespie, Joan, *Algeria: Rebellion and Revolution* (New York: Praeger, 1961).

Kelly, George Armstrong, *Lost Soldiers. The French Army and Empire in Crisis 1947-1962* (Cambridge, Mass.: M.I.T. Press, 1965).

Lacouture, Jean, *De Gaulle* (Paris: Editions du Seuil, 1965).

Meisel, James H., *The Fall of the Republic. Military Revolt in France* (Ann Arbor: University of Michigan, 1962).

Plumyène, J., and R. Lasierra, *Les fascismes français 1923-63* (Paris: Editions du Seuil, 1963).

Taylor, A. J. P., "Fabulous Monster," *The New York Review of Books*, 6 (8), May 12, 1966, 16-18 [About De Gaulle. A perfect gem.]

Viansson-Ponté, Pierre, *Les gaullistes de Rituel et annuaire A a Z* (Paris: Editions du Seuil, 1963).

Werth, Alexander, *France 1940-1955* (London: R. Hale, 1956).

——, *De Gaulle, A Political Biography* (New York: Simon & Schuster, 1966).

Williams, Philip M., and Martin Harrison, *De Gaulle's Republic* (Oxford: Longmans, 1960).

GUERRILLA REVOLUTIONS

Delmas, Claude, *La guerre révolutionnaire* (Paris: Presses Universitaires de France, 1959).

Draper, Theodore, *Castroism, Theory and Practice* (New York: Praeger, 1965).

Galula, David, *Counterinsurgency Warfare* (New York: Praeger, 1964).

Griffith, Samuel B. (ed.), *Mao Tse-tung on Guerrilla Warfare* (New York: Praeger, 1961).

Guevara, Che, *Guerrilla Warfare* (New York: Praeger, 1961).

Heilbrunn, Otto, *Partisan Warfare* (New York: Praeger, 1962).

Mégret, Maurice, *La guerre psychologique* (Paris: Presses Universitaires de France, 1956).

Osanka, Franklin M. (ed.), *Modern Guerrilla Warfare* (New York: The Free Press, 1962).

Paret, Peter, and John W. Shy, *Guerrillas in the 1960's* (New York: Praeger, 1962).

————, *French Revolutionary Warfare from Indochina to Algeria* (New York: Praeger, 1964).

Thompson, Sir Robert, *Defeating Communist Insurgency* (London: Chatto and Windus, 1966).

Trinquier, Roger, *La guerre moderne* (Paris: La Table Ronde, 1961).

————, *Modern Warfare*, transl. by Daniel Lee (New York: Praeger, 1964).

Zinner, Paul, *Revolution in Hungary* (New York: Columbia University Press, 1962).

▣ Index